# Leading Intelligence Analysis

# Disclaimer

This does not constitute an official release of CIA information. All statements of fact, opinion, or analysis expressed are those of the author and do not reflect the official positions or views of the Central Intelligence Agency (CIA) or any other U.S. Government agency. Nothing in the contents should be construed as asserting or implying U.S. Government authentication or information or CIA endorsement of the author's views. This material has been reviewed solely for classification.

Sara Miller McCune founded SAGE Publishing in 1965 to support the dissemination of usable knowledge and educate a global community. SAGE publishes more than 1000 journals and over 800 new books each year, spanning a wide range of subject areas. Our growing selection of library products includes archives, data, case studies and video. SAGE remains majority owned by our founder and after her lifetime will become owned by a charitable trust that secures the company's continued independence.

Los Angeles | London | New Delhi | Singapore | Washington DC | Melbourne

# Leading Intelligence Analysis

## Lessons from the CIA's Analytic Front Lines

Bruce E. Pease

Los Angeles | London | New Delhi
Singapore | Washington DC | Melbourne

FOR INFORMATION:

CQ Press
An Imprint of SAGE Publications, Inc.
2455 Teller Road
Thousand Oaks, California 91320
E-mail: order@sagepub.com

SAGE Publications Ltd.
1 Oliver's Yard
55 City Road
London, EC1Y 1SP
United Kingdom

SAGE Publications India Pvt. Ltd.
B 1/I 1 Mohan Cooperative Industrial Area
Mathura Road, New Delhi 110 044
India

SAGE Publications Asia-Pacific Pte. Ltd.
18 Cross Street #10-10/11/12
China Square Central
Singapore 048423

*Library of Congress Cataloging-in-Publication Data*

Names: Pease, Bruce E., author.

Title: Leading intelligence analysis : lessons from the CIA's analytic front lines / Bruce E. Pease.

Description: Washington, D.C. : CQ Press, 2019. | Includes bibliographical references and index.

Identifiers: LCCN 2018037032 | ISBN 9781506397139 (pbk. : alk. paper)

Subjects: LCSH: Intelligence service—United States—Methodology. | United States. Central Intelligence Agency.

Classification: LCC JK468.I6 P43 2019 | DDC 327.1273—dc23 LC record available at https://lccn.loc.gov/2018037032

Acquisitions Editor: Scott Greenan
Editorial Assistants: Sarah Christensen and
                                    Lauren Younker
Marketing Manager: Jennifer Jones
Production Editor: Veronica Stapleton Hooper
Copy Editor: Diana Breti
Typesetter: Hurix Digital
Proofreader: Barbara Coster
Indexer: Jean Casalegno
Cover Designer: Gail Buschman

# Table of Contents

................................................................

# Preface

∙∙∙∙∙∙∙∙∙∙∙∙∙∙∙∙∙∙∙∙∙∙∙∙∙∙∙∙∙∙∙∙∙∙∙∙∙∙∙∙∙∙∙∙∙∙∙∙∙∙∙∙∙∙∙∙∙∙∙∙∙∙∙∙∙∙∙∙∙∙∙∙∙∙∙∙

This is a book to help the leaders of people who think for a living. All workers think, of course. But I'm talking about workers whose *product* is their diligent, focused thought. These are professionals whose work requires them to make sense of complex issues. They break problems into component parts, assemble data, find correlations, construct hypotheses, and test notions to try to help with decisions that must be made. They produce *insight*. They help national and corporate executives identify threats and opportunities. They try to help navigate the dark sea that is the future.

And for the most part, these "sense-makers" are led by their predecessors. Analysts usually are led by men and women who were analysts themselves—and good ones—just yesterday. Investigators, researchers, reporters, and sense-makers of all types usually are led by those who used to do the job themselves. This makes sense, and it has been the pattern with most crafts throughout history.

But to lead thinkers requires more than experience in the craft. Leading is different from doing. Leading analysis of today's complex issues requires an appreciation for a growing range of analytic approaches—far beyond whatever approach you applied successfully a decade or even a year ago. Leading thinkers requires understanding that there are many different types of thinkers, and most approach their tasks differently than you did. Some form a hypothesis and gather evidence to support or refute it. Some follow a trail of evidence to see where it leads. Some put themselves in the head of a foreign leader, even before that leader has decided what he or she intends to do. And for the first time in human history, some are wielding tools that array millions of bits of unstructured data. Each of these approaches has proven useful for analyzing some questions and failed on others.

Leading such smart people also requires understanding what kind of environment draws out their best work. What brings out their creativity, and when does excessive creativity turn an analyst into Chicken Little? When does pressure bring out their best insights, and when does pressure sap their intellectual energy? What kind of team builds new knowledge, rather than digging the deep rut of groupthink? Do your formulas for leading sense-makers help your team arrive at the right answer? Or do they merely help your team avoid being wrong?

This book tackles these issues, trying to look past some of the easy answers and false assumptions that have deluded countless leaders of news teams, think tanks, investment firms, and intelligence organizations.

My optic on these matters was developed over the course of thirty years as an intelligence officer, first with the US Navy and then at CIA. In working for CIA's analytic directorate, I was part of the most sophisticated production of practical analysis in the world. I saw analytic methods evolve, be tested in the crucible of crisis decision making, and be taught by world-class experts. I saw what worked and what didn't in the leadership of analysis. I saw various approaches to analysis tried, refined, and left behind.

At CIA I started, and thrived, as a military analyst making sense of threats in the Middle East. When I was put in charge of a team of analysts in 1990, becoming their leader and manager, I quickly found a new set of challenges. Drawing the best insights out of others was much more difficult than producing my own. My track record was strong and I rose through CIA's leadership ranks, always working the front-burner crises, with larger and larger cadres of analysts calling me "boss." I led a team of military analysts through the first Iraq war.

Through these experiences I saw an incredible array of analysis. I oversaw political, economic, and military analysis; counterterrorism and weapons analysis; forecasting and warning; strategic and tactical issues. I led the full spectrum of analytic difficulty, from simple reporting of developments to discerning the intentions of Qadhafi, Saddam Husayn, and Usama Bin Laden. I learned that my early impressions of analysis were far too narrow. I was exposed to striking differences between analysts, between approaches to analysis, and between analysis in 1980 and analysis in the twenty-first century. But I also learned there are some things all analysts share—especially the purpose of helping narrow the range of uncertainty for decision makers in an uncertain world.

And since retiring from CIA in 2008, I have learned how much we have in common with knowledge workers outside intelligence—researchers, investigators, data scientists, journalists, experts in our national labs—sense-makers of any stripe who are helping to catalyze smart decisions by others. As more and more corporate leaders see the need for diligent, data-driven critical thinking to help them navigate that uncertain world, teams of various sizes, names, and descriptions are being established to do analysis. Their topics of study usually are different than those my analysts were immersed in, but much of their work is similar. And the leaders of these analysts deal with challenges any analytic leader at CIA would recognize. They make the same mistakes I did, wasting talent here and time there, dictating when we should be listening, and letting short-term needs blind us to strategic imperatives. They also often succeed and will identify with some of the lessons I have put in this book.

Over the last decade, I have also encountered many workers in corporate America doing *analysis*, but not using that word. In this book I will occasionally use the term *intelligence analyst*. But that phrase has to do with the mission and sources of those particular analysts—it doesn't imply that they do some flavor of analysis that is unique to intelligence agencies. And of course, my anecdotes, illustrative points, and jargon come from my career in intelligence, but if you are not of that background, I hope you can translate my lessons to your particular group of sense-makers. I recently taught a seminar to data wranglers for an investment firm, men and women who didn't really call themselves "analysts." But when I showed them my list of "Ten Things Analysts Hate" (you'll find it in chapter 2), they immediately embraced it: "That's us!" When I talked to their leaders about the challenges of politicization (chapter 8), though they are outside the political arena, they recognized the same pressures in their own efforts to serve customers who have their own opinions.

For those of you looking for another memoir by an intelligence insider, this is not that kind of book. I tell some stories from my career, but this is not about my career. Rather, this book tries to make sense of both the successes and failures I experienced. Many times as a leader I guessed right about one thing or another. And like every leader, many lessons I learned the hard way. This book tries to capture the essence—and limits—of those lessons.

Also, for those of you who called me "boss" over the decades, thank you for being my best teachers. Unfortunately, too many of you were the victims of how much I had to learn but hadn't learned fully by the time we worked together. Even worse, some of my own breakthroughs in the struggle to make sense of these matters came only after I retired, when I had the time to reflect and research. You'll find this book advocating some things you'll wish I had done when we worked together. I can only hope you will take it as a sign that I never stopped learning, rather than as simple hypocrisy. However you judge these things, know that I regard you as the most talented and dedicated group of professionals any leader could hope for.

# Acknowledgments

····················································

This book took about six years of fits and starts in the writing, and during that period I amassed a growing cadre of supporters who contributed their time, talents, and knowledge to it. Just as important, they offered their polite impatience as they tired of hearing that it was "almost ready" to submit to a publisher. Beyond those six years, this book was decades in the making, during which I learned from hundreds of bosses, colleagues, subordinates, and customers the impact of various approaches to leading analysis. The list of people I should thank would run as long as the book itself—and would be classified—but you all have my deep gratitude.

As an analyst, I worked for several people who brought out my best work. They showed me how to balance earnest engagement with trusting latitude, hands on with hands off, challenge with support, and confidence with humility. Captain Don Estes, Martha Kessler, Bruce Riedel, Bob Layton, and Tom Wolfe got me hooked on the business and taught me how to both do it and lead it.

Winston Wiley gave me my first job as a leader of analysis—and many subsequently—and began an active mentoring role that continues to this day. He taught me analysis as a business—customers, logistics, production lines, branding, all that. He taught me it takes more than genius—"and you ain't no genius"—to crank out analysis worth a president's attention every day. Another of Winston's protégés, the late Ben Bonk, showed me how to tend to all that in sustained crisis, how to identify the real priorities from the merely insistent, how to make time for the subordinate who needs it, and how to laugh on your worst day. Ben, you never thought of yourself as my coach, and I never thought of myself as your pupil—we were too close for that—but coach you were and pupil I still am.

Several people have held open the door of opportunity for me. George Tenet, Jose Rodriguez, Sue Bromley, John McLaughlin, Jami Miscik, and Dave Cohen repeatedly picked my name out of some very large hats, both challenging me and giving me the experiences that have shown up in these pages. Mary Meyer picked me for my first executive-level job in the business of leading analysis. More than anyone, she taught me that analysts are first people: people with hopes, dreams, and needs, people whom we are blessed to serve. There are many fine books out there on servant leadership. They should all have a chapter on Mary.

I owe a lot to the special people who helped hone material in these pages. Several times in the text I refer to the work of research psychologist Dr. Gary Klein. Much of the time I cite his fine books on insight, intuition, and decision making. But much of the time I am drawing on hours of productive and provocative discussions. He first caught my eye when I listened to a presentation in which he captured the value of experts—when others were finding it particularly hip to denigrate experts. I quickly learned that his own enormous expertise comes packaged with unfailing humility, and he crystalized for me the idea that expertise mixed with humility is a potent combination.

I think there is probably no idea in this book that I didn't try out for size on David Priess. Between kicking around the ideas in conversation and responding to my drafts, David's thoughts made my thinking better. "But what about . . .?" "Have you tried . . .?" "Wouldn't a story help here?" A year ago, he told me that he owed me a debt of burritos—our favorite lunch when we teach together—for helping him with his own excellent book, *The President's Book of Secrets*. Well, friend, the cosmic burrito balance has shifted.

Phil Nolan, Dennis Bowden, and Mark Lowenthal were enthusiastic supporters of the book, generous in reviewing chapters that were not ready for prime time. And I owe Mark special thanks for steering me to the good people at SAGE/CQ. Beth Skubis, curator of cutting-edge concepts on analysis and leadership, was an early and consistent advocate of my project. And she helped crystalize my early notions of the dangers of imbalance in leading analysis. Beth, along with Carmen Medina and Carol Dumaine, also woke me to several of the dynamics I wrote about in the chapter on creativity and innovation in an analytic environment.

The following reviewers are acknowledged for their contributions to the book: Robert F. Alonzo, Texas A&M University–San Antonio; Heather Triplett Biehl, BBN Technologies; Dennis Bowden, Missouri State University; Patty Brandmaier, Momentum LLC; Daniel Byman, Georgetown University; Russell J. Decker, Ohio Northern University; Dennis C. Jett, Pennsylvania State University; Kalu N. Kalu, Auburn University Montgomery; Carmen A. Medina, MedinAnalytics LLC; Gregory Moore, Notre Dame College; James Padfield, Truman State University; Chris Savos; Toshiyuki Yuasa, University of Houston.

One special type of "reviewer" was the freelance editor SAGE/CQ introduced me to. Diana Breti made better every single page of this book, preserving my voice while making me look smarter than I am.

I'd also like to thank an overworked staff at CIA for their help with this book. CIA's Publications Review Board gets the painful task of scouring the manuscripts of CIA employees and annuitants for secrets that should not be released. Too many of us authors treat you as a cat treats its vet—you actually try to help us, but all you get in return is hissing, teeth, and claws. I write in this book about the prospects of analysts being replaced by artificial intelligence. The members of the PRB would be justified in hoping for that day to arrive, but it won't happen in our lifetime. Their work is just as analytic as anything I did or led in my career and just as full of subtlety, art, and expert understanding. They perform a vital task that deserves our thanks.

My career in analysis, of course, began much earlier than my first paycheck. I was raised by two wonderful parents who got me hooked on learning. My mother, Doris, taught me—convinced me—that "Bruce, you can do anything you set your mind to." My father, Edgar, a Navy Chief through and through, would follow that up with, "And what you can do right now is grab a towel and help with the dishes." Is it a surprise that balance is a key theme throughout this book? It was also my dad who instilled in my brother Doug and me the critical thinking skills that made me feel at home in CIA's analytic directorate. An evening at home for me in junior high or high school was frequently a debate over the Cold War, the role of government, bussing, the draft, the Domino Theory, gun control, the space program, or the Lakers' offense. Hours of this debate with Dad and Doug taught me that a weak foundation to an assertion, a sloppy use of evidence, or strained logic are all things to be pitied, and that it doesn't matter if the '68 Lakers are better than the Celtics on paper; they play on hardwood.

Finally, again, balance. I reject the phrase "work-life balance" because there is only life. And critical to my own life and balance are my beloved family. Tristyn and Taylor, I couldn't be prouder of the bright, caring, good people you have grown to be. Some of what I have written in this book are lessons I learned through you. And Betty, the love of my life since 1978, how empty this journey would have been without you. I might have become an analyst, but I would have been a cynical one. I might have become a leader, but I would have been off balance. If the reader can sense any joy in these pages—and in the story of my work—it's because of you.

# About the Author

Bruce E. Pease is a consultant on national security issues and the application of artificial intelligence, and he teaches leadership, ethics, and analysis. For seventeen years, he led CIA's front-burner components, specializing in threats to US security and developing expertise in today's most pressing security issues. In the late 1990s, he led CIA's Office of Near Eastern, South Asian, and African Analysis, providing key policy support during multiple crises in the Middle East. After the 9/11 attacks, he established and led CIA's new Office of Terrorism Analysis and then became deputy director of the Counterterrorism Center. In 2004, he became director of CIA's Weapons Intelligence, Nonproliferation, and Arms Control Center, analyzing the threat posed by weapons of mass destruction and emerging military technologies. His service also includes work as part of the White House staff, when he was director of intelligence programs on the National Security Council, as well as eight years of active duty in the US Navy.

In the mid-1990s, I was director of intelligence programs on the National Security Council, part of the White House staff, and dealing with the entire intelligence community. In the late 1990s, I led CIA's Office of Near Eastern, South Asian, and African Analysis, providing key policy support during multiple crises. Immediately after the 9/11 attacks, I was asked to establish and lead CIA's new Office of Terrorism Analysis. Soon I was promoted to deputy director of the Counterterrorism Center, helping to design and command the campaign against Al Qa'ida. And in late 2003, I began four years as director of CIA's Weapons Intelligence, Nonproliferation, and Arms Control Center, analyzing the threat posed by weapons of mass destruction and emerging military technologies

# Leading Analysis Is Different from Doing Analysis

Too many who lead knowledge workers believe that because they were proficient knowledge workers themselves, the step into leadership will be an easy one. A crack investigator is made head of an investigative team and the team spins apart. An excellent researcher "graduates" into leading a research division, and the performance of other skilled researchers in the division plummets.

Part of what is going on here is almost cliché: Leading is different from doing. Managing workers is different from doing the work yourself. In any field a proficient worker can fail as a manager. A typical reason for failure is that the new manager doesn't understand people. Sometimes the new manager doesn't really understand one person in particular: himself. Sometimes a new manager trips over any of a hundred abstracts that are vital in managing or leading that might have not been relevant—or were different—when she was working on the line: perhaps prioritization, time management, fairness, decision making, bureaucratic savvy, or motivating others. Perhaps the work that you were so good at was like physics, while managing that work is more like chemistry, and leading those workers is more like biology—or, gulp, psychology. The good news is that if you are making this move yourself, there is a vast body of literature on leadership and management in any field, including knowledge work.

However, there is also a reason new managers fail that is particular to those who lead and manage knowledge workers. Knowledge workers produce ideas. Those who lead and manage knowledge workers produce ideas. The line between work and worker can be hard to find, and the line between leader and led even more so. But those lines are real, and they can easily trip you up.

The work itself, producing ideas on a substantive topic, is something most knowledge workers love and many get addicted to. By "substantive topic," I mean the issue or area of study your thinkers are tackling. In intelligence analysis, it might be nuclear proliferation or Al Qa'ida's strategy. In the business world, the topic being analyzed might be consumer trends or the petroleum export market. I don't mean to imply that a leader's business of, say, crafting a strategy for the work has no real substance. But for clarity's sake, wherever in this book I talk about *substance* or *substantive topic*, I am referring to an area of study.

Many of us leading substantive work remain drawn to it. In fact, sometimes there is no escaping it. When the substance is of vital importance, the temptation is even stronger, and sometimes rolling up your sleeves and getting directly involved in substantive idea production will be the right thing to do. Silicon Valley is full of stories of the CEO diving into a thorny problem that is challenging the shop floor, applying his own engineering skills, even writing code, to help produce a breakthrough. The leader who occasionally does this stays in touch with work realities and sometimes teaches, and even inspires, the workers on the production line. *But the leader who does this routinely, who is cranking out the daily product, is ignoring other responsibilities and stifling the workers.*

During my thirty-year career, I saw hundreds of talented analysts move into the ranks of management. One week they were analysts; the next they were leaders of analysts. In general, they made a leap of faith. They moved from work they truly loved into work that is significantly different. Most of them did just fine. But some of them foundered because they didn't grasp just how different the work of *leading* analysis is from the work of *doing* analysis. They did not understand their new *analytic* responsibilities. You are still an analyst, and you do, indeed, still have analytic responsibilities. Choosing where to apply your superb analytic skills will be among your most critical decisions as both leader and manager.

## The Leader of Analysis or the Uberanalyst

Any new manager of analysts has an early choice to make: Who will do the "real" analysis, my subordinates or me? Is my job to enable and support their analysis, or do I want them to be a supporting cast helping *me* do the analysis? Most of this chapter presumes you opt for the former. And for most situations, that is the right answer. But not for all situations.

I have seen wonderfully smart and driven analysts move into a leadership position and succeed as an *uberanalyst*. This was the term we used for the manager who would do the important thinking for the team. (More recently, the term *manalyst* has come into use, and it's not a compliment.) The successful uberanalyst usually moves into management of a unit where he is already an acknowledged expert on the topic. He is intimately familiar with all the important substantive issues and has earned the respect of the most important customers.

Moving into management, this uberanalyst can become like a brilliant movie director. Everybody on the set knows it is his or her job to deliver on the director's vision. And if the director has a flash of inspiration and changes the vision, everyone must go with the flow. In these cases, many subordinate analysts almost become research assistants, working on component pieces of the product. Some of the analysts are sent to work relentlessly on collection issues, developing the evidence the uberanalyst needs.

A few of the most important subordinate analysts retain enough autonomy to do their own analysis, but their work only gets published if the uberanalyst agrees with it.

Some good things can flow from this situation. Teams led by a brilliant uberanalyst can show a focus, a unity of purpose, and an analytic coherence that other teams rarely achieve. They can be an orchestra playing a piece so powerfully and so beautifully that they make other teams look like a garage band.

But the circumstances that suit this approach are limited. Several conditions must exist for the uberanalyst approach to work.

- The unit's analytic scope of responsibility must be limited to what the uberanalyst can personally master. This might be a single question, like "Where is Usama bin Laden?" Or it might be a focused topic like Iran's nuclear threat, which includes several subordinate questions. But a topic like "terrorism" or "Iran" would be too broad.

- The unit must be free to focus on a single project. The director and his team are free to say, "This is the movie we are making *now*." The Special Agent in charge of an FBI investigation can orchestrate his entire task force to conduct *one* investigation. Similarly, the uberanalyst and his team may dedicate themselves to a single worthwhile question—or set of questions—without fear that they are neglecting an array of other substantive responsibilities.

- The uberanalyst must be substantively expert enough and intellectually brilliant enough that the subordinate analysts naturally defer. Think of the character Deputy Marshal Sam Gerard, played by Tommy Lee Jones in the 1993 movie *The Fugitive*. He called himself "the big dog" and his team clearly regarded him that way. They knew he was always thinking two steps ahead of them.

Absent these circumstances, I have never seen the uberanalyst approach work for long. Uberanalysts can fall into the trap of thinking that they are smarter than everyone else—smarter even than the aggregate of their subordinates—and it is only a matter of time until they are proven wrong. Most who try the approach find that they are spending so much time and energy on the substantive analysis that they neglect broad swaths of their managerial responsibilities. Others succeed in a narrow-focus unit but then move to a new unit and fail to adjust their approach. In the new unit they may not have the same substantive mastery, but they still try to dominate the analysis. Still others fail because they produce too many refugees—analysts who flee from intellectual subservience.

# Which Substantive Analyst Responsibilities Carry Over?

Even if you reject the uberanalyst model, managers of analysts must do some substantive analysis. This came as a relief to me when I moved from *being* an analyst to *leading* them. I loved analysis—still think of myself as an analyst today—and did not want to leave it behind for the sake of my new rank. Just as you did as an analyst, you will find yourself spending some energy tracking key substantive questions, honing argumentation, resisting complacency, and asking, "What are we missing?" No matter how high you move in the organization, you will find yourself wrapping your mind around problems that keep your analytic juices flowing.

The difference will be in the depth and breadth of your focus. You will miss the days when you could go as deep as you wanted, the days when you felt you earned the title "expert." When he was CIA's Deputy Director for Intelligence, John Helgerson once commented to me, "The last time I really felt like I *knew* anything was when I was an analyst."

The notion that a manager of analysts should stay involved in the substance is debatable, of course. Some organizations use managers simply to organize work and get the product out the door—those managers tend to care about analysts' productivity, but they care less what the analysis says. We tried that approach once in CIA but had to abandon it. At CIA, besides producing analysis, we produce analysts. We develop them. We expect our managers to be effective coaches, and coaching works best when helping an analyst with the *substantive* issue at hand. A nonsubstantive baseball coach can offer tips about attitude, teamwork, and conditioning; a substantive baseball coach can do all that but also can tell a third-base player that few hitters bunt with two strikes. We also expect our managers to deal directly with important customers and to channel the customers' needs to analysts—conversations that require substantive fluency.

So let's talk about substantive fluency. One thing you probably did as an analyst was to develop a list of the most important issues you are tracking. As an analyst, perhaps you had ten of these. Now you are in charge of a team of ten analysts, and you might have ten important issues you are *fluent* in. By "fluent," I do not mean that you would have the depth of knowledge to replace the analysts on the issue—never forget that they, not you, are the experts. Rather, by "fluent," I mean you will have in your head the ten most important issues and this level of knowledge about each:

- What is our team's analytic line on this issue?

- What are the principal pieces of evidence and reasoning that underpin that analytic line?

- What are we doing to collect more evidence?

- What are we doing to keep ourselves honest on the issue (challenging our assumptions, consulting outside experts, devil's advocacy exercises, etc.)?

- When did we last write on this issue?

Which ten issues? You'll have little difficulty picking the most important based on their innate differences, your customer's interests, your senior's needs, and your common sense.

What about the other ninety issues being tracked by your team? Guess what? You are responsible for them, too. You'll care about them. You'll talk with your analysts about them. You'll occasionally even go deep on one or another of them, getting into an extraordinary level of detail and nuance. But unlike your top ten, you won't work to stay fluent on those ninety; you simply cannot afford the time.

And it does not much matter whether you are an entry-level manager, mid-grade, or an executive leader of analysts. As an office director responsible for hundreds of analysts, I found I could still retain fluency on only ten or so top issues. When events dictated that I needed to get fluent on an issue not on my top ten list, I would have to cram. My focus on this new addition to my top ten list might last for months and make me stale on some of the original top issues. I would have to recover my fluency when I could, and sometimes I would have to adjust my top ten to new realities. Being an office director also meant that I was *responsible* for an increasing number of issues on which I claimed no fluency. I had to get used to saying, "I don't know. I'll put you in touch with someone who does."

Beyond retaining analytic fluency with top issues, it is important for the leader of analysis to analyze things she is in a better position to see. There are several of these:

- Changes in the tone of the group. I recall a time in the late 1990s, for example, when my analysts were debating the prospects for a renewal of the Arab-Israeli war. There was wide divergence of opinion among them, even though none of them thought war was likely. They argued over the evidence, the trends, and the dynamics of the situation. Six months later, they returned to the debate and again argued the evidence, trends, and dynamics. What none of them noticed was that each of them was more pessimistic, more fearful of war, than he or she had been six months earlier, and one or two outliers believed war had become likely. That aggregate shift in position was important and something I, as an observer of the debate, could detect better than those who were in the midst of the debate.

- Changes in the needs of the customer. Teach your analysts to analyze the customer, but expect that the analysts won't be as good at this as you are. First, you are usually more experienced with the customer than they are. Second, the analysts' mental energies sometimes will get completely absorbed in the substance of the issue they are studying. As a customer learns, his needs will evolve. As a customer decides on a course of action, her appetite will change. As a customer makes strategic choices, his need for tactical support of those choices will develop. The leader of analysts must keep a finger on the customer's pulse.

• Are we getting anywhere? It is easy for analysts, or entire teams of analysts, to spin their wheels. Grinding too few pieces of evidence into increasingly fine powder, answering the same basic question over and over. It felt like this was the case in 2001 and 2002 when our analysts were spending great energy on the question of whether Iraq had operational influence over Al Qa'ida. Little new evidence was coming in, so the analysts weighed and re-weighed the same evidence in response to repeated challenges to their conclusions. On other issues, evidence keeps coming in that is relevant to the question but adds no real insight and does nothing to narrow the gap in our knowledge. Analysts often will contentedly examine each new piece of evidence and not think about the gap. At such times, it is up to the leader to say, "Enough!" Then the leader must analyze what might be done to obtain fresh and meaningful evidence.

• What is missing? Sometimes the analysts will be completely absorbed in analyzing a significant volume of evidence, and they neglect to think about evidence that should be there but is not. It will be up to the leader to step back from the picture and be Sherlock Holmes, seeing significance in the dog that didn't bark. Or it will be the leader, seeing her analyst wasting energy speculating about what a customer meant by a particular question, who says, "Did anyone think of simply calling the customer?"

The leader of analysis will also have to analyze this question: Is our approach to this issue sufficient? For example, if I have a team of analysts all studying Chinese foreign policy through the same lens (e.g., they all have graduate degrees in international relations), the team is almost certainly too homogeneous for its own good. Adding an expert in cultural anthropology and another in international finance might spark significant new insights from the team. Similarly, if the team is spending all its time hard at work at their desks, cranking out papers at an impressive rate, they are spending too little time in discussion with outside experts—especially

## A "Black Box" for Analysts?

In chapter 10, "The Tools of Twenty-First-Century Analysis," I speak of the dangerous "Black Box." This is an IT tool that produces useful answers, but nobody on your team knows how those answers are developed. That is a dangerous situation that a leader dreads: the box eventually may produce a flawed answer because its designer did not anticipate something, perhaps never intended the box to field the kind of question you have asked. It is the GPS unit that instructs you to cross a bridge that was washed away in last week's flood. Follow it blindly and you are doomed.

For a leader of an analytic unit that is new to her, the entire unit is a Black Box. She must, and with some urgency, analyze how that unit develops its answers. This will help her understand what kind of questions the unit can field. It will help her assess whether the unit's analytic approach is optimum for today's needs. And it will signal to her unit that she cares not simply that it does its work, but how. She will be like the math teacher who required you to show your work. She needs this level of understanding to lead her analytic unit effectively. The unit needs that level of savvy and engaged leader.

outside experts with whom they disagree. Finally, when a unit's analysis starts to look complacent or stale, a fresh approach is called for.

## No Lazy Thinking

Let's go back to that nonsubstantive baseball coach who talks about conditioning and teamwork. That stuff's important too, right? So what nonsubstantive matters warrant the skills you developed as an analyst?

One strength you demonstrated as an analyst absolutely must carry over into your leadership: disciplined thinking. Discipline in general is key to sustained high performance. Talent is not enough. Details count. Diligence counts. Discipline is required for myriad aspects of your unit's work. From meeting deadlines to submitting travel claims, you will be responsible for building a culture that cares about the little things. And many of these things would feel familiar to someone running a company that produces plumbing fittings. But as a leader of a unit that produces insights, one discipline rises above the rest: *No Lazy Thinking*.

From the time I arrived at CIA, this was drummed into me as an analyst. Lazy thinking has no place in professional analysis. Disciplined thinking to an analyst is as conditioning is to an athlete. Lazy thinking says that because something has never happened it won't happen. Lazy thinking says that because something is scary it is likely. Lazy thinking says that because the evidence was difficult to collect it must be important. Lazy thinking says that because your narrative is elegant your conclusion must be correct. You will encounter these and a thousand other manifestations of lazy thinking among the human beings you lead.

Let me introduce an important nuance here. By *lazy thinking* I do not mean *intuition*. Intuition absolutely has a place in analysis. In chapter 4, I will argue that intuition, especially expert intuition, is essential to analysis when blended with disciplined critical thinking. Lazy thinking would be an analyst blindly trusting his intuition. But lazy thinking also would be to publish logical analysis when your intuition is screaming that it is incorrect.

Lazy thinking is easy to spot with new analysts. Skipping logical steps, overlooking contradictory evidence, coming to conclusions that are too quick and too confident, assertions stated as facts . . . you will spot each of these. And you will be quick to correct them. More important, you will convey a standard with deep cultural significance, saying, "That's not the way we do things around here."

A bigger challenge is spotting lazy thinking among experts. They know so much. They have so many facts at their fingertips. They can so easily marshal persuasive arguments. But they are human and just as prone to bouts of laziness as the rest of us. Enforcing disciplined thinking among your experts needn't be a challenge to their expertise. You can do much with the simple request, "Help me to understand . . ." You can ask them, "What is the weakest part of your case?" In fact, teach them to anticipate that question. And you can establish an expectation among your experts that they have a special obligation to demonstrate an open mind.

In watching leaders over the decades at CIA, I found them generally good—and some of them superb—at rooting out lazy thinking in analysis. The best leaders did not try to do this with a list of rules; they did it by nurturing a culture of disciplined thinking that the analysts themselves enforced.

Where I saw many leaders struggle was when they forgot to apply the discipline to themselves. And it wasn't that they became intellectually lazy on the substantive topics for which they were responsible. Rather, they forgot to apply that same intellectual rigor to other important aspects of their jobs. Deluged by the array of new things to pay attention to, as leaders and managers we often conclude too quickly and consider too lightly. Based on limited experience, based on an anecdote or two that we experienced, we extrapolate principles and guidelines for our decisions. We will firmly conclude such things as "PhDs cling to a writing style that is too academic." Or "Our customers don't respect political analysis." Or "Methodologists will slow you down." Or "Big Data is a big fad." Or "The leadership approach that worked in my last job will work in this one." As an analyst you were trained to resist impressionistic diagnoses of complex human events; apply that rigor to the complex human challenges of your office. Dig deeper for the truth. Test your assumptions. Open your mind to alternatives.

## Setting Standards for the First Time

Just as every manager must enforce discipline, each must set and enforce standards. These are related and overlapping concepts, but one aspect concerning standards is worth special attention here.

Setting and enforcing standards seemed to come naturally to many of the managers I knew in the Navy. But in decades of watching analysis, I noticed that many new analytic managers struggled with this basic function. For a while I suspected that some of them were just too nice and didn't want to deliver the bad news when a subordinate's work wasn't good enough. The real answer, I found, was different and can be seen in the case of a manager I'll call "Emily."

Emily was a terrific analyst. She consistently produced expert, insightful, articulate papers and briefings. She had a natural rapport with customers. She could navigate the bureaucracy effortlessly. And every team she worked on just seemed to work better together. As a student of the leadership literature of the day, I'd talk about Emily's "high emotional intelligence," and how many of the "7 habits" she manifested. So, no brainer, we pronounced her ready to take over a team. And her first year leading analysts was painful to watch.

Emily frustrated the hell out of several of her subordinates. One complained, "Nothing I give her is good enough. I hand her something, she looks at it, and then I see that disappointed face. I got 'the face' on an important paper I gave Emily last week, and then, making me feel even worse, Emily stayed all night to fix it."

Well, it turns out Emily's subordinates were not alone. She was frustrated, too. "They think I am a perfectionist, but I'm not."

Emily suffered from something that plagues many superb analysts when they move into management. Nothing in her experience taught her how to talk about quality standards. She obviously had high standards for her own work when she was an analyst—it was one of things that made her so impressive. But she never thought about those standards. As an analyst, she would tackle a project, mold it, improve it, refine it, massage it until it was the best she could do . . . and then turn it in . . . and it was excellent. At no point did she ask whether it was good enough. Instead, she turned her critical eye on her own work and asked specifically how she could make it better, and she did that.

Now, for the first time in her career, Emily needed to clearly set standards. For subordinates who were not as brilliant as she was, she needed to find the words to convey what standard of performance she expected. They needed help finding the threshold of "good enough." They needed clarity on what fell short when a draft was not good enough. What Emily was giving them, instead, were twenty tweaks to make *this* piece better and an impression that they had somehow failed by not delivering all twenty on their own. She needed to find the words to teach them the difference between *fixing* and *improving* a draft. When I have to fix your draft, it fell beneath my standards. When I improve your draft, I am coaching you on how one might make a good draft better.

Emily wasn't rare in her struggle to set standards. I saw many leaders deliver meaningless slogans as a substitute for clear standards. I couldn't count the number of times I heard a manager say, "I want your best! Anything short of that just isn't good enough." Sounds good, doesn't it? Well, it's nonsense for most knowledge workers and certainly for analysts. A manager needs to set priorities and must recognize that there simply isn't time to do one's absolute best on every task. Doing one's best in analysis at CIA often would mean working through the night and all weekend. Some tasks absolutely are worth that; some are not. An analyst who gives heroic effort on each task will burn out quickly.

Here are some thoughts about "good enough" that served me well for years.

What is "good enough" depends on your customer and your customer's clock. When my customer was the assistant secretary of state for Near Eastern Affairs, I was serving someone who was very smart, very well informed, and personally involved in some of the situations I was analyzing. For him, "good enough" was a paper that would earn an "A" if we were giving grades, unless he had an important meeting the next day and I either gave him a "B" paper or I missed my chance to support him in that meeting. Then, for him, a "B" was good enough *this* time. What was the difference between the "A" paper and the "B" paper? The "B" paper might have been less elegantly written, with a question or two not fully fleshed out and one of the implications not fully developed. And what about a less important customer? Say, for example, a Navy Intelligence lieutenant at the NAVEUR HQ in London (that was me in 1981). Hand Lt Pease a version of that paper just given to the assistant secretary, a paper that now might earn only a "C" because it was not written with Lt Pease's needs in mind, and for him a "C" would be good enough. And for the president, only your best effort to get an "A" is good enough. That is, the product is tailored to his needs and schedule, and the product is the best your organization—not just you—can do. Not all analytic organizations have a customer base as varied as the one I just described, but you can judge the relative importance of your customers. You have your equivalent to the president and you have your own Lt Pease. And your customers have their own deadlines, after which it does not matter how perfect your product was.

Don't take my assertion that "good enough" depends on the customer and the clock as license for low standards. I said that a "C" might be good enough for customer Pease in London. But even for Lt Pease, a "D" paper would not be good enough. What is the difference between a "C" and a "D?" A "C" paper is ok, not great. A "D" piece of analysis has something seriously wrong with it, errors in logic, unchallenged assertions, or flawed use of evidence. You are actually mis-serving the customer with such a product: at best you have wasted his time; at worst you have misled him.

Further, regardless of customer or deadline, always enforce three high standards for every piece of analysis your subordinates produce: (1) It must be clear. I don't care how fast it needs to be written, if your customer has to guess what you are trying to say, you have not served him. (2) The reasoning must be explicit. Your unit is producing *analysis*—why they reach a particular conclusion is as important to the discerning customer as what conclusion they reached. (3) It must make sense to you. Don't expect the customer to buy the analysis if you don't.

## Analyze Everything

Emily's experience as an analyst didn't prepare her to articulate standards, but it did give her the tools to fix this problem. With some help identifying the problem, she quickly became proficient in this area. She *analyzed* questions like, What does the customer need? How much effort can we afford to expend? What is this analyst capable of producing? Then her strong communication skills came into play, allowing her to articulate her conclusions to her subordinates.

As a leader and manager of analysis, you will find your analytic skills serving you on issues well beyond the substance for which you are responsible. You will need to analyze your workforce, their skills, their motivations, their habits, and their mental frameworks. You must analyze the environment in which they work, especially figuring out what elicits—and what diminishes—their trust. You must analyze what your business needs to run well today and tomorrow. You must analyze the moral parameters of the work you have taken on. You must analyze the available approaches to productively tackle the questions your customers need answered. And you must analyze the ever-growing craft that is analysis. This book wrestles with each of these areas, inviting you to analyze your local situation and develop prescriptions of your own. As leader and manager, you have not ceased to be an analyst. Rather, the range of things you must analyze has exploded.

# KEY THEMES

Embrace that leading is different from doing. Your energies—including analytic energies—should be invested in different topics, issues, and priorities than those that earned your promotion to management.

- If you were a successful analyst, think less about how you did analysis and more about how your leaders brought out your best work. Also, what leadership simply got in your way?
- Analyze the individuals who call you "boss."
  - What does each need?
  - How does each think?
- Analyze your unit as a whole.
  - Is it greater than the sum of its parts?
  - How does it develop insights and answers collectively?
- Do your subordinates think you are the uberanalyst? (That is occasionally appropriate, but not usually.)
- Have your analysts teach you enough to be "substantively fluent."
  - What is their analytic line on top issues?
  - What underpins that analytic line?
  - What is being done to get more evidence?
  - Who are their most important customers?
  - Is our analysis "getting anywhere," or have we been chewing on the same hard questions for years?
- Get used to defining and communicating standards (better than your boss did with you).
  - Never tolerate lazy thinking.
  - Be clear about what is good enough and what is not.
  - Although what is good enough may depend on the situation, *every* product must (1) be clear, (2) be based on explicit reasoning, and (3) make sense to you.

# CHAPTER 2

# Understanding Analysts

Every now and then during my CIA career, I used to talk to groups of outsiders about our analytic directorate. I'd start by telling the audience that you know you are among analysts when you hear the question, "Did you see the game last night?" and they are talking about *Jeopardy!* Always got a laugh. Never was true.

Clichés about the analyst's nature abound. We are the academics of intelligence. We read the world news section of the newspaper and ignore what's happening in our neighborhood. We are legendary introverts. We are never happier than in a debate as to whether "move" or "relocate" is the better word. We never met a weasel word we didn't like. We are long on intellect but short on common sense. We were beat up in school.

If you lead analysis, chances are you *are* an analyst, and you know these clichés don't describe you. You know that analysts span the spectra of style, tastes, and personality types. But you also know that *you* can pick out the analyst in any room after about twenty minutes. You know that we earned some of these clichés.

The "academics of intelligence"? More than any group I have encountered outside academia, we analysts loved school. We were good at it. We earned A's and B's and considered a C to be a failure. We enjoy learning and expect to be learning all our lives. We are at home in the world of the mind. We love thinking our way through tough problems. And we even think about thinking.

But we choose a life *outside* academia. We yearn to turn our brainpower into action. Without an interested customer, we feel incomplete. We have various degrees of patience in our quest to produce useful analysis—I have worked with some analysts who could wait a year or two for their research to get into the hands of a customer and others who craved daily contact with a customer. But analysts at both ends of that particular spectrum share a powerful resentment if they suspect their analysis will not be used by some customer to make a decision.

"Legendary introverts"? Well, we have more than our share. By that I mean that compared to the general population, a population of analysts would have a significantly higher percentage. What is the percentage? Surely the CIA's analytic directorate has studied it? Of course not; we were probably afraid of what we would find. Even at the height of the fascination with the Myers-Briggs personality test, which includes an evaluation of the tendency toward introversion or extroversion, I never saw an effort to quantify our overall breakdown. But I'm confident that well over 50 percent of analysts are introverts. I'd bet that also applies to knowledge workers and intellectuals anywhere. Of course, in the intelligence business, put analysts next to our partners—the highly extroverted policy makers and case officers—and we will look painfully shy by comparison.

Obsessed with words? Absolutely. Analysis is useless if not communicated, and words remain our primary communication medium. We labor to find the precise word to convey our meaning. Endless studies of intelligence failure, blaming analysts (rightly) if the audience misunderstands our message, make us work hard at rooting out ambiguous terms.

This obsession is connected also with our reputation for loving so-called weasel words. These are the qualifiers—may, almost certainly, possibly, probably—that litter our products. They are intended to communicate that we are making a judgment rather than stating a fact. They are intended to communicate our level of confidence in that judgment. And they convey our conviction that nuance matters. "It is likely to rain tomorrow" means something different than "It might rain tomorrow." Inexperienced customers of analysis often lose patience over this. "Well, which is it? Rain or not?!" they demand, considering us wimps. I used to tell my analysts that it takes more courage to stand up to such customers than it does to make the prediction. Analysis is no place for wimps.

But as much as analysts yearn to be understood—respected—outside their profession, I have seen them too many times *yearning to be understood by their own leaders*. I have seen many veteran analysts become leaders and founder on their own misperceptions about the men and women they led. It is not that they suddenly forgot what analysts are like. Rather, in the situations I witnessed, I believe these leaders simply didn't take time to think deeply about the nature of their workforce. Over the years, I saw enough leaders (not the majority of leaders, mind you, but too many) fall into the same attitude traps.

# Some Classic Traps

## All Analysis Is the Same

You would think no former analyst would fall for this. A leader of analysis who has been an analyst surely must understand that it is a rich and complex discipline, with distinct approaches to address distinct needs. But leaders of analysis are humans too, and some of them fall victim to the human prejudice that "my experience defines reality." So you might get a new team leader who spent years as a trade analyst flogging his political analysts for more data. "Surely this must be quantifiable!" Or you might get a veteran military analyst demanding that her economists define the economic "center of gravity."

This can go deeper than a simple confusion over terms. When I led the establishment of CIA's Office of Terrorism Analysis after 9/11, we imported many managers to help lead the new organization. Most of these hit the ground running, and I was proud how productive the office became in just weeks. But a few of the new managers struggled to understand that they weren't in Kansas anymore. One came from a career analyzing slow-moving issues, and he struggled to adjust to the front burner. The policy maker appetite for counterterrorism (CT) analysis was unlike anything he had ever dealt with. He was the doctor who couldn't accept the "meatball surgery" normal at the combat field hospital. Another could never seem to grasp that the customers for her targeting analysts were not in the White House. Rather, her analysts needed to identify leads that CT operations officers could follow. In a real way, White House policy makers wanted to understand the enemy, while the ops folks often simply wanted to *find* the enemy. A different analytical approach is required for each.

## All Analysts Think Like I Do

This is related to the "all analysis is the same" mistake, but is both more subtle and more powerful. It can be central to what an analytic leader thinks is achievable in our work.

Two primary approaches to finding answers are rationalism and empiricism. As James Bruce (2008) has written in an insightful essay on epistemology and intelligence,

> In sharp contrast to the rationalist who believes that knowledge is the product of the human mind, the empiricist insists that "sense observation is the primary source and ultimate judge of knowledge and that it is self-deceptive to believe the human mind to have direct access to any kind of truth other than logical relations." Rather than dwelling on reason, the empiricist's focus is on observational data. (Kindle location 2789)

A leader who is principally a rationalist can easily get tripped up dealing with a subordinate who leans toward the empirical. An old joke captures the dilemma. A rationalist and an empiricist share a compartment on a train from London one summer. Looking out the window at a field of sheep, the rationalist notes, "Those sheep have been shorn." With a glance, the empiricist comments, "On *this* side."

Profound differences occur even within the school of rationalism. You will find *deductive* thinkers who draw specific inferences from general principles. (Oranges are fruits. Fruits grow on trees. Therefore, oranges grow on trees.) Or your deductive analyst might say, "Missile programs always conduct a test launch before going into mass production; there has been no test launch of this new missile; therefore, this missile is not yet in mass production." *Inductive* reasoners work in the other direction, drawing a general conclusion from observed particulars. (Every crow we have seen has been black. All crows probably are black.) Or your inductive analyst might reason, "All life we have discovered has required liquid water. To find life on other planets, we should look for liquid water." Other analysts tend toward *abductive* reasoning. Abductive thinkers craft a hypothesis to explain available data. They might infer, for example, "The regime has intervened six times to prop up its currency, but it has taken no action to stem inflation. The regime must be more concerned about revenue from trade than domestic discontent about food prices."

Empiricism and all three types of rationalism have their place in analysis. James Bruce (2008) convincingly argues that the best intelligence analysis comes from consciously and actively mixing the disciplines. But few analysts—and few of their leaders—think about which type of reasoning dominates their own thinking, much less which is most appropriate for the question at hand.

I fell into this trap when I first had to lead military analysts who had been trained as imagery analysts. The world of imagery analysis tends to be empirical. Many imagery analysts will draw conclusions based on what they see and be silent if they see nothing. An imagery analyst's observation, "The tanks are all in garrison," is a powerful reality check for a customer who is nervous about Saddam's immediate military intentions. But as their leader, I would get frustrated when I would ask some of these analysts to judge Saddam's longer-term military intentions. They would ask, "How can we know what is in Saddam's head?" "You are paid to understand Saddam's military thinking," I would reply. And then we'd look blankly at each other. Eventually, I broke out of this trap. The resolution came when we combined our approaches. I would come up with a hypothesis or two about what Saddam might do militarily, and they would think through, "Well, if he wanted to do that, he would need to do *x,* and in its early stages you might see *y.* I'll check the imagery to see if *y* is happening."

I encountered an even deeper division later in my career, when I took over CIA's Weapons Intelligence, Nonproliferation, and Arms Control Center (WINPAC). WINPAC is known for its technical analysts, physicists, biochemists, and many flavors of engineers. My academic studies had focused on political science and history. In the world of engineering, truth is an absolute. Something works or it doesn't. It can or it can't. It is testable and replicable. In the world of historians, the interesting truths lie in *why* something happened, but the truth of "why" rarely can be absolutely established in human behavior. So a political analyst and historian will spend much more energy on reasonable speculation than any engineer would be comfortable with. I learned that I could, with a certain amount of pain, get my engineers to speculate about the future in their areas of expertise. But it was pretty clear that I never convinced them that such informed speculation is part of their job.

## Analysts Are Thinking Machines

There are three manifestations of this trap. I have seen leaders fall into each of them. The first is the leader who seems to forget the analyst is human. The second is the leader who thinks his job is to program the thinking machine. The third is the leader who forgets analysis is as much art as science. Let's examine all three.

The first mistake is to forget that analysts are humans too. Richards Heuer (1999), one of the founders of today's analytic tradecraft, certainly realized that analysts are all too human. He centered his landmark work, *Psychology of Intelligence Analysis,* on the observation that analysts are inescapably human, and they unconsciously will make all the errors of reasoning to which humans are prone unless active steps are taken to compensate. But some leaders believe that once they have taken Heuer's prescribed precautions, the analyst's human nature has been dealt with. These leaders learn the hard way that any group of analysts will have a full set of human emotions, including ambition, jealousy, insecurity, laziness, and selfishness. (Analysts, of course, have all the positive emotions too, but these rarely are problematic.)

The best literature on leadership instructs the leader to understand the human relationship between herself and her subordinates, to bring out the best in them and overcome the worst. I'm not re-creating those lessons in this book. But if a leader of analysts doesn't attend to those lessons, she will lose the trust on which her leadership depends. *You are not leading if no one is following you, and they won't follow you for long if you don't understand human needs for respect, security, fulfillment, and the rest.*

The second dehumanizing mistake is to regard analysts as "thinking machines" to be programmed. I have seen this in leaders who become not just supportive of, but obsessed with, critical thinking techniques. They tend to think that if you teach—and then enforce—critical thinking skills and structured analytic techniques, your analysts will happily crank out sublime products. They also tend to presume that if two competent analysts apply the same fine techniques to the same problem, they will come up with the same answer. Data in; answer out. This oversimplifies analysis and overcontrols analysts. It ignores the reality that people who are paid to think generally resent being told *how* they must think. It also reveals a deep arrogance on the leader's part. He or she thinks, "It is my job to *make you* a good analyst." A healthier mindset is, "It is my job to *help you* become the best analyst you can be." I'll talk more about the upside and downside of prescribed analytic tradecraft and structured analytic techniques in chapter 4.

Connected to the "thinking machine" attitude is the third dehumanizing mistake: forgetting that analysis can be an art. Art is a uniquely human endeavor. Part of analysis is certainly *craft*. Part of improving analysis is to refine the craft. Certainly CIA's definition and refinement of "analytic tradecraft" improved the average quality of our work over the last two decades. But at its best, analysis is *art* too. The art of storytelling. The art of creating an insightful and compelling narrative that will move a customer to useful action. The art of finding the right word, a powerful example, a memorable phrase. Some analysts will only ever be craftsmen. But some will master their craft and go on to become artists. They not only need less guidance from their leaders, they occasionally need to be liberated from guidance. Sometimes they need to be free to produce the unconventional, to occasionally ignore the rules of the craft, to step away from the formulaic. The analyst who is an artist usually does not need a supervisor; she needs a patron.

The art-craft distinction was first evident to me with those imagery analysts I mentioned above. The *best* imagery analysts I worked with didn't struggle with hypotheses like the ones I talked about. Indeed, they were masters at generating their own hypotheses. I considered them "artists" of imagery analysis. And they would bemoan the imagery analysts who were mere craftsmen, limiting themselves to commenting on what they saw. The craftsmen would talk about the *movement* of military units. The artists would talk about the *behavior* of military forces, including the idiosyncratic behavior of certain units that have their own "style."

## I Am Their Most Important Influence

In some situations, this is generally true. And, the more effective leader you are, the *more* true it is. But it is never completely true. In many situations, the analyst's most important influence is other analysts—for good or ill. Ignore this reality at your peril.

What is true in junior high can be true in the world of analysts. As a parent, you like to think your influence guides your kid through his school day. But you know that sometimes peer pressure trumps your best efforts. How does this play out among analysts?

In an analytic organization, the aggregate of analysts' behavior defines the organizational culture. You can influence the culture, but they are its enforcers. If your analysts in general tend to be sloppy, insular, complacent, or arrogant, you have a culture to change. Without active, persistent, multilayered work to develop a new culture, the old culture will enforce its norms. Analysts, being human, want to fit in. Analysts, being analysts, will analyze what this culture rewards and punishes, and they will adjust accordingly.

And I am not simply talking about the analysts' style of behavior. Analysts enforce substantive assessments as well. People presume that it is management that enforces analytic "party lines." This can be true—bureaucracies can try to protect themselves by enforcing a desired consistency of message. But just as often, the analysts themselves enforce their party lines. Experts are particularly adept at this because they can marshal masses of evidence and historical trends to justify maintaining the current line of analysis.

In his brilliant article, "Why Bad Things Happen to Good Analysts," the late Jack Davis (2008) calls this phenomenon "tribal think." He provides a good illustration of "tribal think" at work with the case of a CIA analyst writing before the fall of the Berlin Wall. The analyst argued that the impediments to German reunification were crumbling. As Davis describes,

> This was a bold and prescient departure from CIA's prevailing expert opinion. His well-informed and well-intentioned colleagues each asked for "small changes" to avoid an overstatement of the case here and a misinterpretation of the case there. After the coordination process had finished . . . a reader of the final version of the paper would have to delve deeply into the text to uncover the paradigm-breaking analysis. (Kindle location 2596)

So, what can you do to balance such negative peer pressure among your analysts? Start by determining reality in the situation. Are you dealing with a culture or one bad apple among your analysts? If the problem is a narrow one, breathe a sigh of relief and fix it. If the problem is cultural, you have your work cut out for you. I talk elsewhere in this book about a healthy analytic culture—I won't replay that here. For now, remember a few basic principles. Social media theorist Clay Shirky (2010) points out that a culture is "a community's set of shared assumptions about how it should go about its work, and about its members relations with one another" (Kindle location 1835). Launch a communication *campaign* to challenge the assumptions that are producing the negative behavior. Next, one of the products of a strong culture is a sense of identity. Launch a campaign to implant a new, positive, productive identity in your workplace—a healthier sense of "who we really are." And finally, anytime you are changing a culture, anytime you are taking on *the many*, multiply your influence by enlisting allies. Find analysts whose hearts are in the right place and get them actively displaying the behaviors you want. Try also to enlist a few opinion-makers of the old guard—the owners of the "tribe think." It won't be easy, but if you can get one or two of them to see the sense of change, they can be a powerful force for good.

# Ten Things Analysts Hate

Leaders cannot always make their subordinates happy. There will be times when you need to make choices that ruffle feathers. You will be compelled by priorities that your subordinates dispute. And there will be situations in which you only have unattractive options and your subordinates are firmly in denial.

But the leader should at least be *aware* when he is likely to irritate the people on whom he depends. Avoid doing it needlessly. And when you must anger them, go in with your eyes open. You consciously will make a withdrawal on the bank of trust they have for you, and you must look for opportunities to make a deposit as soon as possible. And make extra time to communicate your reasoning.

Here is a list, by no means exhaustive, of things guaranteed to irritate your analysts.

1. *Being told how to think.* Knowledge workers in general, and certainly analysts, think of themselves as brains for hire. They don't like being told how to use those brains. This is not a rejection of training, although they will be quick to grouse about training they think is beneath them. Rather, it is a rejection of what, in the Navy, we call "rudder orders."

   Normal orders to the helmsman tell him what course to steer. "Come right to course 270," for example. "Rudder orders" are when you not only give the helmsman the new course to steer but tell him how many degrees of rudder he is to use to come to that course. "Right 15 degrees of rudder . . . ease your rudder to 10 degrees . . . ease your rudder to 5 degrees and steady on course 270."

   As with the helmsman in very restricted waters, there will be times when you must tell your analyst what you need him to do and tell him precisely how to do it. This might be the case when a deadline is ludicrously tight, or when some of your analyst's normal array of options for proceeding will backfire. You might have to say, for example, "I need you to analyze the Yemeni president's options. I want it to be a single page examining these three sources. In fact, I need you to open the piece with source number three. And I need this on my desk by 6:30." You can be confident that, hearing this, the analyst will be thinking, "Well, why don't you just do it yourself?" If you find yourself having to give such specific directions, you *must* at least amplify with an explanation of each constraint.

   But such specific direction should be the exception, not the rule. If you are routinely providing such direction, the analyst will hear one message: "I don't trust you." And the analyst will return the sentiment.

2. *Being told the "right" answer.* Analysts are independent thinkers, not your scribes. If you want to do the thinking for your unit, hire a different kind of subordinate to take dictation.

One of your legitimate jobs is to tell an analyst when you are not convinced that he has given you the right answer. You have not found his evidence or reasoning compelling, and he must do more to make his case, or he must broaden his list of possible explanations. This would be a case of you representing the customer and holding your analyst's work to a high standard.

It is also legitimate to fully discuss the topic with your analyst. You will find yourself sitting down with her, listening to her findings, kicking ideas around, and offering your own thoughts and experience.

But it is not legitimate to pronounce the "right" answer and then close your mind to alternatives. That is ideology, not analysis.

3. *A draft stuck in your in-box.* Every analyst has experienced this, and every analyst hates it. She has worked hard to research a topic and to craft her findings into lucid prose. She has regarded this as her most important work, a serious investment of her time and energy that you have endorsed. And now that she has done her best on it, she has turned it in to you for review. And it is sitting there . . . ripening in your in-box. Your excuse—and often it is actually true—is that you are busy with other inescapable priorities. But what she hears is that the least important thing you are doing today is more important than her labor of weeks or months.

There is no single solution to this dilemma. You will certainly have instances where more pressing business prevents you from reviewing the draft promptly. But there are a handful of things that, depending on the situation, may be available to ameliorate the problem. First, communicate. Honestly communicate your best prediction of how soon you are going to be able to turn to the paper. Second, *read* it as soon as you can. Reading it is not the same as reviewing it critically. But that first quick read will tell you whether the paper is ready to be reviewed, or whether it needs more research, a different structure, or clarification of some points. Sometimes that quick first read will serve to immerse you in the paper, and you'll find yourself finished with the review that you had intended to put off. Third, remember you are not the only competent reviewer in your organization. (If you are, that is a business bottleneck you need to fix.) Sometimes you just need to get over yourself and hand the paper to a colleague to review. Finally, deal with the analyst's perception of your disrespect. Find a way to convince her that her product is, indeed, important to you and that she is a valued member of your team whose time you do not regard as disposable.

4. *Not getting credit.* This is also connected to respect. Analysts crave respect. Due credit for their work is both a sign of, and an avenue to, respect.

This is harder than it sounds. The business of analysis generally is the business of supporting someone else who will take an action. The analyst usually is behind the scenes. The action taker—who, by the way, bears the risk—will get the credit or blame for the action. Analysis might be the catalyst for a brilliant action but will rarely be given credit for it.

Another difficulty in handing out proper credit is the team approach to much of today's analysis. The cooperative production of analysis has become the norm in many analytic organizations, with the lone analyst being an anomaly. Doug MacEachon, CIA's senior leader of analysis in the mid-1990s, used to complain that the list of contributors to our papers had gotten so long that he began looking for "Best Boy and Key Grip." With credit being given to a list of names, the name of the principal author or intellectual leader of the project can be lost in a sea of trivial contributors.

The newspaper world deals with this strain with bylines at the top of articles and contributors at the bottom. This approach is unavailable in today's CIA. Although we went back and forth on this point in my career, when I retired the policy was to publish papers without the names of the drafters. The reasoning was twofold. First, the personal security of the analyst was protected in case the paper leaked. Second, our philosophy was that every paper is a product of the organization—drafters, collectors, collaborators, reviewers, designers, and printers—and the whole organization stands behind it.

The final difficulty in giving credit can be found in the schizophrenia of the analysts. As an executive, I frequently called or sent a note to the lead author of excellent papers, telling them how impressed I was with their product. *Every* time I did this, the author demurred. "Oh, thank you, sir, but I can't take credit for this. There were many of us and . . ." Well, bless their hearts.

Despite all these complications, start with the reality that analysts crave respect. Find ways to identify their individual contributions and give them credit accordingly. The single biggest trick in all of this: PAY ATTENTION!

5. *Being misquoted.* This is connected to the analysts' craving for respect and credit but runs in the opposite direction. All analysts fear having something they didn't say being held against them. An intelligence failure happens and this misquote is an albatross dangling from their necks.

   Leaders of analysis are prone to violating this sensitivity. Frequently, we speak for the analysis, paraphrasing its key findings, and drawing them from our imperfect memory. Frequently, we synthesize the analysis, working to find the essence of the thought, the pure idea shed of distracting and (sometimes important) nuance. Occasionally, we prove we are human by completely misunderstanding an analytic line, getting it wrong, but then dutifully giving credit for the incorrect line to the analyst we thought it came from.

   What can we do about this? Make your best effort to quote your analysts accurately. When you are synthesizing their points, consult them. When you strip away their nuance, ask yourself (and them) what you are risking. And most important, establish an environment that *requires* them to speak up when you have been stupid. Finally, my mother's rule: when you have made a mess, clean it up.

6. *Bullies.* There is something deeply psychological in this one, but I'm not competent to diagnose it. I just know it's true. Analysts hate bullies. Deeply. Viscerally.

   And, as in junior high, they encounter bullies frequently. They encounter the rough and ready "men of action" who dismiss them as "some Poindexter" who couldn't survive in the real world. They encounter people of power who press them to give analysis a subservient spin. They even encounter other analysts who are intellectual bullies, using their logic or expertise to beat into silence any who disagree. And of course, they encounter you, their leaders, some of whom brook no dissent. If you are one of those, have no doubt: your analysts hate you.

   What is required of you here? First, help your analysts understand when and how to stand up to bullies. Second, help your analysts thicken their hides and ignore much of the bullying they encounter. Finally, make certain that their analysis is not being influenced by the bullying—that they are not caught up in the emotion of the situation and losing their objectivity.

7. *Having to answer the same question over and over.* In the heart of every analyst is the hard-bitten general, saying, "I hate to win the same ground twice!" They like to feel like they are getting somewhere. Once they feel that they have satisfactorily answered a question, they hate to have to come back to it for the same customer. From my experience, this amounts to "hate" in two situations. One situation arises when the analysts' leader says, "I think it is time to update the customer on this topic." In response, the analyst reflexively chooses from the following menu of responses: (1) We wrote on that just recently; (2) Nothing has changed in the situation; (3) Did the customer specifically ask for this? They feel like your request breaks their momentum and moves them back two squares.

The other situation arises when the customer disliked the answer he got the last time and wants a reexamination. This triggers mild irritation when the analyst suspects the customer is skeptical. It triggers a much stronger emotion when the analyst thinks the customer's mind is closed. "Since you don't believe anything I am telling you, why do you keep asking me?" The analyst smells an ideologue and perhaps a bully.

The leader's best tool here is situational awareness. Ask, What is really going on here? Did we really report on the situation "recently"? My experience is that analysts' definition of "recently" is off by several months. Is the customer hard to convince for a good reason? Then it is incumbent on us to work harder to find the best evidence, to make the most compelling case, and to challenge our own assumptions. Is the customer really trying to bully the analysts? In such cases, at some point it is your job to draw a line and say to the customer, "enough." As I saw DDI Jami Miscik tell senior customers several times, "You have seen our analysis; it hasn't changed; we will update you when significant new evidence emerges."

8. *Having to listen to "idiots."* Oddly, this was especially a gripe of my best analysts. Who are the idiots? Any analyst whom your analysts regard as sloppy, or dilettante, or biased. They are analysts with whom your analyst must coordinate drafts or analysts sending their own inferior products to your customers. At heart, most good analysts wish that these "idiots" were not allowed to publish or speak. You'll hear them complain, "They're just putting noise in the system, confusing our customers!" But as leaders, we not only fail to silence "those idiots," we must require our good analysts to deal with them and their message.

There are several things going on here that you have to teach your analysts to appreciate (or at least tolerate). First, "those idiots" force your analysts to hone their own case, tighten their argumentation, and clarify their points. In the end the customer gets a better product. Second, sometimes the "idiots" are right. Sometimes they simply get lucky, making a guess that turns out to be correct. Sometimes, because of their lesser expertise, the "idiots" are not as fixated on precedent and pattern as experts often are. Third, your analysts are deluded if they think the "idiots" can be silenced. Our customers will always receive analysis or pseudo-analysis from many sources; your analysts must acknowledge, compete with, and sometimes deal with those alternative views, not just wish them away. Finally, your analysts' contempt for "those idiots" reveals an arrogance you need to address.

9. *Monday morning quarterbacks.* These are the people who, after the game, pontificate about what the analyst *should* have seen, or thought, or produced. In the intelligence community, we even formalize the function of Monday morning quarterback, especially after suspected intelligence failures, with the post-mortem review. No analyst whose work has been criticized in a post mortem feels fairly treated. The analyst hears a shrill accusation, "We can't believe you missed *that!*" And the analyst sinks deeper into his cynical self. Reality seems clear, cause and effect seems inevitable, after the fact. But in the middle of the game, nothing is so clear. And unlike on the football field, where just one game is being played, in an analyst's routine, several games are being juggled—other projects and responsibilities are competing for an analyst's attention.

There are several things a leader can do to help in this situation, but the leader *cannot* do what the analysts most hope for: make the post mortem go away. If analysis is going to be a key player in decision making—in other words, if analysis is going to matter—expect it to be held up to scrutiny after each significant failure. And *our own* examination of our work is vital—clear-eyed evaluation of what we did well and what we can improve. So short of preventing the pain, how can a leader help?

The leader can brace the analyst for the inevitable. Just as decision makers cannot hide from the results of their gambles, the analysis supporting them is fair game for judgment. Knowing that such scrutiny is coming can even help keep us honest, can keep our own complacency at bay. At minimum, the leader can help the analysts steel themselves for the experience. Even better, the leader can help the analysts discriminate between the Monday morning quarterbacks who should be dismissed, the ones who should be humored, and the ones who should be seriously engaged.

The leader can establish an environment in which constructive criticism is normal. Some businesses do this well. For example, Pixar employees are expected to give constructive feedback on each other's work (Sims 2011; Sims describes Pixar's effort to build a culture where "there's no penalty for criticizing the work"). Or look at some Army training settings, where a "hot wash-up" happens after each exercise, picking apart what decisions were made and why. Part of the leader's responsibility here is to not tolerate *unconstructive* criticism.

Finally, the leader can embrace and engender an attitude of suitable humility. By "embrace" I mean the leader can visibly step up to his own responsibility for any analytic failure in his organization. By "engender" I mean the leader can consistently challenge the intellectual arrogance to which analysts are prone. By "suitable humility" I mean an attitude open to learning opportunities, dedicated to constant improvement, and acknowledging that our best is all that we can do. I distinguish this from *unsuitable* humility, to which leaders of analysis are often prone. I used to post one rule on the whiteboard at the start of meetings where my staff—all of them leaders—would assess our organization's performance: "NO WE-SUCKATHON!" This addressed a tendency to look at our work and launch into a death spiral of self-flagellation. Try to maintain a healthy balance between humility and pride.

10. *Being out of the loop.* Of things analysts hate, this might be the biggest. It is certainly the one I encountered most often in three decades of working in analysis. There is nothing more inhibiting to an analyst than the feeling that you will look stupid if you say something that others in the room *know* to be wrong because they have a piece of information you do not. If you suspect they know something you don't, you will tend to just shut up. At the same time, you will be seething because they have a secret that hasn't been shared with you. Everybody is playing this game of five-card stud, but you have been dealt four cards. More than feeling disadvantaged, you feel offended.

This is not irritation at having incomplete information. That is the analyst's world. The analyst's job starts with information gaps. And it is not irritation that *someone* knows something you don't. The foe will always know something you do not, and your job is to figure it out.

Rather, it is irritation that someone *on your side* knows something you don't. It might be a collector, it might be a partner, it might be a customer, or it might be the analyst's leader.

In the world of classified intelligence, this is the issue of "need to know." That is, there is a category of collected intelligence that is shown only to individuals with a certified "need to know" that material. Intelligence analysts understand the "need to know" principle intellectually, but they have too often seen it as a way of restricting intelligence to a ridiculously small circle that excludes them. They also resent that "need to know" too often is enforced by people who don't understand the analyst's work well enough to anticipate the analyst's need. They resent that "need to know" is sometimes really "need to plead"; that is, a requirement to beg for what analysts believe is rightfully theirs. And they resent that they cannot even plead for intelligence that they don't know exists.

All of these weaknesses have long been evident to senior leaders of intelligence. Several intelligence community executives, after the establishment of the Director of National Intelligence, said they would replace the principle of "need to know" with one of "need to share." This would put the burden on collectors to err on the side of sharing their information with analysts. Enforcement has been spotty, and at least some intelligence community executives don't use the "need to share" mantra anymore. The WikiLeaks and Snowden scandals show real danger in oversharing.

But the hatred of being out of the loop is not restricted to analysts in the world of classified intelligence. In the corporate world, many analysts encounter not just trade secrets but hoarders of inside information. Also I have participated in dozens of conferences where academic experts with no access to classified information would discuss substance with analysts inside the intelligence community. Almost every time, at least one of the academics would reveal a deep-seated feeling of disadvantage. Almost every time, the academic would ask questions designed to at least discover whether meaningful classified information exists that would change their assessments.

And analysts everywhere bristle when they learn that their bosses had relevant information they did not deign to share. It might be an insight about a conversation with the customer that would have changed the answer the analyst developed. It might be a boss's knowledge of a changing landscape that makes obsolete the analyst's approach to a project. Or it simply might be the boss who knows, but doesn't articulate clearly, what he or she wants the analyst's project to achieve.

So what can you do about your analysts' hatred of being out of the loop? First, as with so much else in leadership, *communicate, communicate, communicate.* Don't be the boss I just described who knows what he or she wants from the analyst but doesn't tell the analyst. If you have to make a "need to know" decision that rules against the analyst, communicate your reasoning and make a commitment to reevaluate the situation as it develops.

Second, be a loop-opening champion of the analysts. Work visibly and relentlessly to help your analysts get access to information that can help them. Bring your analysts with you to meet with customers face to face. Talk to your analysts about what the "front office" is thinking and planning. Work to get your analysts into decision-making meetings so they can see the impact (or absence of impact) of their analysis.

Third, expect that the analysts will hate anything short of perfection in this area and that you will be unable to deliver perfection. Your only obligation is to do your best to deliver progress.

All of this amounts to being attentive to the complex human individuals who call you "boss." It is about being sensitive to analysts' tendencies and diversity—what they crave and what they hate. It doesn't require pandering to their pettiness or selfishness or spoiling them in any way. And it doesn't involve protecting them from the world's harsh realities. It amounts to stepping out of your head and into theirs to bring out their best and stem their worst. They are by far your most precious asset. Motivating them, earning their trust—in simplest terms, *leading* them—requires understanding them.

## KEY THEMES

Avoid these misconceptions about analysis and analysts:

- All analysis is the same.
- All analysts *think* like I do (they use my approach to reasoning).
- Analysts are tools—*thinking machines*—for you to use.
- I am their most important influence. (Sometimes that's true, but sometimes their peers or the workplace culture will dominate.)

Here are ten things you can expect your analysts to hate. (You don't control all ten.)

- Being told *how* to think.
- Being told the "right" answer.
- A draft stuck in your in box.
- Not getting credit for their ideas/insights.
- Being misquoted.
- Bullies (you or anyone).
- Having to answer the same question over and over.
- Having to listen to "idiots" (people whose reasoning they have dismissed).
- Monday morning quarterbacks (people who have the benefit of hindsight).
- Being out of the loop.

Don't think you are going to protect your analysts from everything they hate. Some of these things (like bullies) come with the territory. You can help your analysts respond maturely and productively. But if you trigger these irritations needlessly and repeatedly, one of the things they hate will be you.

# 3

# Shaping the Environment

I f you are leading analysis, you are responsible for more than the analysts whom you lead. You are responsible to nurture an environment that brings out their best. This is one of the greatest challenges you will face. There are many ways to get it wrong, and how to get it right can be a moving target. And there is much that is counterintuitive for the high-achieving, hardworking leader.

Don't get me wrong here. It's not about the physical environment. I've seen analysts thrive in wartime Baghdad and Kabul. It's not about pay and incentives. I've seen GS-10s in the basement outperform GS-15s with a window office. It's about nurturing an environment that maximizes the potential that your analysts will think the thought—hatch the analytic insight—that makes a difference.

I will not provide you a formula for establishing the optimum analytic environment. I have never discovered one that applies across situations. But I will point out approaches that I have seen that are consistently counterproductive. And I will give you this advice: always, always, always keep your eye on balance.

## Nurturing Trust Is Job 1

Leading involves moving people to do what they wouldn't on their own. Nudging them when they are stuck on idle. Heading them in a direction they didn't think of themselves or one they disagree with. Leading requires telling a worker what he just delivered is not good enough. Coaching, correcting, challenging, critiquing. Leading requires deciding between two subordinates who advocate opposite views, picking winners and losers on an issue about which they care deeply. Leading requires firing people who are not right for the organization. I have done all of this and been thanked and respected—even by those on the losing end—because they trusted me. I have done all these things and been bitterly resented—even by those on the winning end—because they didn't trust me. What a delicate, tricky business is earning and keeping peoples' consent to be led.

There are no simple formulas, but there is a simple starting point. Start with your workforce. If you have recruited the right analytic talent, you have a force of smart, driven, hardworking people who want to do work that matters. If you haven't hired such talent, it doesn't matter what you do, you won't get excellent analysis from them—the best you might get are decent assistants who can help *you* do analysis. But if you *have* hired real talent, they should be a joy to lead. If they are not, *you* are doing something wrong.

I say start with the workforce rather than individual workers. Trust is given or withheld by each of them, and you will always have to navigate your relationship with these individuals. But you lead a spectrum of individuals. Some are naturally trusting. Some are cynics. And if your organization is large enough, it almost certainly contains individuals who do not deserve *your* trust. But the workforce, not the individuals—the macro situation—should determine your default setting. For a workforce of talented, dedicated, bright analysts, *your default setting should be that you trust them enough to give them a lot of latitude.*

To some extent, our challenges are not unique. In their article for *Harvard Business Review,* "Leading Clever People," Rob Goffee and Gareth Jones (2007) discuss the special challenges of managing "people who don't want to be led and may be smarter than you." Such people are the norm in an analytic cadre. Goffee and Jones advise, "If you try to push your clever people, you will end up driving them away. As many leaders of highly creative people have learned, you need to be a benevolent guardian rather than a traditional boss."

I have seen too many leaders of analysis pay lip service to what a talented workforce they have and then demonstrate a fundamental lack of trust. Beyond training and coaching, they will tell the analyst what to do and how to do it, how to think, and what to say. They will hold the analysts' work to a standard they cannot always articulate and imply that anything short of that standard is not just imperfect, but sloppy. Some will provide endless formulas for the work and then complain that the analysts are not thinking for themselves. Soon the workforce proves that trust is a two-way street; they begin to demonstrate their own distrust of the leader. They will complain about every decision and policy, inflate every leadership lapse into workplace legend, and channel at least some of their analytic talent into exquisite whining. If that is the behavior you are getting from your analysts, you are probably thinking, "What's wrong with them? They are so childish!!" What might be wrong is that you have an environment that treats them like children, and they have responded accordingly.

Frequently, what is wrong is that these leaders were oblivious to any of the "Ten Things Analysts Hate" I listed in chapter 2. Here's the list again:

1. Being told how to think.

2. Being told the "right" answer.

3. A draft stuck in your in-box.

4. Not getting credit.

5. Being misquoted.

6. Bullies.

7. Having to answer the same question over and over.

8. Having to listen to "idiots."

9. Monday morning quarterbacks.

10. Being out of the loop.

Remember that you won't always be able to protect your analysts from these irritations. But violate them frequently and your analysts will feel violated. Trust cannot be established against that backdrop.

It is certainly not enough for a leader to trust the workforce and let them fly. The analysts—regardless of their talent—need leadership. They need direction and channeling; they need strategic priorities and connection beyond their community. They need challenge. They need standards and correction. But they won't accept any of these things if they don't trust you, and they won't trust you if you don't trust them.

I have seen a few deluded leaders of analysis take the position, "I don't require their trust. I simply require their compliance." They tended to be tough-as-nails commanders of analysis, quick to say, "Don't give me that crap about how you *feel*; we don't pay you for your feelings. We pay you to *produce*." That might work if analysis were a formulaic business—take these steps, follow this procedure, avoid these pitfalls, and produce answers to the customers' questions. Compliance and formulas can make the analysts generate products, but they cannot make them generate insights.

Eliciting insightful analysis requires more. It requires the leader to draw the analysts' best from them. It requires engaging the analysts' emotions, initiative, and energy. It requires that the analysts care enough about the issue that their mind is chewing on the toughest parts even when they are off work. XPRIZE founder Peter Diamandis says it well: you need to capture their "shower time." "What are they thinking about in the shower? If they're working in an exciting place, they're not thinking what they're going to do over the weekend. They're thinking: How do I solve that problem? It's capturing their subconscious time" (McGregor 2015).

Surprisingly, superb analysts can deepen the hard-nosed leaders' delusions. Consider a terrific analyst I'll call "Nell." Without the leader doing anything to bring out her best, Nell gave her best anyway. Chances are something else was driving her. Perhaps the mission was so important she overlooked her boss's innate distrust. Or perhaps her pride ran so deep that she needed no external factor to elicit her best effort. Whatever drove her, her performance was superb and the leader would point to her and say, "See! That's what I want from all of you! Why can't you all give that level of effort and quality?" What the boss was really doing was pointing to the one person who didn't really need his leadership and complaining that everyone wasn't like her.

There is nothing like honest communication—talking *and* listening—to enlist the trust of your analysts. Honest communication includes your acknowledgment that you don't have all the answers—that you need them to come up with many of the answers themselves. Honest communication includes showing that you are a real person with strengths and weaknesses and problems with which they can empathize.

And honest communication includes your explanation of *why*. Analysts analyze your behavior; they want to figure out why you did this and not that. Analysts—and knowledge workers in general—are always interested in getting past the face of a thing to the underlying truths. So never expect it to go well when you give them an order and simply expect them to follow it. Tell them why you are *asking* them to do something. ("Because I said so!" is no answer.)

Once you have a nurtured an open and trusting relationship with your analysts, everything becomes easier. Without trust, your guidance will be taken as dictatorial, your coaching as micromanagement, and your correction as perfectionism. With trust, the same guidance, coaching, and correction will be taken as wise and helpful. Without trust, you will never have an analyst come to you and confess that he just doesn't understand something. With trust, both you and your analyst will be comfortable confessing limits, and working together you will blow by them.

## Taking the Pulse

There are some things you can easily examine to help you gauge whether you have a positive, productive, trusting environment. Are your best people enthusiastic or angry? Does the general population of your analysts feel energized or stifled? Is a flow of analytic insights coming from them? Are your subordinate leaders—including the informal analytic leaders—taking initiative? How does the attrition look? Are the wrong people leaving the organization? These are straightforward questions, and it should not take you long to determine the answers. If the answers all look bad, you have a serious environment problem.

In assessing the health of your environment, be careful of flawed indicators. You'd think analysts would be good at smoking out invalid indicators, but a few are powerfully seductive. Here are flawed indicators I have encountered:

- Are people happy? Yes, you must concern yourself with your subordinates' happiness. If they are *unhappy*, you have a problem. But you'll find the state of "happy" damnably hard to identify and not always a relevant indicator of the health of your organization. Take, for example, the analysts I worked with in counterterrorism after 9/11. Happy? No . . . they were grimly determined. They were outraged by what Al Qa'ida had done and were driven to help defeat it. The closest they came to "happy" was their sober satisfaction when they saw their work paying off. My job wasn't to make them "happy"; my job was to help fix things that made them visibly unhappy, which quite simply was anything that got in the way of their effectiveness.

- Are people busy? As with an unhappy workforce, an un-busy workforce is a bad thing. As a leader of analysts, you are wasting your most precious resource if they are watching the clock. But a workforce that is busy doesn't mean that your resources are being well spent. Their day may be filled with activities, but that tells you nothing about the value of those activities. Or they may *look* busy because they are good at not letting you catch them looking idle. The other thing wrong with busyness as an indicator for analysts is that you cannot always detect it. The analyst staring out a window might be busy thinking. The analyst reading *WIRED* magazine might be on the verge of hatching a truly fresh insight. You must give them room for such seemingly "inactive" activities.

- Are people productive? Just as you cannot afford an unhappy or un-busy workforce, you cannot afford an unproductive workforce. But a high volume of production, by itself, is an insufficient indicator of health. Even a high volume of high-quality production might be insufficient. What you require is a high volume of high-*value* production. High-value production either helps an important customer today or it helps grow the expertise of the analyst for tomorrow.

Part of taking your unit's pulse is analyzing what pulse best suits your mission. If your unit is providing crisis support to high-stakes decision makers, expect your unit's activity to be frenetic. Your challenge will be to consider how best to generate fresh and useful insights despite what might be an exhausting workflow. Or perhaps your unit is one with the mission of discovering new insights hidden in masses of data. That mission requires much trial and error, following many leads that turn out to be dead ends, and coping with the reality that you rarely know you are close to a discovery until you have discovered it. Your challenge might be to contrive ways to keep your crew energized when they are having a streak of fruitless explorations. Or perhaps your unit's principal responsibility is warning. Your challenge here might be to create an environment resistant to the powerful temptation to cry wolf.

It is also important to realize that your unit's mission is probably dynamic, so the environment that suits it well in one phase of its work might not suit another. When I led Iraq analysts in the 1990s, for example, we were a high-performing crisis team. Supporting senior policy makers in repeated, high-stakes confrontations with Saddam was our norm. I used to think that running to a White House meeting on Christmas Eve was simply nature's way of saying I work on Iraq. A big challenge for me was dealing with the gaps between the crises. We could never know how long those gaps would last. Those periods required me to consciously build a different work environment. I wanted analysts to get a chance to rest up for the next crisis. But I also wanted them to take advantage of the quiet by launching fresh research and by developing analytic notions they had hatched but could not pursue during the last crisis. The single hardest challenge was that extended crises tended to build analysts who were almost exclusively reactive. In the gaps between crises I struggled to coax them to take creative initiative. I learned to anticipate the fluctuations in our battle rhythms. I learned to ask my analysts in the crisis, "What do you wish you had time to do?" They answered with interesting analytic notions, like "I'd dig deeper on the interests of tribes." Then, in the quiet between crises, I could bring them back to that notion and say, "Start your research on tribes, even if you might not be able to finish it."

## Four Critical Balances

The mission will determine the optimum balance for your unit's work environment, but the operative word here is *balance*. No matter what your unit's mission, no matter how exquisitely your analysts trust you, to nurture a healthy analytic environment, you will have to establish a healthy balance in each of several pairs of tensions:

- Imaginative vs. pragmatic analysis

- Breadth vs. depth of expertise

- Eliminating mistakes vs. generating insights

- Reacting (to events and customer needs) vs. initiating (analysis)

These are not tensions between good and bad. These are tensions between business requirements that frequently pull in opposite directions. You will need to produce pragmatic *and* imaginative analysis, for example.

You will need breadth *and* depth. But what it takes to deliver more of one element often comes at the expense of its mate. Each pair of elements affects the DNA of your organization. *And in all cases, the extremes are to be avoided.*

## Imaginative vs. Pragmatic

The 9/11 Commission faulted CIA analysis for a "failure of imagination" (National Commission on Terrorist Attacks Upon the United States 2004). The Weapons of Mass Destruction (WMD) Commission blamed CIA analysts for, in effect, imagining a threat that was no longer there (Commission on the Intelligence Capabilities of the United States 2005).[1] Yes, the irony was not lost on us. And yes, both commissions produced seriously flawed reports. But they point to a significant tension in our business. Analysis can fail from too much imagination or too little.

You must tend the balance in your unit between imagination and pragmatism. In chapter 5, I will discuss the related issue of nurturing creativity in your organization; I'll go into more detail there about why there is a natural tendency among analysts to "get real." As they do in reaction to genuine creativity, hard-nosed analysts can too easily dismiss imagination as flights of fancy, with no place in our business. Their first retort to a genuinely imaginative hypothesis usually is, "Oh, puh-lease . . . there is no evidence for that!"

Don't get me wrong. Even the most pragmatic analysts use imagination. They imagine models that explain the data. They imagine outcomes that extrapolate from the current trends. And they imagine straight lines that connect dots. But the most imaginative analysts are comfortable going far beyond this. They are much more likely to ask, "What if . . .?" They are not intimidated by a dearth of evidence. Indeed, they are much more willing to spend time or collection resources looking for evidence that they are not sure exists. The imaginative analyst is much more willing to toy with fresh models that might explain available data. The imaginative analyst might come up with a double helix as the structure for DNA, when the pragmatic analyst never will.

This is not just a difference *between* individuals who are more naturally imaginative and others who are more naturally pragmatic. Every *individual* has imaginative days and pragmatic days. You need both tendencies in your analytic organization. You need the freshness that imagination brings. You

---

[1] In the Overview of the Report, Introduction, it states: "On the brink of war, and in front of the whole world, the United States government asserted that Saddam Hussein had reconstituted his nuclear weapons program, had biological weapons and mobile biological weapon production facilities, and had stockpiled and was producing chemical weapons. All of this was based on the assessments of the U.S. Intelligence Community. And not one bit of it could be confirmed when the war was over."

need the people who can imagine tomorrow looking significantly different than today. You need people who can find new evidence by first imagining that it exists or that it is hiding in a place we never thought to look. And you need the practicality that refuses to let you ignore the evidence in hand—the pragmatism that is not afraid to point out that most trends *do* follow past patterns most of the time.

In thinking about this balance in your organization, ask these questions: Is the analysis feeling stale? Does the unit seem uncomfortable discussing new hypotheses? Does the unit recoil from challenges to the consensus? Do your formats for writing look rigidly formulaic? Does the unit act hamstrung by absence of empirical evidence? Each of these requires you to do something to inject imagination into the organization.

Alternatively, does the unit have trouble bringing anything to closure? Does it engage in endless "what if" conversations? Does it have a reputation of frightening every audience with catastrophic possibilities? ("My hair is on fire and I won't be happy until yours is too!") This unit is desperate for some practical parameters and grounding truths.

## Breadth vs. Depth

This is another inescapable tension in every analytic environment. You need substantive experts—people who have deeply studied the issue at hand. You also need generalists—people who move from issue to issue to issue, picking up insights and skills along the way.

Have only experts, and you have a set of analysts who are very wedded to the trends and dynamics they understand so deeply. (Nearly all the famous intelligence failures had genuine experts on the job.) Have only experts, and when a crisis erupts in a backwater, you will have little flexibility to respond to it. Your experts will tell you explicitly, "I have been studying nuclear weapons for 15 years. You can't waste me by putting me on a political crisis in Haiti!" Generalists, people who are comfortable moving around and people who bring fresh perspectives to every issue, will help in all these situations.

Have only generalists, and you have analysts who will be quickly productive on that Haiti crisis. They may have seen political crises elsewhere and can translate what made sense in Honduras to what should make sense in Haiti. But their sense-making will necessarily be shallow. They will not have insight, say, on how voodoo influences Haitian politics. Have only generalists, and your customers will look elsewhere for expert input.

In any analytic organization, the combination of experts and generalists can be powerful. The experts bring deep knowledge and credibility and the generalists bring freshness, relevant new knowledge, and task flexibility. But what balance is appropriate?

Clearly that depends on your mission. If the issues your unit studies are deeply technical, you may need 80 percent of your analysts to be technically expert. If the issues are highly dynamic and short-fused, perhaps 70 percent of your analysts are generalists. Whatever the situation, avoid the extremes. One hundred percent experts or 100 percent generalists is always the wrong answer.

But whatever balance you think best serves your mission, look at the balance from several perspectives. The terms *expert* and *generalists* will help you judge the balance between breadth and depth in your entire organization, but you will need to look deeper.

### Personal Expertise

I mentioned the "generalist" who moved from a political crisis in Honduras to one in Haiti. That analyst actually might have built personal expertise in political instability in Latin America. Or you might channel his assignments in a way that helps him become an expert in coup aftermaths, if you think that specialty could be useful for your organization. An expert in, say, nuclear reactors might have a broad understanding of Third World industrial practices. And both analysts might benefit from readings in, say, cultural anthropology.

Your analyst will benefit from discussing with you how she might usefully broaden *and* deepen her knowledge. Start with her personal tastes and tendencies and channel those into experiences and training that serve the organization today and tomorrow.

### Skills Mix on Tasks

For each analytic project you assign, bring in the most varied skills you can afford. Even when you have a single analyst drafting a paper, invite analysts with a range of relevant other skills to critically comment on the draft. When the topic is a high-stakes one, you'll need more than several analysts involved in review. You probably will need several analysts involved from the beginning, and you'll need to ensure that those analysts are as diverse as possible (see chapter 2, "Understanding Analysts," about the diversity of approaches to reasoning among analysts). On high-stakes issues you will want a mix of empiricists, inductive reasoners, abductive reasoners, and deductive reasoners.

### Breadth of Exposure

Expert or generalist, every analyst who I sent to work directly with the customer came back a more effective analyst. Every analyst who had a wacky hobby, went on sabbatical, moved desks for a year, tried to write poetry, or spent six months on the night watch picked up something that helped with his primary job. Analysts learn for a living and they learn quickly from such experiences. Analysts are thinkers for a living, and at some unconscious level, they are mulling their analytic challenge even when their brain is relaxing with that wacky hobby. The only difference between analysts in this respect is that you need to force some into broadening and refreshing experiences, while others are addicted to them.

The benefits from a broad exposure are so evident, of course, that it can be overdone. Every staff and commission that examines analysts in the intelligence community mandates broader exposure. Their prescription for building analysts almost looks like a Mad Lib: *The analysts should be required to do (length of assignment) to (another intelligence agency, a collector, a policy shop, the military, an embassy, industry, academia, language immersion, a congressional staff).* Don't get me wrong; these prescriptions have merit. But add all the "required" exposure-assignments together and there is no time left in an analyst's career to do analysis. In my function as a senior leader of analysts, I would make sure individuals from my organization were on each of these types of rotation at any given time. In aggregate, the analysts developed a highly useful breadth of knowledge. This aggregate breadth of experience was powerful as long as the analysts were communicating with each other. But no single analyst would be allowed to be on a perpetual tour of such assignments. Indeed, we recognized something about the individual analysts who signed up for every "out of body" assignment available: they did not really want to be analysts.

## Eliminating Mistakes vs. Generating Insights

Every organization that has been chastised for making a big error reacts by generating mandatory procedures to prevent its recurrence. They used to tell us in the Navy, "Our safety rules are written in blood," meaning "You are required to wear goggles for this job because some poor sailor lost an eye doing it."

At CIA's analytic directorate, our error prevention procedures are broadly termed *analytic tradecraft.* We lifted the term from our espionage directorate, which had long taught "operational tradecraft" practices intended to keep our officers and assets effective (and alive) in a dangerous environment.

Analytic tradecraft began to be built around the groundbreaking work of Dick Heuer and Jack Davis to address chronic weaknesses in analysis. They showed that analysts, being human, come with a full set of biases, mindsets, and assumptions. Although those biases help them filter data and make sense of a complicated world, they occasionally lead analysts to serious error. Heuer, Davis, and others crafted techniques and disciplines to address that vulnerability and to refine critical thinking. Tradecraft also came to include prescriptions for communicating effectively with busy customers (e.g., "Put your bottom line up front").

Analytic tradecraft was in place in the directorate before the Iraq WMD intelligence failure but was refined and reemphasized after it. Greater emphasis was put on the need to make our reasoning explicit—with customers more skeptical than ever, we needed to show them *why* we believe something. We also needed to show the customers the strength (or weakness) of our sourcing. As Director of WINPAC, I knew analytic tradecraft was critical to our effort to rebuild the trust of our customers. This work on analytic tradecraft has been—and still is—vital.

But analytic tradecraft has its limits. Usually, it only prevents us from being *wrong or misunderstood*; by itself, the tradecraft doesn't make us *useful*. The goggles prevent the Navy Machinist's Mate from taking a metal splinter in the eye; the goggles don't grind the valve. What makes analysis useful is *insight*. We generate an insight that helps a customer make a good decision. Tradecraft might require that your analysis contains—even highlights—an insight, but it rarely generates the insight.

Insights can come from several places. A seasoned analyst might see patterns others miss. An expert might weigh factors and variables differently than other observers. A source might deliver a critical piece of evidence. A data scientist might discover a valuable truth hidden in a mass of data impenetrable to others. A new analyst might see relationships or parallels that the experts were blind to. Or several analysts in dialogue might put thoughts together that spawn a brand new idea. Chapter 5 discusses the commonalities between insight, creativity, and innovation and explores the kind of environment that encourages all three.

But is there a tension between analytic tradecraft and the spawning of insight? Rigor need not stifle insight. Indeed, it can make the insight more convincing. Occasionally tradecraft might even trigger an insight. For example, application of Heuer's Analysis of Competing Hypotheses technique might force you to consider carefully an alternative you had previously glossed over, allowing you to see that a bit of evidence you had missed before makes all the difference. So what is the problem?

Gary Klein (2013: 156) captured the problem when he introduced the very useful concept of "up arrows" and "down arrows" as components of performance. In *Seeing What Others Don't,* he provides this equation:

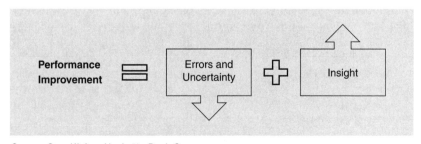

*Source:* Gary Klein – Hachette Book Group.

This means that improving performance is a combination of reducing mistakes (the down arrow) and generating insights (the up arrow). He notes that organizations frequently fall into the trap of obsessing with the down arrow (easy to articulate procedures for reducing mistakes) and ignoring the up arrow (elusive elements of generating insight). And he particularly points to the intelligence community's analytic tradecraft as being all about the down arrow. "The intelligence community has a unit to enforce tradecraft, the Office of Analytic Integrity and Standards. Its job is to reduce mistakes and unsupported conclusions" (Klein 2013: 158).

Imbalance arises when you, as a leader, obsess with one element at the expense of the other. The error can be made in either direction. The leader obsessed with tradecraft can unintentionally convey that the most important thing is for his analysts to avoid mistakes. Or that leader might sap his analysts' energy following prescribed tradecraft procedures, leaving no energy for creative thought. He might edit out insight because it seems half-baked or hide an insight behind a meticulous airing of all possibilities.

On the other side, a leader obsessed with insight can also be destructive. Never attend to rigor (analytic tradecraft), and you will find your analysts—being human—getting sloppy in their reasoning and their communication. Their writing often will be littered with hyperbole. Publish a string of half-baked insights and your busy customers will start to conclude they haven't time for analysis that is merely speculative. Or you might deliver a product that is brilliantly insightful and compellingly reasoned, sweeping the customer along and provoking the customer to make an expensive decision, only to have the case collapse the next week with the arrival of contrary evidence.

In assessing the appropriate balance for your unit, be mindful that tradecraft has some natural advantages over insight in the competition for your analysts' energies. First, it is easier to teach tradecraft than insight. It is easier to teach procedures than creativity. And most institutions examining an intelligence failure will find that the analyst did something "wrong," presume that the mistake caused the failure, and promise to never let that mistake be repeated. If your bureaucracy is one that tends to push tradecraft, you might have to even the balance by stressing insight.

Your particular analytic institution might not even use the term *tradecraft*, but that does not mean the concept is alien. Your organization might refer instead to quality control, rigor, due diligence, analytic standards, journalism standards, or critical thinking techniques. They are all getting at the same concept: measures intended to reduce mistakes.

Regardless of the bias of your institution regarding mistakes or insights, your job is to attend to both things at once. Your job is to reduce the mistakes and maximize the insights coming from your analysts. The "up arrow" *and* the "down arrow."

Be clear about what a "mistake" is. It is not a mistake, for example, if you published a prediction saying there was a 90 percent chance of rain and it did not rain—as long as it rains 90 percent of the times you make that prediction. It is a mistake, however, to publish that it *will* rain tomorrow— with no indicator of uncertainty—if it does not.

In attending to *insight*, be clear that not all insights are created equal. Your analyst will occasionally write something like, "Whoever wins the final point will win the tennis match." (For those of you who don't play tennis, that is why they call it the "winning point.") Even if that reality had never occurred to you before, it has no predictive value. But if your analyst casually mentions that this tennis match is on a clay court and one of the players only has experience on asphalt, your job is to recognize that as an important insight and highlight it.

## *Right* and *Wrong* in Analysis

Leaders of analysis need to be clear about what they mean by the terms *right* and *wrong*. They need to help customers understand what analysis can realistically deliver, and they need to help analysts understand what is expected of them.

The complexity of the issue can be captured in a simple story: I look at your bald tires and tell you I think you are going to have a blowout on your long drive home tonight. You drive gently and arrive safely home but notice that one of your tires is now nearly flat. Was my analysis "wrong"? You certainly did not have a blowout. But my analysis was useful; it might even have saved your life. The impact of my analysis was to change your behavior, and that might have averted disaster. We cannot know for sure. But it's a good bet that you are glad I looked at your tires and provided my analysis. Both you and I can consider this an analytic success story.

It could have gone otherwise. Had I looked at your tires and pronounced them fine for another thousand miles, I would have been *wrong*. Had I looked at your tires and concluded a blowout was likely but said nothing, I would not have been wrong, but I would have failed my responsibility. Had I examined your tires and pronounced, "Four tires never blow at the same time," I'd have been *right but useless*, another failure.

Of course, another scenario is conceivable: Say I warned about a blowout and you disregarded my warning, drove normally, and no tire suffered at all. In this situation, I'll probably conclude that you were lucky, and

*(Continued)*

(Continued)

you'll probably conclude that I don't know what I'm talking about. My grim consolation is that my warning probably will be vindicated soon.

As a leader of analysis, you also must be clear about the kind of error you cannot tolerate:

- To state something as a fact that is incorrect.
- To hold one level of confidence but communicate another.
- To ignore contradictory evidence.
- To be useless.
- To be unclear.
- To be sloppy in thought or presentation ("lazy thinking").

Outside of such errors as these, you will have to tolerate the fact that your most brilliant and diligent analysts will not always be "right." Punish them for not having a crystal ball and you will soon have analysts afraid to do their jobs.

## Reacting vs. Initiating

The fourth and final critical balance is that between your unit being reactive and being self-initiating. I mentioned the reactive nature of my Iraq team in the 1990s. Events—frequent and dramatic crises—tended to drive them. This also is a common feature of analytic task forces—they are gathered in reaction to a clearly defined challenge, something that feels like a crisis. Even without a crisis you might have a reactive environment. I have seen several analytic organizations completely absorbed by the need to react to questions their own leader was posing. I have seen others that felt they had no time to do anything other than respond to a steady stream of questions and tasks from an insatiable customer.

I have seen other organizations that were almost exclusively self-driven. The analysts were given an "account," a broad topic to work on, and they decided for themselves which analytic question they would write about. Generally the analysts decided when they had something interesting enough to say to warrant their customers' time and attention. Sometimes these self-initiators allowed themselves to be too cut off from their customers. Some even developed a blindness to the customer's appetite. In the interest of best serving the customer's *need*—for what does a customer need more than insightful, fully developed, value-added analysis?—they were dismissive about the customer's *want*. The customer wanted to know what was going on, and the condescending analyst responded, "If there were something significant going on, I would have told you."

Clearly, both extremes are unhealthy. Some units inevitably will tend to be more reactive while others will tend to be more self-driven. But being completely one or the other means shorting the customer. If I am always responding to an insatiable customer's questions, I am not standing back and thinking about what the customer might need to know but has not asked. Nor am I taking the time to think deeply about *anything*—not even the customer's explicit question. If I only am initiating, I am not having a sufficient dialogue with the customer. Only by frequent contact with my principal customers can I get an adequate sense of what they know, what they are trying to do, and what they really need from me.

And too often, it is you, the leader of analysis, who has produced the imbalanced environment. I have seen analytic leaders whose style was to treat everything as a crisis. "Let's get on it!" "What are you waiting for?" "What is taking you so long?" "Yes, you could take another day to write the report, but why not man up and have it on my desk by the time I come in tomorrow?" At the other extreme, I have seen analytic "leaders"—and I am using that word very loosely here—who ceded all initiative to their analysts. "The analysts are the experts; they will tell me when they have something to say."

The key to getting this balance right is to listen attentively to *both* your analysts and your most important customers.

Listen to your analysts for these important indicators that your unit is too reactive:

- *"You* (the leader) never say no to any request!"

- *"I* don't have time to think."

- "I'm busy answering questions, but not the questions that matter."

- "We are just spinning our wheels analytically."

- "I never get a chance to analyze what *I* want."

And listen to your most valued customers for these signs of frustration:

- "I'm flying blind here!"

- "I'd rather have a short list of possible answers now than the right answer next month."

- "I'm sure your analysis is good; I just can't remember seeing any."

Once you have thought about these critical balances, you will find yourself nudging the pendulum to the right or left. Among other things, you'll convene meetings to consider or announce the adjustment you need. Here is another great opportunity to shape the environment.

Think about what you need from the meeting. Do you need more information to decide whether to shift a balance (or make any other change)? Do you need a decision to arise from the meeting? Do you need to announce a change you have already decided? Don't confuse the three.

Think about what your team needs from the meeting. Start with the fact that they are analysts (i.e., smart, independent thinkers who want to look deeply at any issue presented to them). Be prepared to share with them all the information you have, including the balance issues and business drivers that are relevant. The issue is not, for example, a simple choice of picking breadth or depth; it is how to slightly adjust the balance between breadth and depth. These business choices usually will be outside of their substantive analytic experience, but not beyond their analytic capacity, and certainly not beyond their appetite.

Usually, if you are clear about what you need from the meeting and sensitive to what your team needs from the meeting, you won't feel a tension between the two. They will appreciate that you are sharing mission and business imperatives with them and that you are listening to their input. They will be better equipped to make their own decisions as they affect the business environment. They will feel more trusted and trust you more.

The more skeptical readers are saying here, "You are giving analysts a lot of credit for rising above their self-interest." Yes, I am. I am also crediting them with the ability to weigh their own short-term and long-term interests, including their interest in being part of a highly successful enterprise. Finally, I also credit them with the ability to see through manipulative leaders who only pretend to listen.

## Stress in the Environment

One important feature of the reactive vs. self-initiating spectrum is stress. It is tempting to think that the stress exists in the reactive environment and disappears in the self-initiating environment. It is also tempting to think that stress is bad for analysis. That is just too simplistic.

John Medina (2008) is a developmental molecular biologist and director of the Brain Center for Applied Learning Research at Seattle Pacific

University. In his book *Brain Rules,* Medina notes, "[N]ot all stress is the same. Certain types of stress really hurt learning, but some types of stress *boost* learning" (172). He amplifies,

> If the stress is not too severe, the brain performs better. Its owner can solve problems more effectively and is more likely to retain information. . . . If the stress is too severe or prolonged, however, stress begins to harm learning. . . . Stressed individuals do not generalize or adapt old pieces of information to new scenarios as well as non-stressed individuals. . . . Specifically *stress hurts declarative memory (things you can declare) and executive function (the type of thinking that involves problem solving).* (177–78; emphasis added)

Declarative memory and executive function are two of the most vital functions in an analyst's brain.

What does this mean for you? First, recognize that you lead individuals who react to stress individually. Just as some individuals skydive for recreation, you have some analysts who get a rush from crises. (I was a crisis junky for twenty years.) Other analysts will burn out quickly from crisis support. Telling the latter to suck it up simply adds to their stress.

Regardless of individual tolerance, watch for this phenomenon, again described by Medina (2008: 187): "The perfect storm of occupational stress appears to be a combination of two malignant facts: (a) a great deal is expected of you and (b) you have no control over whether you will perform well." The more stressful the environment, the more you will have to give them a sense of control over *how* they do their job and the more you will have to engage them in discussions about what they *feel* they need (space, tools, time) to succeed. And the more explicit you will need to be in defining success, so they do not set the bar unachievably high.

Medina's "two malignant facts" also hold a clue as to why the team that is completely self-initiating may also feel stressed. Although they seem like they have a great deal of control—they initiate their work, after all—they may not have a sense of control over whether they will perform *well.* They may feel cut off from the customer who could validate that they have performed well—that they have provided useful analysis. Some analysts simply are not comfortable in the ivory tower.

Let's return for a moment to the notion that if "the stress is not too severe, the brain performs better." This is an important phenomenon for the unit that is naturally slow-paced. The unit might be studying an issue that changes slowly. Or they may work an issue that is on the customer's back burner. There is no imperative to get the product to the customer today; tomorrow or next week will be just fine. It is easy for such a unit to become intellectually lethargic. They can get locked in a mindset that "nothing ever happens here" and dismiss indicators that something big might be brewing. Like the TSA supervisor who occasionally puts a knife or gun on the scanner screen to keep inspectors alert, you might need to introduce some heat into your unit's environment, some level of challenge. You might enforce expedited deadlines. You might give the equivalent of pop quizzes ("Give me a one-page analysis of *x* by close of business today"). You might stimulate some good-natured competition within the unit. Keep it light-hearted and realistic, lest your subordinates dismiss you as a martinet. But don't apologize for cranking the pace up a notch. You will know you have gotten the balance right if you see your subordinates walking quickly. You will have gotten the balance wrong if they are walking away.

## What Else Might Help?

To elicit your analysts' best, you must attend to both the positive and negative in their environment. Worry most about the things in your control. On the positive side,

- *Keep an eye on bedrock values.* For example, serving a customer is more important than providing beautiful prose, so giving the customer something worthwhile but imperfect today may be better than giving the customer something dazzling the day after the decision meeting.

- *Let them see your human side.* Your analysts don't expect you to be a genius or a hero. They will forgive many flaws if they see you as a real person doing his best, especially if they see you as a person who cares about them. You'll be amazed what they will do for you if they genuinely like you and don't want to let you down.

- *Embrace trial and error.* Connected to the *fact* that you don't have all the answers will be the *reality* that you will make some mistakes. Show your subordinates that you have the grace and humility to acknowledge your mistakes and that you learn (and learn quickly) from them. Then they may start to accept that they, too, can make well-intentioned mistakes without fear. The analysts and managers who are making no mistakes are taking no risks and pushing no frontiers. You cannot afford that. You need your analysts trying some approaches that do not pay off.

- And, as one senior and very wise analyst told me, *don't believe everything you think.* Too many leaders—including me—have added up all the relevant factors, calculated the pros and cons, and then pronounced (what we have convinced ourselves *must* be) the only right answer. We teach analysts to be humble about their conclusions; we need to be humble about *ours.*

And you must attend to the negative factors as well, especially the ones in your control.

- *Attack the ludicrous.* Into every bureaucracy creeps stupidity. Never accept it as just part of the background noise. There used to be a men's room in a CIA facility that had a formally printed sign, "Do NOT put paper towels in the urinals." What I was really looking at was a sign saying, "Stupid people work here." Not an advertisement I would tolerate at the CIA.

- *Minimize the distractions.* I bet your analysts are filling out some administrative form for a person long retired. Sure it takes only five minutes. But to your analysts, nothing is more important than their time. Kill that requirement and you have conveyed to your analysts, "Every minute of your time is precious to me."

- *Corral the cynics.* Nothing puts a damper on a new idea or insight faster than the vocal cynic. Your organization needs fresh ideas and insights—in matters of both substance and process. Put some work into winning the cynic over—as an ally, their active support can be powerful. But if you cannot enlist them, do what you must to prevent them from poisoning the environment.

- *Clean up after yourself.* Even good leaders produce collateral damage. Your decisions will have consequences beyond those you hoped for. As I mentioned before, your decisions sometimes produce winners and losers. You must not let that reality freeze you into inaction. But you can do amazing good by spending time with the losers. Acknowledge their grief, correct anything that needs correcting, adjust course as you go along, and stay humble. They will walk away from the loss without walking away from you.

## KEY THEMES

Your job is to build an environment that brings out the best in your analysts: their energy, their discipline, their most impactful insights. It all starts by building trust. With trust, your constructive critique is taken as welcome coaching. Without it, it is taken as perfectionism and micromanagement.

- Give them your candor, including candidly admitting when you don't know.

- Give them your time; listening is usually the hard part.

- Always tell them *why*. You only hire people smart enough to dig for the truth. Give them yours.

- Pulse the environment regularly. Trust these indicators of health:

  o Are you seeing initiative, creativity, energy, and self-discipline across your workforce?

  o Are good people asking to join your team?

  o Are people leaving your team for the right reasons?

- Keep an eye on these critical balances. **You need both elements in each pair**, but the pressures of your business will often push you toward one end of the spectrum:

  o Imaginative vs. pragmatic analysis

  o Breadth vs. depth of expertise

  o Eliminating mistakes vs. generating insights

  o Reacting (to events and customer needs) vs. initiating (analysis)

- Monitor stress in your workplace. A little stress can bring out the best in people. But stress becomes toxic when people feel they are being held responsible to deliver something they cannot.

- Let your workforce see your vulnerable, human side. You are going to make mistakes, but if they see that you are driven by solid, selfless values, they will forgive you. If you are an insecure, pompous, know-it-all, they will be watching for every mistake.

# Choosing the Best Approach and Techniques

They'd come into my office glowing. Analysts returning from stints in Baghdad and other parts of post-Saddam Iraq were energized by a "new way" of working. They talked about the clarity of the mission. They talked about playing to their strengths. They talked about unprecedented collaboration with their ops partners and sometimes their foreign partners. They talked about the liberating feeling of being "far from the bureaucracy" and having "nobody trying to tell me *how* to do my job." They talked about having an impact, unaided by layers of review. With greater or lesser diplomacy, they all found a way to say, "We should work that way back here."

Several of their supervisors would talk to me about the "Baghdad glow," too. "I'm so tired of hearing how they did it in Baghdad," they would complain, "I finally had to tell them . . . you know . . . get over it; you're not in Baghdad anymore."

Surely our war-zone veterans were on to something. It wasn't just the Iraq experience. Our analysts who had been to Afghanistan were speaking the same way. They shared a feeling of "being unleashed" to do work that was "too important for bullshit."

What they discovered was that there is more than one approach to managing analysis. The irreducible truth of their enlightenment—which we ignore at our peril—was that their tolerance for bullshit had plummeted. They had a heightened sense of mission and a reduced patience for anything that seemed to get in the way. Like the World War II veterans flocking to universities on a new GI Bill, they weren't willing to quietly tolerate long-standing school procedures simply because "that is the way we have always done it here."

Our response to their experience, at a minimum, must be to scrub our systems of the plaque buildup that clogs the arteries of any bureaucracy. We must repeatedly ask ourselves what exists in our management of analysis that no longer has a compelling purpose? What procedures perhaps made sense once but no longer add value? Or add insufficient value for the cost they incur? When the procedures add value that is real but not apparent to the analysts, the burden is on leaders to communicate the compelling justification.

Beyond this minimum level of response, we must take seriously the revelation that there is more than one approach to managing analysis.

I am not talking about different types of analysis. Clearly, the geospatial intelligence analysts use a different approach from political analysts who use a different approach from S&T (scientific and technical) analysts. I am talking about different approaches to managing analysis. You have a growing menu of choices, some of which arrived as a feature of the information revolution.

Get the approach right and it will make it easier to, as discussed in chapters 3 and 5, nurture an environment that brings out the best in your analysts. Get the approach right and they will see themselves producing impactful insights at the highest level, evoking that sense of mission and purpose seen in the "Baghdad glow."

For most managers of standing analytic units, there seems to be only one approach: the one they inherited. Unless the unit is clearly dysfunctional, few incoming managers consider something transformational. When do those managers try something different? When they are put in charge of a large ad hoc unit. This might be a task force responding to a crisis; or a group trying to crack a single, tough analytic problem; or a unit directly supporting an operation. The unit is seen as temporary, brought together for a clear purpose. For efforts such as these, the manager becomes a leader and thinks more clearly about the assignment—the mission—than she did when she was in charge of a standing unit. The leader can see success (and failure) more clearly and looks for the optimum way *we* can work together *now*. The "Baghdad glow" I mentioned before was often the result of such a task force experience.

Certainly, I also have seen ad hoc units poorly managed and led on occasion. Too many times I have seen a chief think that the purpose of his task force was to have a task force. Too many times I have seen resources thrown at a large ad hoc analytic unit with greater regard to evenly distributing the manpower levee than to mission need—and unsurprisingly, many of the draftees complained they were left in the corner with nothing to do. Too many times have I seen leaders from one work culture unable to take advantage of talent from a different culture.

But when the ad hoc units worked well, they had much in common with those war-zone experiences I mentioned. They had **clarity of purpose**. They usually had a **short line between producers and customers**. They had a **drive to get the job done**. And they had a prejudice to take advantage of the **diversity of talent** available.

None of these success elements is unavailable to the leaders of standing units. The problem is that standing units, over time, accumulate more and more definitions of success and more and more complexities, responsibilities, and distractions. Standing units develop a momentum that, to weak leaders, seems unalterable. For leaders of ad hoc units, there is no escaping the need to focus on both mission and resources. For leaders of standing units, it requires a force of will.

In this section, I'll lay out some of the basic choices we have when considering which approach to analysis might be most productive. By calling them choices, I don't want to give the impression that they are mutually exclusive—like an à la carte menu, feel free to mix to taste. Also, I'll talk about them as if they were all equally available to you, but I know that is not true. Your choices will be constrained by some realities you cannot disregard. The skills and patience of the people who already call you "boss" will be the most powerful of these realities. They cannot simply apply a new approach without learning it, and learning it requires an investment of time. Also, if you are a first-level line manager, you will not have the array of options and flexibility that is available to your boss's boss. But whatever level you are, you have more flexibility than you imagine. Only victims are prisoners of the status quo.

# Evolving Approaches: Three Paradigms

Your most strategic choice is how to organize for analysis. You face three basic paradigms or approaches that have grown over the decades.

- **Intelligence analysis used to focus on "what do *I* know?"** The expert figured out what was going on in a situation and what was likely to happen from that point.

- **Then analysis moved to an emphasis on "what do *we* know?"** Teams of analysts became producers of more important insight. Drawing expertise and knowledge from across disciplines often delivered richer, more meaningful understanding and predictions.

- Now, in the digital age, the focus is again shifting. **The focus now increasingly is "what is *knowable?*"** In using cutting-edge tools and methods, we are fracking insights out of previously impenetrable data shale.

## What Do *I* Know? The Solitary Analyst

When I started in the CIA in the early 1980s, there were teams of analysts that shared resources and ideas. But actually *doing* analysis was very much an individual craft. The default setting would be one paper, one author. The only time that default would be set aside would be when you had *two* co-authors; for example, you might have a military analyst and an economist collaborating on a paper about a country's military industries. The products that had several contributing analysts were often disdained as assembly line references, like the *CIA Factbook*. In this environment, the default personality for an analyst was introvert. I was very much at home.

## What Do *We* Know? The Analytic Team

But over the next two decades, teamwork became a more normal analytic approach. Papers might have five authors. A challenging analytic task might be kicked off with a brainstorming session involving a dozen analysts. I'd frequently see papers with the seals of three or more agencies on the cover. The extroverts in CIA's analytic directorate came out of hiding (I like to think they aren't lonely anymore).

The rise of team analysis was driven by many things. First, we leaders of analysis could see the powerful impact of true analytic collaboration. A paper on, say, Chinese stability produced by a political analyst, a cultural anthropologist, and an economist was bound to be richer and more sophisticated than one produced by a solitary analyst of any flavor. Analysts working hand in hand with collectors frequently secured evidence of a higher quality and relevance. Second, as the world emerged from the Cold War and into the globalized information age, our policy customers had to deal with a level of complexity beyond most individual analysts. Third, communications and IT tools allowed unprecedented secure collaboration among analysts. Drafts and drafting could be shared among analysts on different continents. And because it was now *possible* for an analyst in Washington to get a timely input from, say, a US Army intelligence captain in Baghdad, we began to *require* such partnership. Fourth, the American education system was having an impact. Our new analysts were taught teamwork and collaborative problem solving from elementary school, and they were good at it.

With this evolution from solitary to collaborative analysis, another dynamic frequently arises. In the 1990s, even though they were collaborating more often, most analysts still could quickly revert to a solitary role and be quite productive. But in the next decade, we saw more and more specialists whose contribution was unique and important but did not stand alone. Their work was integrated into a team product. An expert in weapons modeling, for example, might have little to say to a customer, but his work will be essential in a team product on a country's chemical weapons threat.

And occasionally, we would see teams in which nearly everyone was a specialist. That type of team is more than just collaborative—it is truly interdependent. It is less like a basketball team, in which any combination of players can put together a fast break, and more like a baseball team, in which the pitcher would never consider donning the catcher's face mask.

## What *Is* Knowable? The Big Data Team

Big data teams are even more truly interdependent. In this emerging field, it is not unusual to have an expert in a particular data mining tool, a specialist in quantitative analysis, someone who excels in writing algorithms, and someone skilled in composing a lucid narrative all applying their skills to a problem. In other models, an individual data specialist might be added to a more traditional team, to mine for data that can help with some of the team's standing issues.

These big data specialists and teams are finding useful information in the volumes of data that come with the digital age. In many cases, the volumes are so enormous that they would be impenetrable to individuals working without specialized tools. As an analyst in the 1980s, I could wrap my mind around columns of data on a spreadsheet, eventually spotting trends in one, perhaps two dimensions. But make the columns long enough, and multiply the numbers of columns, and I would be lost. And, of course, all these data in columns were the product of enormous inputting work done *before* I could be confident they would be useful. Now, big data tools can handle staggeringly large volumes of data, discovering subtle patterns and relationships. And data scientists are finding value in information that wouldn't even have been considered "data" in the 1980s.

Walmart provides a simple illustration. Consider this question: What should Walmart stock up on when a hurricane is approaching? As an analyst in the 1980s, I would have guessed milk, diapers, flashlights, and batteries—and, oh yes, beer please. And in time I could have collected a couple thousand Walmart purchasing records during relevant time periods and tested my guesses. Today, Walmart data teams already have purchasing data from millions of transactions—data that simply flow through their system—that enable them to quickly confirm or refute my guesses. But most important, they are able to say, "Yes, but what sells before hurricanes that is *not* obvious?" The answer, according to a Walmart team anticipating Hurricane Frances's approach in 2004: strawberry Pop-Tarts (Provost and Fawcett 2013). The answer is there in the data, but even if I had access to the data, I never would have found it because I never would have guessed to look for it. Today's data teams do this routinely. In areas trivial and consequential, they are expanding the definition of *what is knowable.*

In this progression from solitary analysis to interdependent data team, the previous paradigm has never been rendered obsolete. The individual analyst, obsessed with a problem, acting primarily alone, still plays a vital role. That person often is a catalyst for analytic breakthrough. Neither is the information revolution rendering obsolete the collaborative team of mixed expertise working much as they did in the early 1990s. Rather, each stage has given us approaches that can be used—must be used—*too.* We add to our repertoire but continue to find worth in the time-tested approaches we were raised with.

As leaders of analysis, our job is to stay current on this expanding menu of approaches. We must thoughtfully match the analytic approach to the situation we are in. What question are we trying to answer? What information is available? What can our customer use? What resources are available? These things help determine which approach to analysis will provide the most useful insights.

Too many leaders of analysis are blind to the choices available to them. They get locked into a complacency that *this* is how you do analysis—*this* being whatever approach yielded good results before. Too many simply play the hand they were dealt, custodians of whatever analytic approach they inherited. You will hear them say, "Well, this is how we do analysis here." Certainly there is a cost to changing approaches. Generally, the approach that has been the norm achieved that status for good reason: it was successful. If your two choices are cling to the tested approach or abandon it, your hesitation might be wise. But rarely are your choices that stark. And you can broaden your choices by nurturing healthy attitudes toward experimentation and growth.

## Why Not the Very Best?

Some observers of analysis are baffled when they examine any approach to analysis that appears to suffer from obvious limitations. I have heard some say, for example, "I just don't understand why we have single analysts working alone on anything, anymore. We know that mixing many experts is better—and exploiting big data is better still." Those observers are doing something you cannot afford to do as a leader of analysis: ignoring resources.

The very best analysis might involve the mobilization of huge resources against one question. Say the question is, *How can we best help the current regime in Afghanistan survive a departure of US troops?* I would put my leading Afghanistan expert on the issue. I would put a large team of other experts together as well: political analysts, economists, leadership experts, cultural anthropologists, insurgency experts, and instability experts. I would give them the best designers of predictive analytic tools to identify relevant data from the past and stability patterns of the present. I would assign at least a couple data scientists to look for subtle and deeply hidden data that others missed. I would hive off a few experts to do independent alternative analysis. I would send several analysts to work directly with the collectors. And if this were a moonshot, I might build a NASA (National Agency for Serious Analysis).

But of course, building a NASA to answer one question is impractical. First, it ignores that, in today's world of fast-moving issues, nimble teams are usually more able than ponderous ones. Second, analysis can become expensive. Exploitation of big data, for example, requires much up-front preparation before any insights flow. Common sense suggests we should put more resources on the most important questions. On other questions, you will know that you can only afford to invest one analyst.

Neither can we simply allocate resources across *today's* questions. We build an enterprise that is going to have to answer tomorrow's questions as well. We do our best to anticipate tomorrow's questions, but we make educated guesses and place our bets. We also need to delve for insights and information where there is no explicit question. By that I mean that sometimes, by simply *exploring* we learn things of value; in those cases, our discovery is the result of our exploration, not our development of an answer to a question.

Your own examination of analytic choices will have to embrace realities of budget, manpower, and time. You will have to consider the costs of change, training, and retooling alongside the costs of the status quo. You might start with, "What is the best approach to analysis that I can imagine?" But very quickly practical concerns will frame your choices, and the question becomes, "What is the best approach to analysis I can produce right now?"

# Picking Your Paradigm

So, among the three paradigmatic choices (What do *I* know? What do *we* know? What is *knowable?*), how might you balance cost and gain? The first choice, the lone analyst attacking an issue, is the cheapest and very versatile. A bright and trained analyst can bring value to a topic very quickly, even without prior expertise on that topic. Analysts are "quick studies" by profession. One can quickly develop and deliver useful insights simply by focusing on a question, conducting focused research, and understanding a customer's needs. Certainly we saw this rapid learning and quick productivity after 9/11, when we surged many analysts to counterterrorism. Managers talk about "fungible analysts" who can be moved from issue to issue as needs arise. Fungible analysts are the key to dealing with a world where a coup can take a country like Haiti from the back burner to presidential priority overnight.

A variation of the lone analyst, but even more impactful, is the lone *expert.* This is an analyst who has developed a deep understanding of a topic over time. It will be the deep expert on Haiti who is most likely to sense that events in Haiti have entered a pre-crisis stage. The new analyst will see that the Shia and Sunni are clashing in several places in the Middle East. The expert will "feel" that the clashes are different this time—that they have not been this intense or widespread in the past century.

"Experts" seem to come in for more than their fair share of criticism. Observers like Daniel Kahneman (2011) and Philip Tetlock (2005) have written convincingly that simply being expert shouldn't earn uncritical acceptance of what one says, especially when the expert is talking about the future. Certainly the list of intelligence failures is full of examples of deep experts being the last to accept that radical change is underway on their topic. But more common (though less famous) is that experts see things no one else can, including subtle indicators of change. They will not get right every analytic call they make, but in my experience, they produce analysis more sophisticated, more insightful, and more impactful than other analysts. The "experts" Kahneman and Tetlock tend to disparage often are those I think of as the "pontificators": overconfident windbags who are eager to dole out pearls of wisdom but not eager to do the hard work of challenging their own conclusions and keeping an open mind. The leader of analysis must watch each expert for signs that he is becoming intellectually lazy, becoming a pontificator. Especially on issues that change slowly over time, it is easy for any expert to become complacent and overconfident. But across the issues I led over the decades, by far the more typical experts were those who had both deep knowledge and the confidence to say, "I don't know." They were the analysts senior customers would ask for by name; they were the analysts I would put in front of the president. (I'll say more about the value of experts later in this chapter when I address the precious resource expert intuition.)

Producing or recruiting an expert is expensive for any analytic organization. On complex topics and issues, it takes years, often including things like lengthy travel, language training, or doctorate-level technical training. It often also takes conscious career management by both the expert and her supervisor, choosing tasks and experiences that continue to grow and challenge the analyst but avoid either burning her out or letting her grow bored with the routine.

At some point as the leader of analysts, you will face the need to make one of these deep experts a fungible analyst. A major crisis will arise, and you will need to "throw analysts at the issue." This is very expensive. Yes, the analyst will be a quick study and soon be productive on the urgent new topic. But she will need years to develop the level of sophistication she brought to her old topic. Meanwhile, she is not working at her peak. And if she doesn't completely see the need to make this personnel move, she is angry to have her expertise "wasted." A better choice, if you have the resources, is to nurture breadth in some analysts and depth in others. Any large population of analysts will have plenty who naturally prefer one or the other. You can tailor their training and work experiences to emphasize flexibility of assignment or substantive depth. You try to mold the healthy balance between the breadth and depth I mentioned in chapter 3.

The second paradigmatic choice is the team of analysts working on a question together. And here I am not talking about the kind of team in which you have several analysts working mostly independently on different questions related to an issue—say, five analysts working on five questions related to Russia's economy. On balance, those analysts fit better in the lone analyst paradigm because each does his primary work alone. Rather, I am talking about a team of analysts working *interdependently* on a single question. You might have several analysts with different substantive skills—say, macro-economist, micro-economist, statistician, and trade specialist—working on a single question or a single study related to Russia's economy. Beyond those differences, one member might be the most effective researcher, one the best writer, one a specialist in data presentation, and you try to play each to his strengths. Such a team usually can outperform the lone analyst. They often can find and weave together more information faster than a lone analyst. If they have a deep substantive expert on the team, that person often can be a force-multiplier, bringing substantive sophistication to many aspects of the project.

In his book *Collaborative Intelligence*, J. Richard Hackman (2011: 27) notes, "Teams should be used only when there are good reasons for them, reasons that can be explicitly named." But if the mission is important enough to warrant the investment of a team, it is important enough for you to do the work to get it right. Here are some considerations:

- Hackman lays out how vital it is to launch a team properly—get this wrong and you have wasted precious time (27). Key is embracing their diversity from the beginning and making sure you (and they) communicate across their various professional cultures. You will be disappointed if you assume that, say, the macro- and micro-economists will play well together because they are both economists.

- Homogeneity misses the point. If you form a team of analysts who are similarly trained and think alike, you'll be pleased just how harmoniously they collaborate. But the point of a team is to bring disparate skills and perspectives together. If it is not disparate enough to produce some friction, it is not disparate enough. As one senior analytic veteran put it, "Friction produces heat, and heat produces light" (John Helgerson, then-CIA Deputy Director for Intelligence, pers. comm.).

- Some creative tension is a good thing on the team and passionate debate will be normal. But the manager must ensure that the tension does not turn counterproductive. If a team fails, it is a more expensive failure.

- Take measures to identify and protect the dissenting voice. If team analysis comes to you with no sign of dissent, you will have to work to unearth it. Analysts might all learn to nod their heads on cue, but they never agree on everything.

- Identify the team's storyteller. This analyst will write and brief with a clearer vision and more coherent message (because it was not drafted by committee).

All this points to one reality: molding a highly functioning interdependent team takes more sophisticated management. A leader of a team of solitary analysts focuses on *how each works*. A leader of an interdependent team does that, too, but spends as much time on how they work *together*. With sophisticated management, the highly functioning team *usually* can deliver a quality result faster than the highly functioning lone analyst. For *high stakes questions with an urgent deadline*, the interdependent team—under a strong manager—is usually the better way to go.

Most of these interdependent teams are built around just such issues or questions: high-stakes, front-burner questions that require you to do your best fast. The right mix of analysts is brought together and each plays to his strengths. And when the task is finished, they usually disband. Although it was an educational—often exhilarating—experience for the analysts, they developed their expertise elsewhere and often go back home when it is done.

Some such teams, however, are kept together. They go on to apply their team approach to other questions. They become the "pros from Dover," brought in to crack tough problems. The upside is they develop and refine an elite, highly effective approach. Their growing pains are behind them and they work efficiently. They do an effective, sometimes excellent, job analyzing a range of questions. The team might develop a cross-cutting specialty. They might, for example, become specialists in political instability, or insurgency, or fledgling democracies. One downside is that deep experts tend to not like traveling from issue to issue. Depth in something—say political instability—comes at the expense of depth in something else—perhaps Egyptian politics. When the team moves from Egyptian to Honduran instability, the Egypt expert probably will remain behind. And the Honduras political expert may well resent that this team of strangers has arrived to "handle" his issue. These challenges are manageable, but they must be actively managed.

This brings us to the third paradigmatic choice, the analytic team established to take advantage of big data. These data teams themselves can take remarkably different approaches.

Some data teams *explore*. They might focus on a particular information stream to determine what useful insights it contains. You explore the data to find something of worth—and until you find something, you are not certain your effort will pay off. Can tracking phone card purchases in Africa tell us anything of national security interest? Can Google determine anything useful from the stream of queries that flow through its servers? Can Twitter feeds tell us what is on the minds of large populations? To some extent, the answer to all three of these questions is yes, thanks to big data.

- African telecom CellTel data showed that "massacres in the Congo are presaged by spikes in the sale of prepaid phone cards" (Siegel 2013: Kindle location 2528). The reasons underpinning this correlation are not exactly clear, but the trend is clear enough that policy makers interested in thwarting the massacres should take notice.

- In a much more famous example, one of Google's teams started paying attention to searches containing symptoms and medications associated with various flu strains. Google discovered that it could track the spread of flu in "near real-time" faster than the Centers for Disease Control and Prevention (CDC), and it did so for several years (Google Flu Trends Data 2015; see also Butler 2013; Bilton 2013). (I find this a particularly illuminating case and will come back to it at the end of this chapter.)

- Other teams work to see what they can make of information flowing through Twitter. Twitter might provide a form of instant opinion polling unthinkable a decade ago, but these teams have to determine the validity of their messy data. They also are discovering what is *too* messy and what is *messy but exploitable*.

Other data teams start differently. Rather than exploring a stream or repository of data to see whether it contains something useful, they start with a problem or issue and go looking for data that can help. This is what intelligence analysts and analytic teams have always done, but with a difference. Part of the analytic team will focus more on collection than analysis, that is, gathering data from a range of sources and linking it together to make it analyzable. The data might not appear immediately relevant to the question in an obvious manner, but it is gathered in volume in the hopes that subtle but relevant trends and linkages might be discovered. The team accepts that a high volume of slightly relevant data might contain more valuable insights than a few bits of pristine information exactly on topic. Another part of the team—and a key to making these data teams productive—constructs models and algorithms. Data miners—and sometimes data scientists—will build the programs to identify subtle data patterns and make them visible to the analysts. Once the algorithm can reliably identify correlations and trends, its use as a prediction tool can be tested.

An early example of this type of data team—in which the question or issue is identified first and the data is brought to it—comes from the field of meteorology. The basic question is, "What will tomorrow's weather be?" Data relevant to weather—temperature, humidity, winds—had been collected all over the globe for more than a century. As computers became powerful, that historic data could be used as never before, comparing it to freshly collected data on today's conditions. First simple, then highly sophisticated models were built to help the "analyst," the meteorologist, tell you whether to carry your umbrella tomorrow. Now, no weather forecaster would work without these models and none trusts a single model blindly. The complexities of the weather system are enormous, and these data tools have remarkably improved the performance of the average meteorologist. I think this example also holds some good news for intelligence analysts: the data and the models *help* the meteorologist achieve unprecedented predictive accuracy, but they do not *replace* the meteorologist.

To make a thoughtful choice about whether a data team is the most useful approach for your mission, you will need a better grasp of this evolving arena. I'll try to provide that in chapter 10, when I examine twenty-first century tools. We'll look a bit deeper at what types of questions are suitable for data analysis and what kinds of information are now being treated as data. For now, let me simply assert that, before your career as a leader of analysis is over, you will look back and wonder how you functioned without big data and predictive analytics. You will be like the meteorologist who cannot imagine the business without these tools.

## Blending Approaches

The three paradigmatic choices are not as distinct as I make them sound here. The lone analyst is never alone. She must be connected to other experts. The interdependent team might include analysts who are working basically by themselves on aspects of the bigger question. And everyone, including the lone analyst, will be taking unprecedented advantage of the tools and techniques of the big data world, just as watching a baseball game today means being hit by an avalanche of statistics (. . . *the Nationals have won 73 percent of home games when they score two runs by the third inning . . .*)[1]. Analysts watching an insurgency today may not think of themselves as a big data team, but they are engaged in a data-heavy endeavor. They keep score on such parameters as attacks by weapon, location, date, and lethality. By developing such data, analysts under all three paradigms

---

[1] I made this "statistic" up. Do not place any bets based on it.

are in a position to discover such subtle and intriguing insights as, say, "Insurgent attacks in any province drop by 90 percent the week before the deputy security minister visits that province."

Whichever of the three paradigms dominates the approach of your unit, you must maintain a healthy respect for the other two. As a leader of lone analysts, you must ensure your unit is constantly trawling for data. Even without the depth of a big data team, your individual analysts can employ some of the simpler big data tools. Some will be able even to code some simple if-then logic trees to sift and sort data. You and your analysts must be ever on the lookout for new sources of even messy data that might contain useful information. And you must sometimes force yourselves to be open to the revelations that come from dedicated big data teams playing in your sandbox.

Similarly, if you are the leader of a big data team, you must ever be sensitive to the value of those lone analysts, especially the lone analysts who are deeply expert. It is easy for big data teams to convince themselves they have found the keys to true insight. It is powerfully seductive for a data team to set themselves the challenge, "Let's prove we can beat the experts!" It is easy for them to dismiss an expert's opinion as "feelings" and label their own product the weightier sounding "findings." "Our *findings* are based on real data; don't bring your *feelings* into the debate until you can back them with data!" Often, the big data team can find meaningful correlations in masses of material impenetrable to a single analyst. But just as often, the lone analyst can weigh meaningful factors, dynamics, and context that are beyond the focus of the data team.

The leader of analysis today simply cannot afford to be stuck in an organizational rut. To find the best approach for your current situation, you need to be clear about the strengths and weaknesses of each and nimble enough to mix and match as you go along. This is not to say you must be highly expert in leading all the available approaches. A superb leader of individual experts might not be as skilled in the challenges of leading an interdependent task force. And an experienced leader of data mining might not be ready to edit the prose of a lone expert. Every leader will be best at one of the paradigms. But none of us today can be Johnny-One-Note, oblivious to, or even contemptuous of, the range of other approaches to leading analysis.

# The Expanding Menu of Analytic Techniques

Once you have decided how to organize your analytic effort, you can turn to the array of analytic techniques the unit might apply. The default choice is timeless and productive: you simply tell your analysts to do their thing, that is, to apply their skills and expertise to a particular issue or question. "Study this and let me know what you think." You don't prescribe how they should think through the problem. Rather, you let them attack the problem, and through dialogue and review you help refine their product. This default approach can be applied to lone analysts, to teams working interdependently, and big data teams. The bigger the team, of course, the more management is required to organize everyone's best contribution to the effort. But for the most part, you are still letting everyone apply their expertise and critical thinking their own way.

Don't let the simplicity and casualness of this approach lead you to suspect you aren't providing your analysts enough management. If they have been trained in disciplined thinking and rigorous research, this approach is usually productive. And your analysts will greatly appreciate that you trust them enough to think for themselves. After assigning the work, your most important contribution is in coaching and facilitating. There is a strong temptation to *overmanage* their work. If you find yourself telling your analysts how to organize their research, which analytic formula to apply, and what evidence to weigh most heavily, you might think you are merely being efficient and making the final product predictable. (What manager doesn't want that?) But really you are thinking *for* them—wasting the talent you have assembled.

Even if you are blessed with the most skilled analysts, those who need the least help from you, there will be times when it is wise to go beyond this default approach. Besides allowing them to apply their own best approach to analyzing a question, sometimes you will *also* (*not* instead) ask them to apply a specific analytic technique, to step out of their own heads for a bit and consider the question from another angle. There will be times when you want your entire team to array their evidence and arguments together on a whiteboard, to see what new thoughts emerge and which assumptions appear shakier with age. And there will be times, especially on issues they have worked for years, where you sense that they could use help freshening their imagination and creativity. Each of these situations is one in which you suspect that complacency might be settling in among your analysts and a Structured Analytic Technique might be warranted.

## Structured Analytic Techniques

In the past two decades, there has been an explosion of Structured Analytic Techniques (SATs) to help in such situations. When speaking with SAT evangelists, I find myself being critical. SATs can be overused and misapplied. When speaking with expert analysts, I find myself defending SATs—they are the best techniques that I know for (1) nudging analysts who have become complacent and (2) demonstrating an open mind to a customer. Like so much else in leading analysis, balance is key.

SATs are an important addition to the analyst's toolkit. They force the analyst to step out of her mindset and look at a question from a different perspective. Some, like "Outside-In Thinking," at least give you an opportunity to climb out of your cognitive rut. Others, like "What If? Analysis," force you to give due attention to possibilities you hadn't thought of or dismissed too soon. Others, like "Alternative Futures Analysis," can be a spur to the imagination and can help you identify key drivers that will at least frame an unpredictable future. Most of them give you a visual take on the problem, literally putting key elements (including key unknowns) in front of your face. All of them shine a bright light on the weaknesses of your current thinking. All of them help you adjust your analytic confidence to a more appropriate level. The US Government (2009) published a good introduction to SATs in *A Tradecraft Primer: Structured Analytic Techniques for Improving Intelligence Analysis*, available online.[2] By far the best manual I have seen for actually using a wide range of SATs was written by Richards Heuer and Randy Pherson (2010), *Structured Analytic Techniques for Intelligence Analysis*.[3] Leaders of analysis can use this manual to choose the structured technique most suitable to the question at hand. The analyst can use it as a "how-to" guide.

As valuable as SATs are, they are not a good replacement for what I described as the default, the analysts applying their expertise and good critical thinking without a prescribed structure. *SATs are a useful aid to thinking, not a better way of thinking.*

After two decades of advocating SATs to my subordinates, I rarely caught an analyst using one on his own initiative. The most common excuse is, "SATs take too long and I simply didn't have time." That excuse is usually a sign of inexperience with SATs. I have seen SATs applied in the middle of war and crisis, actually saving time and discussion by getting analysts quickly focused on the most important evidence, arguments, and possibilities.

A more valid reason they don't leap at the opportunity is that, in a real way, SATs feel unnatural to an analyst. A new analyst might appreciate you suggesting a structure for thinking, but a veteran analyst does not.

---

[2] This paper describes "What If? Analysis" as a technique that "assumes that an event has occurred with potential (negative or positive) impact and explains how it might come about," helping the analyst focus on how an event might occur rather than prematurely dismissing its likelihood (24). The paper describes "Outside-In Thinking" as a technique "to identify the full range of basic forces, factors, and trends that would indirectly shape an issue" (30). This technique focuses on factors outside the situation, such as globalization or social media, that might influence the situation. Analysts are quicker to focus on the internal dynamics of the situation. The paper describes "Analysis of Competing Hypotheses" as the "identification of alternative explanations (hypotheses) and evaluation of all evidence that will disconfirm rather than confirm hypotheses" (14).

[3] By way of full disclosure, I have done some consulting for Pherson Associates over the years and have used this handbook, but I had no role in its production or sales.

A veteran analyst has developed an approach that has worked for him for years, and he is not attracted to any manager who frequently disrupts that approach. His own time-tested approach to critical thinking feels natural, while a SAT's prescribed structure often feels forced. And it is worth remembering my list of "Ten Things Analysts Hate" (see chapter 2): Being told *how* to think was number 1.

Although a strength of SATs is that they force the analyst out of a rut, when used to excess, they don't allow an analyst to get on track. An analyst who *only* has applied a SAT—or even several—to a question will typically present his findings with, "One could argue that . . . ." An analyst who has first applied her own critical thinking to the question usually will instead begin her presentation with, "I believe . . . ." The former approach feels more like an academic exercise. The latter invests the whole analyst.

Lest I sound schizophrenic about SATs, remember it is all about getting the balance right. At either extreme—rejecting SATs or using SATs instead of analysis—you are off balance. What is the right balance? Of course, that will depend on the question being analyzed. But in general, think of SATs as a safety net for analysts, not a prescription for analysis.

## Tapping the Intuition of Experts

There is another reason to allow analysts to *start* working on a problem their own way, without applying a SAT: *you must allow the expert analyst's intuition to play a role.* The intuition of experts has been a longtime focus of research psychologist Gary Klein (2003). In *The Power of Intuition*, he describes high-stakes situations in which experts apply intuition effectively and rapidly. Studying such experts as veteran firefighters and neonatal intensive care nurses, his team found them making the right decisions but often unable to articulate their thought process. They had built up a store of tacit knowledge that allowed them to quickly, often unconsciously, recognize patterns. They were keenly sensitive to departures from typicality—anything subtly unusual. They were diagnosing complex situations and modeling options to improve the situation without ever thinking of it as analysis.

I certainly have seen this many times among expert intelligence analysts. Ask them how they got an important call right, and they often stutter, abashed that maybe they just got lucky. But dig deeper, ask them to reconstruct how they began thinking about the issue, and they will point to details they focused on, details a rookie would have missed. Ask them about other details that were also present, and they often can tell you why they considered those less relevant. The more you pick at this, the more you find an expert insightfully triaging the available information, sorting the useful from the distracting, and looking for things that, if he is reading the situation correctly, should also be evident. They usually don't shed the feeling that they "just got lucky" when they got a call right—they certainly know their thought path sometimes leads to a dead end. But the expert's intuitive read of a situation is the product of years of experience. It generates intuitive notions—hunches—that are key both to picking a productive thought path and to picking an alternative if the first path is fruitless.

This intuition at work is so often productive that you, as a leader of analysis, must value it as an important resource. It allows your analysts to work efficiently, saving real time in most projects. If you routinely push against it—if you always demand documentary evidence for their judgments—you will often provoke resentment. "Why do you want an expert if you dismiss my expertise?" Or if you always instruct an analyst to start thinking about a question by applying a SAT, they often will think you are wasting their time, delaying the start of their "real" analysis.

But what about the analyst who is not yet expert? Klein (2003: 284–86) addresses this situation, too, and provides some very useful tips I'll quote here. He says, "We can use intuition even if we don't have a chance to build up much expertise. In fact we always have to rely on intuition when faced with unfamiliar challenges. We learn as we go along. Here is some advice for making better use of intuition even in these cases.

- *"The first option you think of is likely to be the best.* That's not a guarantee, just an observation backed up by research evidence. . . .

- *"Use analysis to support your intuitions.* That means being aware of what your intuition is suggesting to you before applying your intellect. . . .

- *"Don't confuse desires with intuitions.* . . .

- *"Think ahead.* Intuition can help us think ahead of the curve by creating expectations, by connecting the dots, by flagging inconsistencies, or by warning us of problems. . . .

- *"Consult the experts.* We should trust the intuition of experts more than our own if we are in unfamiliar territory."

For the expert or the novice, Klein (2003:3) is clear in his warning that intuition is insufficient—even dangerous—when used alone. "Our intuitions aren't always reliable. Usually they guide us in the right direction, but sometimes they are mistaken." The key words are "usually" and "sometimes." Klein endorses Kahneman's (2011) conclusion that *both* "system 1" (the lazy mind thinking fast) and "system 2" (the analytic mind thinking slow) are necessary. It is the effective blending of intuition and analysis that can be powerful.

## Tapping the Wise or Knowledgeable Crowd

In 2004, James Surowiecki published his acclaimed book, *The Wisdom of Crowds*. His thesis goes beyond the intuitive concept that there is much knowledge to be harnessed out there. Rather, as he says, "when our imperfect judgments are aggregated in the right way, our collective intelligence is often excellent" (xvii). "This intelligence," he goes on, "is at work in the world in many different guises. It's the reason the Internet search engine Google can scan a billion web pages and find the one page that has the exact piece of information you were looking for . . . and it explains why, for the past fifteen years, a few hundred amateur traders in the middle of Iowa [in the Iowa Electronics Market founded by the University of Iowa's College of Business] have done a better job predicting election results than Gallup polls have."

In subsequent years, Surowiecki's catchphrase, "wisdom of crowds," has been at times conflated with the notion of "crowdsourcing." This latter term more appropriately refers to an open call to a large pool of self-identified individuals to contribute their knowledge to an issue or project. Wikipedia is such an enterprise. Two other highly productive examples of crowdsourcing are OpenStreetMap (http://www.openstreetmap.org/about) and Google Maps,[4] both of which tap volunteers' knowledge of local geography to produce high-fidelity street maps for nearly any place on the globe. Need a detailed current street map of Bujumbura? Both can help you.

Neither crowdsourcing nor tapping the "wisdom of crowds" is right for every situation. Surowiecki (2004: 477) says, "Bubbles and crashes are textbook examples of collective decision making gone wrong. In a bubble, all the conditions that make groups intelligent—independence, diversity, private judgment—disappear."

But I find a troubling dismissiveness among intelligence analysts and most of their leaders when it comes to harnessing the crowd. This dismissiveness goes beyond analysts' reputation for introversion. It has roots in their training, standards, and experience. Analysts are properly trained to pay close attention to the pedigree of sources (i.e., a source's access, expertise, agenda), and crowds have no pedigree. Intelligence analysts have a standard that says, the closer we can get to direct, first-hand sourcing, the better, and many in the crowd are at the other end of the spectrum. Intelligence analysts will cite their own topic of substantive expertise and then point to inaccuracies in a Wikipedia entry on that topic as a reason to "never trust Wikipedia."

---

[4] Google Maps' program to incorporate local knowledge used to fall under its "Mapmaker" program. Mapmaker has since been absorbed by the Google Maps and Local Guides programs. See http://www.google.com/mapmaker.

What intelligence analysts and their leaders must allow for is that *sometimes* the crowds are insightful. Sometimes crowdsourced products are not only good enough, but good indeed. Let's examine a couple of examples of when tapping a crowd produced good results.

The jelly bean jar at the state fair provides perhaps the most cited example of the "wisdom of crowds." The challenge is to guess the number of jelly beans in a large jar. Each person *independently* submits a guess. Surowiecki (2004: 42) stresses the importance of independence.

When groupthink takes over a crowd, biases multiply, but when the opinions are truly independent, biases often cancel each other out. The independent guesses are then aggregated and the average guess sometimes proves accurate.

What is there for the leader of analysis to learn from the jelly bean jar experience? One positive thing that is going on with the jelly bean example is that the methodology provides a way forward when

- Many people have *some* knowledge (e.g., "It looks like several thousand beans to me")

- No one has overriding precise knowledge (e.g., the full and empty weights of this jar and the weight of an average jelly bean)

- The correct answer is simple (e.g., 3041 beans)

- The correct answer will never be found in the extremes (it is neither 6 beans nor 6 million beans)

Has such an odd array of conditions ever arisen in intelligence analysis? It has for me. I'll change the details here to keep this unclassified. Borostan was a front-burner threat country, with a wide array of analysts plying their various forms of expertise to assess it. These analysts had been arguing strenuously over how close Borostan was to a particular breakthrough that would advance its military capabilities appreciably. At one end of the spectrum, I had experts arguing that Borostan was within five years of the breakthrough. At the other end, equally impressive experts were confident that fifteen years was likely. This debate had been going on for a year, with opinions becoming entrenched. The debate, though frustrating, hadn't been fruitless. It showed me vividly the limits of our current information base.

Then one day, we received some powerful new intelligence. Borostan just had achieved a milestone toward that threat breakthrough. The new intelligence, as so often is the case, was not an established fact; it was a credible source's claim. We needed to report the new intelligence and its implications to the White House. I gathered the relevant experts to discuss it. By the time I arrived, they had filled the conference room and were already arguing. And their argument sounded exactly like it had the month before. One side was yelling, "They are way closer to the breakthrough than you think!" The other side was wagging their fingers and saying, "These breakthroughs are much harder technologically than you think!" I rolled my eyes and dove in.

I silenced the room and handed out 3″ x 5″ cards. "On your card, I want each of you to characterize your confidence in this new intelligence. Is it low, medium, or high?" They were done in a minute. Then I told them, "On the other side, write your *best guess* for the number of years before Borostan's breakthrough." That was tougher and took five minutes. I had to keep telling them that I wanted a single number, not a range—they hated that. We gathered the cards and chatted for a few minutes while one of my economists did the math. The result was that the aggregated confidence in the new intelligence was medium-to-high. The average guess for breakthrough was seven years, with the range of views being three to nine years. Remember, the range before had been five to fifteen years! I proposed to the group that we inform the White House of the new reporting, our assessment that it was probably true, and that the range of our views had both narrowed and moved forward, standing at three to nine years for a breakthrough. Straying from Surowiecki, I also decided we would not report the average guess (seven years), afraid that a single digit might imply a precision none of us felt. Consensus was instant! We had captured the significance of the new reporting. We had narrowed our uncertainty while faithfully reporting that it was still significant. We had captured the wisdom of an array of experts (a small crowd) without a fruitless afternoon of point and counterpoint. Surowiecki's key ingredients, diversity of thought and independence of judgment, were preserved, and a very simple methodology for producing a group "answer" could be applied.

My very simple application of tapping the wisdom of a crowd might, of course, appear too simple. And few challenges for intelligence analysis equate to the jelly bean jar. The basic principles of tapping the independent thoughts of diverse individuals—letting their individual biases cancel each other out—have great value for more complex questions. The hard part quickly becomes picking a methodology for aggregating their views into a single answer.

Look, for example, at another success Surowiecki recounts. Drawing on an account from the book *Blind Man's Bluff* by Sherry Sontag and Christopher Drew, Surowiecki (2004: xxix–xxxii) points to the remarkable instance of USS *Scorpion*. The submarine had disappeared in the Atlantic in 1968. The Navy had its last reported location, but searching was turning up nothing. Naval officer John Craven assembled a "team of men with a wide range of knowledge, including mathematicians, submarine specialists, and salvage men." He didn't ask them to team up and develop a likely location of the downed submarine. Rather, he asked them to independently guess the likelihood of scenarios for "why the sub ran into trouble . . . its speed as it headed to the ocean floor . . . the steepness of its descent, and so forth." Then, Craven applied his magic and produced a location just 220 yards from where the wreck was found.

The important part here is not what "magic" Craven used. Surowiecki notes that it was a heavy application of Bayes's theorem—which is a good approach to keeping the latest data that an event *seems to have happened* from overshadowing the statistical probability of such an event happening. (It is a way to stay sane when your latest PSA test shows positive for prostate cancer.) But a lot of choices, assumptions, and calculations were involved. The important part here is that this is several orders of magnitude beyond the complexity of averaging all the jelly bean guesses. This is a case of the leader of analysis, Craven, applying his own sophisticated analysis to produce a useful aggregation of the group's inputs. Collecting the views of the crowd was relatively easy; turning it into "wisdom" was Craven's own, highly sophisticated analysis.

Now, imagine you are Craven's customer. The admiral is going to have to decide whether to move search ships to Craven's datum. Craven himself cannot know that he is correct. He can only recount the methodology he used and say that this is the location it produced. The admiral is likely to ask, "How many times previously has a downed sub been found with this approach?" "None, sir." He'll care how expensive it will be to check Craven's guess. He'll weigh whether Craven's location is counterintuitive or "makes perfect sense." Craven, on the other hand, will wish he had an established track record of success using this methodology, to encourage the admiral to give him the benefit of the doubt. And even if the sub is found where he said, Craven probably would wonder, like our experts often do, "Did I just get lucky?"

I am not telling you not to bother trying what Craven tried with your own analytic issues. Start with the earlier tests I mentioned for whether the wisdom of the crowds pertains: many people in your "crowd" have *some* knowledge; no one has overriding precise knowledge; the correct answer is simple; and the correct answer will not be found in extremes. All these conditions existed for Craven and for my Borostan example. Then decide whether *you* have the ability to collect and aggregate the independent guesses into something meaningful.

This is all much easier *if you have issues that repeat.* Here is where the data scientists would speak up. They would tell you to develop your best calculation method (the algorithm), refine it, and then test it against data it hasn't seen before. This is relatively easy if you have a situation that recurs. As you see the event recur, you will learn whether to trust your methodology. The data scientists would tell you not to place great bets on the algorithm working the first try on any problem. Even with the simple jelly bean challenge, don't bet the farm that the mathematical average of the guesses will be correct with the *next* jar. What you can tell over time is whether that approach provides a more statistically accurate tally than any other approach you might use.

And don't think having a willing crowd obviates expertise on every question. Remember, Craven assembled people with professional knowledge—they were diverse, yes, but still carried relevant expertise. In *Crowdsourcing*, Jeff Howe (2008: 143) states this usefully, saying, "[T]he crowd must have some qualifications to solve the problem at hand. A random collection of subway commuters could hardly be expected to outperform a group of nuclear engineers at designing a more efficient nuclear reactor." Someone who has not been to Bujumbura is going to be useless when you need that map.

## Keep Your Eye Out for New Choices

A central lesson of this chapter is that analysis is not a static craft. The craft you lead is changing before your eyes. The approaches to organizing it and conducting it are expanding. Some principles of analysis are timeless—the ancient Greeks and Romans contributed lessons that all critical thinkers apply today. But our unprecedented abilities to think together, to think with machines, and to weigh masses of data offer options for analysis that are multiplying. Between modern thinkers about analysis, thinkers about the human mind, thinkers about information, and thinkers about machine intelligence, we have a mix of relevant insights richer than any leader of analysis has enjoyed in history.

One recent example of blending of approaches captures much of today's analytic dynamic. I mentioned earlier in this chapter that the wizards at Google found a way to monitor the spread of flu. Examining queries flowing through its search engines, one of Google's teams started paying attention to searches containing terms associated with various flu strains. Google discovered that it could track the spread of flu in near real time faster than the CDC (see, e.g., Ginsberg et al. 2009). In a bit of bragging, Google's Flu Trends website used to show its track and the CDC track side by side, with the CDC track visibly lagging by about two weeks.

But Google's model was jolted by some quite public failures, exaggerating the likely flu. In the winter of 2012/2013, it appears that a media-fanned flu scare prompted many Google searches based on fear rather than the actual spread of the flu. Writing for Nature.com, Declan Butler (2013) notes that Google's "estimate for the Christmas national peak of flu is almost double the CDC's."[5]

---

[5] Butler writes, "Google Flu Trends has continued to perform remarkably well, and researchers in many countries have confirmed that its ILI [influenza-like illness] estimates are accurate. But the latest US flu season seems to have confounded its algorithms. Its estimate for the Christmas national peak of flu is almost double the CDC's . . . and some of its state data show even larger discrepancies."

If there was ever a company that respects data, it is Google, and they adjusted to this significant new information. Here's what they posted in the Google Research Blog:

In the 2012/2013 season, we significantly overpredicted compared to the CDC's reported U.S. flu levels. We investigated and in the 2013/2014 season launched a retrained model (still using the original method). It performed within the historic range, but we wondered: could we do even better? Could we improve the accuracy significantly with a more robust model that learns continuously from official flu data?

So for the 2014/2015 season, we're launching a new Flu Trends model in the U.S. that . . . takes official CDC flu data into account as the flu season progresses. (Stefansen 2014; see also Stefansen 2013)

The final chapter of this journey appeared in another Google announcement. In August 2015, Google said, "Instead of maintaining our own website going forward, we're now going to empower institutions who specialize in infectious disease research to use the data to build their own models" (The Flu Trends Team 2015).

The entire experience is, to me, emblematic of what we are seeing with analysis today. A creative use of big data made the previous state of the art appear obsolete. Then the big data approach let the customer down. Then a mix of new and old approaches produced value that surpasses what either approach could have achieved alone. Any leader of analysis can learn from the creativity, open-mindedness, and nimbleness demonstrated by Google here. And any leader of analysis should also see a cautionary tale here: however successful your approach or technique may be for a while, you would be wise to frequently ask yourself, "Is this still working?"

As you lead analysis, don't get hung up on trying to pick the one optimum approach or technique to be applied to each situation. There is no static, single "optimum." A single approach to analysis is a rut. It will work for a while—else you wouldn't use it—but something slightly or significantly better will become available. Be open to that reality. While your experts are focused on the substantive analytic issue you have handed them, reserve at least some of your analytic energies for something else. Analyze what is new on the menu of approaches to analysis that might render insights faster or deeper than what your experts are producing today.

Do this well, and your customers will notice your team is producing more useful analysis than other suppliers. Your team's impact will increase. And the analysts on your team just might take on that "Baghdad glow."

# KEY THEMES

The best analytic units I have seen had several traits in common: They had clarity of purpose. They usually had a short line between producers and customers. They had a drive to get the job done. And they had a prejudice to take advantage of the diversity of talent available.

But they didn't share a particular approach to analysis. They were seized with finding what works in *this* situation, not applying some formula that worked for them before. And they never disdained an analytic innovation (e.g., advanced data analytics or gaming) as "not our way."

- The default approach to analysis has shifted from the single expert working alone (*What do I know?*) to cross-discipline teams working together (*What do we know?*). Now, analytic units are awakening to crowd sourcing, big data, algorithms, machine learning, AI, and machine-human partnership (exploring *What is knowable?*). None of these approaches makes the previous approach obsolete. Instead, all are available to apply to the appropriate problem.

- Expertise is precious—build it. Observers love to catch experts being wrong, or to point at the so-called expert who is closed-minded, stuck in the past, or too arrogant to listen. But give me a self-critical, always-learning expert and he or she will elevate any approach to a hard analytic problem.

- Diversity of thought, skills, and approach catalyzes analytic insight. Such diversity often makes your job harder, as you may have to referee discussions of, say, your inductive and deductive reasoners. But it's worth it.

Beware of an analytic unit getting stuck in its approach or overconfident in its judgments. Structured Analytic Techniques can be one great way to look at a problem from a different optic. But nearly every new approach to your unit's work is a significant resource investment. It will usually be you, as leader, who has to say, "Let's try something fresh." Rarely will your analysts gamble their precious time with such trial and error.

# Nurturing the New Idea

## Creativity, Insight, and Innovation in Analysis

*Originality is fragile. And, in its first moments, it's often far from pretty.*

Ed Catmull, President,
Pixar and Disney Animation Studios (2014)

In his wonderful book, *Brave Dragons*, Jim Yardley (2012) writes about the Chinese passion for basketball. Thanks to YMCA missionaries, basketball was introduced to China very soon after its 1891 invention. In American basketball, the point guard is a creator. No matter how large the team's playbook, our point guards are encouraged to spot opportunities and improvise. Some of their best highlights show maneuvers the coach never dreamt of. By contrast, as Yardley puts it, "the job of a Chinese point guard is to please the coach." In the Chinese system, the coach tends to be a dictatorial disciplinarian and practice is dominated by endless drills. And while the Chinese basketball system has produced world class athletes, it has never produced an NBA-caliber point guard and it has never won a medal in the Olympics.

It is not that China lacks creativity. The Beijing Olympics, where the Chinese basketball team was again shut out of the medals, produced the most creative and breathtaking opening ceremonies I have ever seen. It is that the Chinese approach to organized basketball chokes the creativity out of the players.

This can happen with analysis. If you are one of those leaders who rigidly insists on sticking to the "playbook," you can be pretty sure that your unit's analysis is formulaic and risk averse.

And the suffocation of fresh ideas doesn't have to come from the leader—it can also come from the players. One of my CIA co-analysts in the 1980s decided to color outside the lines and write a different kind of a paper. He told the reader he was going to provide a dialogue with a fictitious taxi driver in a particular Middle Eastern country, as a way of presenting the local political and economic sentiment. The analyst was true to the body of reporting he had seen, but he was telling "the story" in a holistic and highly readable way. Other analysts in our office howled at what they saw as unprofessionalism. "This isn't what we do. This isn't intelligence analysis!" Fortunately, the office director was not as stodgy as those analysts, and he published the piece despite their offended sensibilities. His attitude was that as long as we did not mislead the reader, this was worth a try. The analyst, by the way, was John Brennan, who decades later would be director of CIA.

In chapter 3, I argued that it is the leader's responsibility to shape an environment that brings out the best in her analysts. By "the best," I mean a stream of the most useful insights they can hatch, delivered in a way that resonates with the customer. This chapter zooms in on an aspect of that environment: the extent to which it promotes or stifles new ideas.

There are three manifestations of "the new idea" that I will be dealing with here: creativity, innovation, and insight. They are not interchangeable; they are, indeed, different things. But all three involve a new idea, and all three are necessary in analysis. And that which promotes or inhibits one element tends to have the same effect on the other two. The dictionary definition of *creativity* is the "ability to transcend traditional rules, patterns, relationships or the like, and to create meaningful new ideas." *Insight* has to do with discerning a meaningful underlying truth. An insight, to me as an analyst, will be the "aha!" thought that occurs to me—the new thought that changes the whole picture. It is also delivering an insight to a customer if it is a pivotal notion new to *him*—his "aha! moment"—even though it might be old knowledge to me. *Innovation* has to do with putting a new idea to work with a new approach—in analysis it might be a new way of unearthing insights or a new way of presenting them to the customer. The point is not to nurture creativity for its own sake. The point is to put creativity *to work* in your unit; nurture an environment in which creativity is welcome, and your analytic unit will produce more insights and innovations.

Over the years I have seen several analytic environments, with varying levels of comfort with new ideas. When I worked in the intel shop at the Navy headquarters in London, it was made clear to us that our job was to communicate the expertise *of others* to the admiral. We lieutenants were discouraged from presuming that our own insights would be of interest to him. The unspoken question to us was, "What do the experts think?" Creativity in analysis among lieutenants was unwelcome. Cutting and pasting was expected.

When I worked in CIA's Counterterrorism Center (CTC) after 9/11, I saw the other end of the spectrum. The analytic environment there was driven by desperation. We had to beat Al Qa'ida and its allies as quickly as possible, and we were quite willing to try new things to see what worked. We quickly hatched such efforts as a new approach to gauging strategic progress in the war, several new threads of targeting analysis, and the famous "Threat Matrix." We threw into the mix analysts who had never worked terrorism before and saw new ideas emerge. Some of these efforts worked and some did not, but all were welcome.

So . . . were CTC analysts just *genetically* more creative than those in that Navy intel shop? I don't think so. In studies of twins, researchers judged that only about 30 percent of creativity appeared to come from genetic predisposition (in contrast with 80–85 percent of intellect). This strongly suggests that the greater determinant of creativity is nurture, not nature (Dyer, Gregersen, and Christensen 2011: 21–22). *I* was certainly more creative in CTC than I had been in London. Many of our new analysts in CTC were being more creative than they had been in their previous offices. The difference was the environment.

In Ed Catmull's (2014) *Creativity, Inc.,* one of the best books on leadership I have ever read, he describes this dynamic superbly. He tells the story of when he and John Lasseter took over leadership of Disney Animation in 2006. He encountered the same types of creative people he had grown used to in Pixar Animation but in an environment that put their ideas through a bureaucratic wringer. "There seemed to be undue emphasis put on preventing errors; even when it came to something as small as office décor, no one dared to put themselves out there, or to make a mistake." The environment produced a drought in hits by the legendary studio. Catmull and Lasseter set about overhauling the stifling bureaucracy at Disney Animation. Among many other things, they reversed the 2004 business decision to shut down hand-drawn 2D animation—the Disney executives believed that Catmull's own Pixar studios demonstrated that 3D computer animation was the business formula for the future. But Catmull and Lasseter shifted their focus from the formulaic approach (the business formula was to replicate the ingredients of the last success) to emphasize that Disney's greatest animation successes had stemmed from its innovation and creativity. Two-dimensional animation movies would not be dismissed by the audience if they were fresh and creative stories brilliantly animated. Soon Disney studios were producing animated hits again—both hand drawn and 3D.

# Creative Analysis?

What do I mean by creative intelligence analysis? Clearly, the intelligence analyst cannot make stuff up. An intelligence analyst creating his own "facts" would be drummed out of the corps. Further, we cannot tolerate "creative" use of evidence that cherry-picks some bits and hides others to create a slanted picture for the customer. We also cannot tolerate an analyst being so creative in his presentation that he loses the customer. It doesn't matter how profound the analysis is, we will not allow it to be presented in haiku, for example. So professional intelligence analysis will always, to some extent, be bounded creativity.

I am not dwelling here on the most trivial forms of creativity in analysis. Writing is always to some degree a creative process, so even the least creative analyst "creates." Every analyst creates at a basic level when he thinks of the perfect metaphor to describe a situation. And analysis itself usually involves an analyst thinking thoughts she didn't have before, so each new thought is, to her, a "creation."

Rather, by *"creative analysis"* I am referring to developing new ways of narrowing the range of uncertainty in the issues we study. The most striking examples of creativity in intelligence show up as innovation. As I mentioned before, innovation is creativity put to work. Here are just a few examples I have encountered over the years.

- CIA officers worked with the Office of Naval Intelligence in 1961 to discern identifying features of crates carrying Soviet military hardware to overseas clients. The shape of crates could help analysts tell, for example, that MiG-21 aircraft and Komar missile boats were being shipped. The approach, termed *cratology*, played a role in identifying the Soviet buildup on Cuba culminating in the 1962 missile crisis (Goodell 2002).

- In the 1980s, a team of analysts gleaned decades of indicators of state instability to identify nations most at risk.

- After the 1998 East Africa embassy bombings, an analyst compiled data from several actual terrorist explosions to build a model for safe perimeters to protect different types of structures against varying sizes of truck bombs.

Or the analyst might come up with a creative way to communicate his message. One of my economists in the 1990s presented a paper digitally and allowed the reader to adjust certain variables on his economic tables to display ways to influence the situation. This would be no big deal today, but it made several of us say "wow!" at the time. And over the last decade, I have been impressed by how many analysts are telling more and more of their "stories" through imaginative and interactive graphics.

But I recoil when my friends in CIA point to such examples and say, "See how creative our analysts are? See what imagination we have displayed over the years? We just don't get enough credit for our creativity. And we clearly do the most innovative analysis in the intelligence community." Such pride is like bragging you are the funniest person on the Supreme Court. A much more telling critique came from an analyst who told me, "They tell me to be creative, but some editor is always there to make sure I color inside the lines."

I've had some analytic leaders tell me, "If you really want us to be creative, we are going to have to hire different analysts." I disagree. Beyond the twins studies I mentioned, which demonstrate that only a small part of creativity seems to be genetic, I frequently saw creativity finding an outlet in our workforce. CIA has a thriving community of spare-time novelists and poets. One office I led did hilarious holiday party skits that are talked about—and quoted from—twenty years later. And more than a few retired analysts enter the civilian world to become artists or entrepreneurs.

So, if we have demonstrably creative people and creative analysis occasionally happens, what is the problem? The problem is that creativity in the analytic environments I have seen was too rare. I encountered too many analysts passively "waiting for someone to collect the intelligence I need." Every time one of my analysts produced something truly creative, I made a point of telling my bosses about it. This rarely occurred more than a few times a year. To us, creativity in analysis was an unnatural act.

A signal that things are not fine is the repeated conversation I had with the *most* creative people I found in analysis. In CIA's analytic directorate, they were not hard to find—they seemed to be *different* from most analysts. For years, I made a point to take their pulse. Time and again they told me, "Well, I'm hanging in there, but I don't know if I'll still be here next year. I'm getting tired of getting nowhere." All thought they had paid a professional price for trying to press their creativity. And one who stayed for decades told me her secret: "I deactivated my care button."

# Stifling Creativity and Innovation in Analysis

There is a dark strain in us analysts. In movies and on TV, we have a reputation for obsessing to find an answer, usually the answer to the question, "What is *really* going on here?" That is close, but off. The question we obsess over most is, "What is wrong with this picture?" We are trained skeptics. For many of us who have warning among our responsibilities, we obsess over, "What bad thing could happen?" I'll talk about the ethical ramifications of this—and its link to the analysts' disease, cynicism—in chapter 8, "Ethics in Analysis."

With us excelling in the game of "What is wrong with this picture?" every truly creative notion we hatch is met with immediate and daunting critique—sometimes one's own. In his excellent book, *Where Good Ideas Come From: The Natural History of Innovation,* Steven Johnson (2010: 75) points out that "most good ideas come into the world half-baked, more hunch than revelation." Analysts are masters at lacerating the half-baked idea. It takes a force of will to resist the temptation.

We carry our "What is wrong with this picture?" attitude to the function of editing. Give me a fresh draft, and I am instantly looking for its weaknesses. Make me the second reviewer of the draft, and I am sure I can find something the first reviewer missed. What has the author gotten "wrong" in logic or tradecraft or word choice or sourcing? Where might the reader be unconvinced? What might the reader find confusing or needlessly off-putting? Is the reader going to find a surprise in the analysis—a fresh insight—too surprising? The unfortunate result, all too often, is dry and formulaic writing.

A State Department friend once critiqued CIA's writing this way: "It's like hospital food. It's nourishing, but all the flavor has been extracted!"

We showed our mastery at "flavor extraction" during the administration of President George H. W. Bush. One of his senior aides asked whether, occasionally, we could include a little humor in the President's Daily Brief, an appropriately serious intelligence periodical. I will gladly put the analysts of CIA up against any organization—even the staff of *The Daily Show*—for wit. We have some analysts who can consistently make me laugh until it hurts. But put our wit through the editorial chain, and it is doomed. Several truly funny offerings to the "humor section" of the PDB were submitted, but before they were published, anything that would produce more than a wry smile was simply drained of all life. In abject embarrassment, we soon abandoned our pathetic effort.

Another powerful factor stifling *innovation* is the prevalent attitude toward failure—it scares us to death. Psychologists talk about two basic attitudes toward failure, and you can see them clearly in children. One child regards failure as something to be avoided. She tends not to enjoy trying challenging things she is not already good at. The other child doesn't even focus on failure but tends to keep trying until she succeeds. All children take the latter approach when learning to walk, but by elementary school the two groups tend to diverge—some kids dive into new challenges and others hang back. Analysts overwhelmingly were the students who excelled at school, never getting an "F" on a report card—indeed, they would have been horrified by the concept. It wasn't that we were great at everything in school—nobody is. It was that we avoided things we were not confident we would succeed at.

This individual abhorrence of failure can be mirrored in any organization's culture. For example, Chet Huber, a retired General Motors executive, described his "company's crippling propensity to over plan. . . . Ironically, in attempting to minimize risk and reduce errors, GM's emphasis on regimented systems stymied innovation" (Sims 2011: 15–16).

In an analytic organization, some failure is inevitable. Regardless of our talent and professionalism, some nasty surprise eventually will occur, and we will wallow in the aftermath of yet another "intelligence failure." For a failure-averse culture, this is agonizing. And I believe one result is that our executives can sometimes compensate for this, perhaps unconsciously, with a balancing mechanism: "If we are going to fail, let it be on something beyond our control. But for anything within our control, including our initiatives, failure *must* be avoided." When we consider big change, first we blanch, and then we study the issue to death. And just as individual abhorrence of failure can aggregate into an organizational mindset, the organizational mindset sits like a wet blanket on the individual analyst who might be contemplating trying something new.

But innovation requires a comfort with error. As Steve Johnson (2010: 137) writes, "[E]rror is not simply a path you have to suffer through on the way to genius. Error creates a path. . . . Being right keeps you in place. Being wrong forces you to explore." Innovation researcher Peter Sims (2011: 7) echoes this and describes failure as not just a catalyst to creativity but a normal part of innovation. He says, typically, "Experimental innovators must be persistent and willing to accept failure and setbacks as they work toward their goals."

A third and more subtle factor inhibiting creativity—and by extension, innovation—in analysis can be found in the nature of the business. Analysis, when done right, requires diligent critical thinking. The dictum I mentioned in chapter 1, "No Lazy Thinking," means that real work is required. Real mental energy is spent in the process. It requires what psychologist and Nobel laureate Daniel Kahneman (2011: 60) refers to as "cognitive strain." This is a state in which, he says, "you are more likely to be vigilant and suspicious . . . and make fewer errors." These are all vital to an analyst's credibility. The problem comes with the cost of cognitive strain. Kahneman points out that in the state of cognitive strain, you are also "less intuitive and less creative than usual." This is connected to a critical balance I mentioned in chapter 3: the balance between trying to generate insights and trying to eliminate mistakes. We tend to think of mental work as not burning calories, but Kahneman makes clear that brain work is, indeed, energy consuming. Your analyst's diligence can literally leave her feeling spent before the creative thought sparks.

I don't believe this third factor is as stifling as the big two. "What is wrong with this picture?" and fear of failure actively push against creativity and innovation. They are like driving with your brake on. The fact [or idea] that diligent critical thinking can sap energy otherwise used in creativity is more like driving with your air conditioner on—in times of strain, the engine might not be able to both power the car up a hill and keep you cool. Nevertheless, it is worth keeping an eye on the dynamic. At the very least, it means that in times of greatest "cognitive strain" for your analysts, you can expect less creativity than usual.

## And What of Insight?

Creativity, innovation, and insight are different things, but they overlap. Indeed, *creativity* and *innovation* overlap so much that the burgeoning literature on them often uses the terms interchangeably. You can see that in just the last few pages. Insight is similar but more distinct. As I said earlier, that which promotes or inhibits one is likely to have the same effect on the other two. But unlike creativity and innovation, *insight* is a normal part of analysis. Nearly every day at CIA, I saw insightful analysis. This needs some explaining.

As I mentioned, *insight* has to do with discerning a meaningful underlying truth, a truth that changes perspective on an issue. That is very much what analysis strives for. We spend significant mental energy trying to come up with the key to the puzzle box. We strain to hatch the idea that will suddenly make a situation make sense. And we suffer from a visceral frustration when something just doesn't make sense to us. Not every piece we write is insightful, but string too many "blah" pieces together and we are miserable.

So how do the dynamics that inhibit creativity and innovation inhibit insightful analysis? The two big stiflers—"What is wrong with this picture?" and *fear of failure*—are at work here, too. Insight is often born vulnerable— Steve Johnson's "half-baked" new idea. We have all seen the seed of a profound analytic insight tossed into an analytic debate, only to be burned up under the lasers of merciless experts. They find a weakness in the idea, hold the weakness up for everyone's contempt, and toss the idea aside.

Similarly, our fear of failure plays its part. In some cases, we won't invest the time it takes to fully bake that idea, fearing that after hours or weeks of work, it still might turn out to lead nowhere. In other cases, the fresh analytic insight is truly pivotal, changing the paradigm for our understanding of a situation. In those cases, the new insight may mean that our old understanding was wrong—a failure we will hesitate to embrace. In still other cases, we might invest so much attention to our analytic tradecraft— which, as described in chapter 3, largely is designed to prevent us from being wrong—that we are intellectually spent before we arrive at insight.

These inhibitors are not strong enough to stanch insights as effectively as they stanch creativity and innovation. Our powerful sense that it is our *job* to produce insights prevents that. But the inhibitors have their sorry impact. They slow our production of some insights, kill others in the cradle, and bury still others in an avalanche of qualifiers and alternatives.

You may be asking, If insight happens a lot in analysis, why doesn't that define the environment and, by extension, encourage creativity and innovation? You can find your answer in our remarkable capacity to compartmentalize. Part of analytic rigor is to separate things that are even subtly *different*. We are good at that. What is *different* in this case? In our minds, it is our *job* to produce analytic insights. Too many of us simply don't think of it as our job to be creative or to innovate. Our production of analytic insights can be narrowly focused on our *substance*—Iran's nuclear program, or China's development of a satellite, or Al Qa'ida's latest campaign. Creativity or innovation is usually connected to our *processes*—how we develop or display information, how we connect with our customers, or how we approach a topic.

# Promoting Creativity, Innovation, and Insight
..............................................................

With so many things inhibiting creativity and innovation in analysis, and at least slowing breakthrough insights, it is not sufficient for you to simply be receptive to them when you see them. **The leader must be an active advocate and champion of creativity, innovation, and insight.** You can do this in several steps.

## Step 1: Start with Your Own Demeanor

First, stop being part of the problem. If you are a master at playing "What's wrong with this picture?" restrain yourself. Set a receptive tone in your meetings by restraining the other wet blankets as well. A simple statement can work wonders when someone is trying to introduce a creative thought into the discussion: you can say, "This is interesting; I want to hear more."

If you are horrified by failure, screw up your courage and hide your fear. If you are naturally risk averse, push yourself well out of your comfort zone. If you reward only the consistently successful analysts, broaden your definition of success to include the productive failure. And demonstrate that you embrace the occasional dead-end project that was worth a try.

Take heart in all of this examination of your own demeanor. You don't need a personality transplant (probably), but you can channel your instincts productively. Once you have made it safe for analysts to air creative ideas—once you have made it safe for the half-baked idea to see the light of day—your skills at critique can be channeled constructively. Critique is essential, but make sure it doesn't stop the conversation. Acknowledging that an idea is half-baked, you might help ensure that it becomes fully baked. If the idea has a weak point, identify it and see if you can strengthen it or work around it. Not every new idea is a good one; far from it. As Catmull (2014) confides, "[E]arly on, all of our movies suck." You will quite properly leave most ideas on the cutting room floor. But if you consistently leave *everything* on the cutting room floor, your negativity is in charge.

Similarly, embracing failure as a normal part of any dynamic business doesn't mean you need to start ignoring it. For failure to be productive, you must recognize it as failure and learn from it. Sloppy efforts that lead to failure should never be tolerated. It is not the failure you will be condemning but the sloppiness. The serious, diligent efforts that fail usually include something worth salvaging and building on—including the dignity of those involved.

Don't let your inner abhorrence of failure make you too slow in declaring failure when it happens. Too many failed experiments are continued months or years past their productive life because no leader had the heart to say, "Enough!" Peter Sims (2011), in *Little Bets*, talks about "failing quickly to learn fast." Or consider design firm IDEO's mantra, "[F]ail soon to succeed sooner" (Dyer, Gregersen, and Christensen 2011: 170). Unless you have the courage to declare failure, the subsequent success stays over the horizon.

And overriding your risk aversion does not mean ignoring risk. A healthy attitude toward risk is one that acknowledges it cannot be avoided. There is risk in maintaining the status quo. A healthy attitude toward risk allows the risks of both action and inaction to be weighed. You should have little trouble identifying the difference between smart and stupid risk. You also should have little trouble calculating potential consequences—good as well as bad. You needn't risk the health of your company when you can risk the time of a single team—experiments and pilot programs often are a sensible way to move forward when the stakes are high.

## Step 2: Tend the Mix and the Mixing

Now you are ready to move beyond your own interactions with analysts and actively build an environment that breeds healthy interactions with each other and outsiders. New ideas tend not to hatch in a vacuum. They usually are the product of existing ideas bumping into each other. Build an environment where that happens a lot.

As a molecule can only combine with the molecule next to it, an environment that puts one idea next to another allows them to combine into something new—a creative thought, insight, or innovation. Again Steve Johnson (2010: 30): "The scientist Stuart Kauffman has a suggestive name for all those first-order combinations: 'the adjacent possible.'" In human history, the wholly new idea emerging without such contact is rare, but fresh ideas emerging from the contact of component ideas is common. Johnson goes on to describe an environment where ideas naturally flow, bump together, and combine as a "liquid network." History pivots on periods when information flow became more "liquid": the rise of cities, the invention of movable type, and today's Internet. Each of these brought ideas together at an unprecedented rate, stimulating an explosion of new ideas. Author Frans Johansson (2006: 2) argues that creativity and innovation blossom most at intersections. He says, "When you step into an intersection of fields, disciplines, or cultures, you can combine existing concepts into a large number of extraordinary new ideas." He names this "the Medici Effect," pointing to the Medicis' Florence in the fifteenth century as a magnet for artists and thinkers and a source of explosive creativity.

Chris Anderson (2011), curator of the TED conferences, talks about this mixing in reference to what he calls "Crowd Accelerated Innovation." Anderson says,

Innovation has always been a group activity. . . . Most innovation is the result of long hours, building on the input of others. Ideas spawn from earlier ideas, bouncing from person to person and being reshaped as they go. . . . So Crowd Accelerated Innovation isn't new. In one sense, it's the only kind of innovation there's ever been. What is new is that the Internet—and specifically online video—has cranked it up to a spectacular degree.[1]

Steven Johnson (2010) cautions that this appeal to mixing is not the same as the oft-heard appeal to tap the knowledge of the collective. That has its place, as discussed in chapter 4, but it is a different thing. Johnson notes that the so-called "hive mind," a collective consciousness, tends not to be a generator of innovation. "It's not that the network itself is smart," Johnson says, "it's that individuals get smarter because they're connected to the network" (58). Similarly, Anderson's (2011) "crowd accelerated innovation" is not the same as the so-called "wisdom of crowds." Remember, that concept is to tap the *independent* opinion of many individuals, aggregated into an answer to a specific question (Surowiecki 2004). Rather, Anderson (2011) is talking about "crowds" of interested individuals sharing ideas and feeding off each other—sometimes competing with each other—to hatch new ideas. The existence of the interested crowd *accelerates* innovation.

How do you promote this mixing in your analytic unit to maximize the production of new ideas? Attend both to the mix inside your unit and the interaction with outsiders. Bring into your unit a diversity of skills, approaches, and analytic disciplines. Teach them—and enforce—productive critical debate and constructive criticism. Teach them to take new ideas seriously, building on them, strengthening them, and protecting them from

---

[1] Anderson goes on to explain that this dynamic requires three ingredients—a crowd, light, and desire—each of which the leader of analysis needs to pay attention to:
"A crowd is simply a community, any group of people with a shared interest. . . . The community needs to contain at least a few people capable of innovation. . . . [O]ther necessary roles:
• The trend-spotter, who finds promising innovation early.
• The evangelist, who passionately makes the case for idea X or person Y.
• The superspreader, who broadcasts innovations to a larger group.
• The skeptic, who keeps conversations honest.
• General participants, who show up, comment honestly, and learn."
Light
"All members of the community need to be visible; each needs to be aware of what others, particularly the most talented members, are up to."
Desire
"Active learning is hard work. And in most cases, what drives all that work, whether we will admit it or not, is the prospect of recognition for what we've done."

premature dismissal. Rein in your intellectual bullies. And spend enough time in their debates to make certain their "arguments" leave them feeling stimulated rather than enervated.

Having this rich mix of analysts in physical proximity to one another will not always be sufficient. You must also tend carefully to their communications. In the summer of 1990, I was a new manager in a group focused on the rising Iraqi threat to Kuwait. Saddam had moved forces near the Kuwaiti border, and we were trying to figure out whether he was just saber rattling or intended to invade. Our military analysts noted that the forces had, for the most part, arrived without their supply units. No supply support, no invasion. This reality reassured our political analysts, who also noted, given Iraq's strength and Kuwait's weakness, Saddam could probably extract significant Kuwaiti concessions without resorting to force. In the middle of this, I had to take a quick trip. When I returned, I went to the analysts' desks to get the latest. I started with the military analysts, who were deeply disturbed that the missing Iraqi logistics units had arrived on scene. The Iraqi Army appeared fully ready to mount an invasion, but the military analysts were reassured that the political analysts were still seeing Iraq-Kuwaiti negotiations that could win Saddam significant concessions. Then I spoke with the political analysts. They told me the Iraqi "diplomacy" appeared even more insulting than usual, almost designed to elicit a Kuwaiti rejection, but these analysts were still reassured that the military forces *lacked logistics support*. I was amazed. These political and military analysts sat within thirty feet of one another. They *liked and respected* one another. But the crush of the crisis in-box had interrupted their normally healthy exchange of information. Once we put the two teams together to tell each other what they had just told me, together they pivoted to an assessment that invasion was likely.

Look also to the interaction of your analysts with outside experts. By expanding the perimeter of your analysts' contact, you are expanding their "liquid network" and enabling more "adjacent" possibilities. Depending on your unit's culture, you might have to force this to occur. You might think this odd, presuming that excellent analysts would have a natural appetite for expert input. Yes, they have that appetite, and it generally is acute. But several things can inhibit their outreach. First, many of us earn the analyst's reputation for introversion. Approaching strangers is a psychological burden. Second, outreach is usually inefficient. For a busy analyst, it takes a leap of faith to spend a half day or more to get maybe fifteen minutes' worth of genuine insight from an outside expert. Conferences of several experts might seem more efficient, but the analyst doesn't control those conversations and can get frustrated with how academic they feel. One cynical analyst once confided to me, "The only thing worse than a roomful of academics is a roomful of academics with me in it." Third, analysts with security clearances always find interaction with "uncleared" outside experts a bit awkward. Some of those analysts simply have not been taught how to have an unclassified conversation. But even if they are good at unclassified conversations, they know they will have to disappoint the outside expert who is naturally hoping for an even give-and-take. For all these reasons, many analysts will feed their appetite for outside expertise by reading the book rather than meeting the author. They don't consciously renounce direct contact with the outsiders; they simply decide not to spend that time *today*. Your intervention will be required to change this situation.

## Step 3: In All This Mixing, Protect the Individual

Johnson (2010), Johansson (2006), and Anderson (2011) focus on interaction between people as a catalyst for new ideas. Research psychologist Gary Klein (2013) has done an extremely useful study, looking in the other direction. He has looked closely at what tends to occur *within a single mind* that allows the insight to be born. It is always, after all, within a single mind that a new idea is hatched. Looking at more than a hundred breakthrough ideas, ideas that altered paradigms, he determined the "aha! moment" is not a simple thing. Indeed, the "aha! moment" is not the critical thing, although it feels good when it happens. Rather, he digs for what underlies the "aha! moment": the journey that leads the thinker to that point. So many thoughts are mixing within the mind—together with unconscious activities—that there is no simple recipe for producing an insight. Instead, there are several ways that insights typically are born in the individual's mind.

Klein's (2013) research shows that one trigger for insight is *contradiction*. The thinker, evaluating a situation, comes across a discrepancy that simply offends the brain, and it cries, "Tilt!" "Wait a minute . . . this thing cannot be true if *that* thing is true!" This "Tilt!" reflex is common among analysts, I believe, being a natural cousin to the "What is wrong with this picture?" reflex. While one analyst would simply dismiss the new element that is challenging his old model, another analyst will obsess over this misalignment. He will chew on it long enough to consider that his old mental model might be flawed. Then he starts the critical process of reexamining assumptions, reweighing evidence, and reconsidering relationships. Sometimes unconsciously, his mind will be trying new models that might explain both the new and the old facts. The "aha! moment" comes when he arrives at one.

Another typical foundation for insights, according to Klein's (2013) research, is making a *connection*. Klein is quick to point out that this is not the cliché of connecting the dots, a description that offends analysts because it trivializes the process of determining what is and isn't a dot. Rather, Klein is referring to a mind, sometimes unconsciously, finding a link between two things so far apart or so subtle that others don't see it. He points to Admiral Yamamoto seeing the successful British raid on the Italian fleet at

Taranto, in November, 1940, as an indicator of the American fleet's vulnerability at Pearl Harbor. Interestingly, Klein notes that Yamamoto wrote about this connection before he was even aware that Japan and America would be going to war.

A third catalyst Klein (2013) talks about is the humble *coincidence*. Coincidence is often disdained because so often, it's "just coincidence." For an analyst to develop an insight triggered by a coincidence, she needs to notice a subtle correlation between two things. She then needs to resist the temptation to dismiss it as "*just* coincidence," and do the mental labor of hypothesizing what could explain the coincidence. All this is a tall order for a busy analyst who has seen many coincidences collapse under scrutiny. It is important for analysts to remember that patterns frequently begin life as coincidence. Spotting and assessing patterns is a classic and honored analytic function. The human brain is practically wired to spot patterns. Your brain will be happy doing this with a coincidence as well, if you take time to dwell on it.

Klein (2013) points to *creative desperation* as the other frequent trigger for insight. The thinker is trapped in a problem that must be solved. Out of frustration and desperation he starts to treat key assumptions as no longer sacred. He asks, "What if . . .?" more frequently and more wildly than usual. And one of those "what ifs" turns the key that unlocks a new solution. Early in this chapter I described the post-9/11 Counterterrorism Center as an environment rich in creativity and innovation. Creative desperation was certainly what we felt.

However the insight is catalyzed, *your job here is to protect the analyst gestating it*. What is going on is special; in the world of analysis, it is nearly sacred. You almost need to hang a sign on the situation: INSIGHT BEING BORN!

Do your best to identify what the analyst needs for this birth. Do your best to clear his decks. Lesser tasks—distracting meetings, the in-box—can wait. Does the analyst need to think out loud with some interested and interesting colleagues? Set that up for him. Does he need to be protected from the distraction of interested and interesting colleagues? Hang the "Do Not Disturb" sign on him.

And do your best to set aside *your* imperatives for the analyst. Resist the temptation to say, "But you are not working on the question I gave you!" Hand someone else that question for action. Or perhaps he is working on exactly the question you gave him, but you are seeing your deadline go out the window. Your customer probably will prefer to wait a bit for a new paradigm—remember, insights often change paradigms—than to make a decision based on a flawed old paradigm.

You may also need to resist your prejudice for action. If the issue being worked on is very important, you may be tempted to be an activist—to *make* the insight come. It doesn't work that way. At most, you might be able to have an occasional conversation with the analyst, letting him think out loud and offering a suggestion or two. But you cannot accelerate insight by command. You cannot increase its chances of arriving by lecturing your analyst on how important this is, or making him work through the weekend, or reminding him his promotion panel is meeting next week. You might be tempted to try to induce that "creative desperation" Klein talks about. Let go of that. A boss making an analyst desperate is more likely to trigger a defensive shutdown than a catharsis. (Recall my discussion of productive and counterproductive stress in chapter 3.) All such interventions are more likely to hurt rather than help the process—they distract the analyst's focus.

And make room for disappointment. There simply will be some times when, after all this effort, a significant insight doesn't come. How long you allow the gestation process to drag on should largely depend on the importance of the issue. For something really high stakes, you can protect the analyst from distractions for months, even with no guarantee of a breakthrough. The occasional gusher more than makes up for a string of dry wells.

All this implies a long labor and delivery. That is only sometimes the case. Many times the analyst will hand you an insight in a flash, generated almost effortlessly. Whichever way it arrived, your job now is to protect the insight itself.

If the insight is fresh enough, other analysts will bristle at it. They will quickly brainstorm why it must be wrong, perhaps find weaknesses in it, and minimize the validity of the supporting evidence. This is the "What's wrong with this picture" reflex kicking in. Then, as a last resort, they may allow that the insight is correct but deny that it is significant.

If the insight changes important paradigms, it is by its nature disruptive. Disruptive ideas will often provoke pushback not just from other analysts, but from institutions—including the one in which you serve—and from your customers. As a leader, your bureaucratic shoulders are broader than your analyst's. You will need to shepherd his important insight past any wolves.

## Step 4: Nurture an Innovative You

Most of what I have been talking about is you nurturing the creativity, innovation, and insights of your analysts. Your responsibility doesn't stop with them. You also need to attend to your own new ideas. And, if you have managers working for you, they need nurturing, too. Innovation researchers Jeff Dyer, Hal Gregersen, and Clayton Christensen (2011) write that "disruptive innovators" tend to have five key skills: associating, questioning, observing, networking, and experimenting. Their book, *The Innovator's DNA*, can help you hone your skills in each of these areas. Analytic leaders tend to be strong in these skills, but they can easily apply them to analysis rather than innovation.

Pay attention to your own interaction with outsiders. In intelligence analysis, the substantive issues your team analyzes are seductive and monopolize your outreach time. When I led our Middle East analysis, I invested time and travel connecting with outside experts on Middle Eastern affairs. When I led strategic weapons analysts, I engaged in regular dialogue with thinkers at Los Alamos, Sandia, and Lawrence Livermore National Laboratories. This was essential but insufficient. It helped me interact more productively with my analysts as well as my senior policymaking customers. And this was typical among my fellow leaders of analysis. But only after I retired did I invest real time on other types of experts—experts on cognition, data science, business leadership, and information technology. Very quickly I realized what my outreach had been missing all those years on the job.

In one of my seminars recently, I encountered an analytic leader who most vividly demonstrated his neglect of this kind of outreach. We were talking about IT tools to help analysts do their work, saying we needed to streamline the process of installing apps on analysts' desktops. This executive came up to me during the break and said, "Ok . . . what's an *app*?" His whole world was the substance of the foreign issue he led. But there was another world passing him by.

Pay attention to your inner gambler. Your organization and your subordinates need you to take occasional risks. For a dynamic organization, you need to experiment and frequently move forward with a gamble that is "worth a try." If you are never taking such initiatives, you are being too conservative. If you never *fail* at some of these initiatives, you are being too conservative.

As a thoughtful gambler, you will be gambling with your analysts' time and attention. These are, indeed, your most precious resources. But beware of regarding them as *too* precious. You cannot be the general who regards his soldiers as too precious to risk in battle. You need to invest their time and attention wisely but expect that not every investment pays off.

What might your gamble look like? Your innovation might involve throwing your analysts at a question that so far has eluded answer. Or you might put analysts together in an unconventional team, mixing skills that others think of as oil and water. Or perhaps you will have your analysts look at an issue using a structured analytic technique, to see if it catalyzes a new insight. Or—if you are truly innovative—you will come up with something fresher than any of these.

In your enthusiasm for innovation, be careful of being a half-baked innovator. Don't forget you work in a "What is wrong with this picture?" environment. It will not tolerate thoughtless enthusiasm. Writing for *Harvard Business Review*, innovation specialist Scott Anthony (2012) called out leaders whom he labels "the Four Worst Innovation Assassins." Each of these is an innovation enthusiast but weak leader:

1. **The Cowboy** . . . says something along the lines of, "No boundaries! Just great ideas!" . . . But every company has a set of things it simply will not do. Saying innovation has no bounds when it does just leads people to waste time working on ideas that—honestly—have no hope of being commercialized.

2. **The Googlephile** . . . asks everybody to spend a bit of time on innovation. . . . This approach feels participatory and inclusive. But it rarely works, unless the company has sophisticated systems to select and nurture ideas. Too frequently these efforts lead to a long list of suggestions that never get implemented.

3. **The Astronaut** [urges] "We need something big, people! What is our moon shot?" It's great to think big, of course, but pushing for big ideas often leads to proposals with sink-the-company risk. . . .

4. **The Pirate** . . . says "We don't have a fixed budget for innovation—but we don't need one. We find the money when we need it." While that statement sounds entrepreneurial, it can make the innovator's life a nightmare because it signals a lack of clear rules for obtaining resources. This often means endless meetings with a varying cast of stakeholders. No one quite says yes, and no one quite says no, either.

## Big Idea Leaders and Requirements Leaders

A keenly insightful observer of the practical application of creativity is Bran Ferren (2008), who for years led Disney's "Imagineers." He cautions that each executive-level leader must also pay attention to the mix of "requirements leaders" and "big idea leaders" on the management team. Speaking at the Harvard Center for Public Leadership in 2008, he noted that the "requirements leaders" are the most typical in large bureaucracies. They are the people who make certain the product is delivered. They get things done. They tend to build teams to study and recommend and build processes to achieve defined requirements. They are essential. Ferren then describes the "big idea leader" as more like the movie director; he is selected because of a record of successes, and a team is built around him to execute his evolving vision.

*(Continued)*

(Continued)

You need *both* types of people on your management team, and you can expect them to not get along well. Ferren (2008) says, "Ultimately, I think the only organizations capable of succeeding over the next century are going to be those that are capable of doing big idea thinking to generate vision, and then using the requirements process for a large organization to execute that vision and make it work."

If your analytic organization is large enough and has a tight relationship with customers, almost certainly its managers are overwhelmingly of the "requirements" type. The productive analytic cadre develops a customer service loop in which the analysts feed a nearly insatiable appetite for expert insight. Answering the last question and getting on to the next one—and sustaining this at a fast pace indefinitely—becomes dependent on leaders with high delivery skills. It is easy for the successful analytic organization to nurture and promote *only* these "requirements leaders," applauding vision when it happens but not expecting it. But with the analytic challenges of today, that approach is insufficient. The executive will have to nurture vision at all levels of the leadership chain and also teach the "big idea leaders" and "requirements leaders" to productively collaborate.

## Step 5: "Nurture" Your Boss!

Deliberately nurturing the analytic *environment you preside over* should result in a notable increase in the flow of creativity, innovation, and analytic insights. Now you have to tend to something else: the *environment that your unit operates in*. It is easy for your unit to get out of alignment with either the bureaucracy in which your unit operates or the customers your unit serves.

If, for example, your unit does not control its own publishing, it might be easy for you to get crosswise with those who do. Perhaps your analysts have created a truly fresh graphical way to convey a complex technical story to the customer. You submit the dazzling product to the editorial staff and one of them says, "That's not the way *we* do things here." Unless you personally champion this new idea, bureaucratic inertia will kill it and deflate your innovative analysts in the process. At the very least, you should expect roadblocks in the path of anything new. Be prepared for that reality and expect to spend real energy overcoming them.

Even better than bracing yourself for the inevitable pushback is to get ahead of it. Almost every organization is led by people claiming to value creativity and innovation. *Surprise* them with something different and they may reflexively recoil. Tell them *ahead of time* that your unit is trying something creative, and usually you will enlist their better angels. They will instruct that editorial staff to be flexible, at least on a trial basis.

It is also possible for your unit to make a leap that is simply too great, leaving behind either your bosses or your customers. For example, if brilliant analysts had argued in 1981 that, "based on all the trends and data in Soviet politics and economics, we anticipate the collapse of the Soviet Union by the end of 1991," they simply would have been dismissed.[2] In an interview, Kevin Kelly, author of *What Technology Wants*, explained the dynamic this way:

Ideas that leap too far ahead are almost never implemented—they aren't even valuable. People can absorb only one advance, one small hop, at a time. Gregor Mendel's ideas about genetics, for example: He formulated them in 1865, but they were ignored for 35 years because they were too advanced. Nobody could incorporate them. Then, when the collective mind was ready and his idea was only one hop away, three different scientists independently rediscovered his work within roughly a year of one another. ("Kevin Kelly and Steven Johnson" 2010: 122)

Too big a leap is, simply, too big a leap. Peter Sims (2011: 7) turns this rule of thumb into a deliberate strategy in his book, *Little Bets: How Breakthrough Ideas Emerge from Small Discoveries*. In examining many cases of entrepreneurial success, he notes that most commonly, "creators use experimental, iterative, trial-and-error approaches to gradually build up to breakthroughs."

Sims's (2011) research, by the way, turns up a finding that leaders of analysis should find highly encouraging. He says, "The most productive creative people and teams are rigorous, highly analytical, strategic, and pragmatic" (13). Hey! Sounds like he's talking about us!

---

[2] I do not, by the way, believe that a credible prediction along these lines was possible in 1981; key variables like Gorbachev, Yeltsin, and Afghanistan were by no means clear in 1981.

# KEY THEMES ●━━━━━━━━━━━━━━━━━━━━━━━━━━━━

- *Creativity*: the "ability to transcend traditional rules, patterns, relationships or the like, and to create meaningful new ideas" (from Dictionary.com)

- *Insight*: discerning a meaningful underlying truth

- *Innovation*: putting a new idea to work with a new approach

Bring enough smart, clever people together and you will find many who are creative. But bring them together in a business unit, and creativity can be stifled by processes, standards, and the need for predictability. All leaders say they want creativity, but the ones who see it frequently are those who actively protect it from these stifling imperatives.

In the business of analysis, the point is not to nurture creativity for its own sake. The point is to put creativity *to work* in your unit. Nurture an environment in which creativity is welcome and your analytic unit will produce more insights and innovations. Watch for several things:

- Analysts are trained skeptics—they need to be. But their skepticism can often kill the new (usually half-baked) idea before it is fully developed.

- Veteran analysts are masters at killing the new ideas of their juniors. Restrain this.

- Many analysts—good students all their lives—suffer an acute fear of failure. Fear of failure prevents innovation.

- Analysts often burn most of their intellectual energy on making sure they are not wrong, leaving little energy for creativity or innovation.

Make sure you are not part of the problem.

- Do you tend to pick apart new ideas too soon? Instead, help strengthen them.

- What subtle cues are you giving that you don't like the "error" part of trial and error?

- Have your subordinates ever seen you celebrate a failure (when someone tried his best)?

Encourage *mixing*. New ideas often result from two ideas bumping into one another.

- Never assume your analysts are talking to each other.

- Bring outside ideas into your unit.

- Send your analysts to meet outsiders more frequently than they prefer.

But also protect *incubation*.

- After the mixing, the new idea usually hatches in one person's mind. Sometimes that person needs some isolation from distractions for the idea to come together.

Keep an eye on your competition. There is no greater incentive to innovation than seeing theirs.

- Nurture your own boss. She also says she wants innovation, but you know she hates surprises. Telling her about your unit's experiments brings out her better angels.

# CHAPTER

# 6

# Asking the Right Question

A nalysis starts with a question. You don't always know it. When I started at CIA, they told me I would be working on an *issue*. "You'll be working the Libyan Military account," they said. My job at CIA had started, but my analysis hadn't. My analysis started the next day, after I had found the coffee pot, the men's room, and my desk. That second day, it was made clear to me that, from then on, I would be working on one overarching question: "What is going on with the Libyan military?" With that one vague question, I began analyzing.

Very quickly, the vague question was replaced by specific ones. (Remember, this was back when Ronald Reagan seemed to think of Qadhafi as his personal enemy.) I began analyzing questions like, Where is that submarine headed? What is Libya's capability to invade Tunisia? How will Qadhafi enforce his bluster about the "Line of Death"? How (and why) did Libya mine the Red Sea? How much farther will Libyan forces push in Chad? Each of those was a driving question, and each included a long list of subordinate questions.

That was the start of literally thousands of questions for me at CIA. I cannot think of a day in my career when I was not actively analyzing—or helping others to analyze—at least one question.

As a manager, I learned another dimension about questions. Every analytical question I asked a subordinate became an investment. I was investing my analyst's time and attention. I was focusing him or her on an issue I considered important. This was not an imaginary or metaphorical investment. By focusing on the question I asked, the analyst was not focusing on something else, and he or she might even become blind to something else. I learned not to be casual about this. Especially after I had earned the respect of my analysts, I learned not to vocalize a question simply because I was curious—they would take my question more seriously than I had intended and spend time to dig up an answer. More than this, I learned I could guide and coach them with my questions. And I learned some questions have no useful answer.

## Toxic Questioning

Let me talk about Waylon. Waylon is not his real name. But Waylon characterizes one managerial approach I saw many times.

The morning team meeting starts and we take turns reporting the most interesting material we encountered in the overnight intelligence traffic. It comes to "Linda's" turn and she hesitantly reports a violent demonstration in the Third World country she analyzes. She thinks this demonstration might be the start of something big, but she doesn't want to sound alarmist. She says, "I'm monitoring a demonstration on the west side of the capital. Reports are sketchy, but both demonstrators and police were hurt."

Waylon swings into action. I can see Linda cringe because she knows what is coming. "How do you know this?" Waylon asks, his tone full of challenge.

"Both the opposition press and the Embassy reported it," Linda replies.

Waylon fires his next salvo, "Do you *believe* the opposition press?" It's a straight question, but Linda hears, "Why would you trust a biased source?"

"Our Embassy talked to people on the ground and is sending in a video of the demonstration. But the video is still from an opposition source," Linda responds, getting tense.

"Well, this could *mean* something," Waylon asserts, clearly changing direction on the issue and now implying to Linda that she is underestimating the potential gravity of the event.

"I'll keep an eye on it," Linda says, "but an isolated demonstration doesn't mean much by itself."

"Revolutions start with such developments! Why *couldn't* this shake the regime?" Waylon is in full cross-examination mode now, asking Linda to prove a negative. Linda now has gone from thinking the demonstration might be significant—which was why she raised it in the first place—to praying it fizzles so Waylon can't launch another "I told you so" in her direction. The meeting ends with Linda feeling like she has been through the Inquisition. Waylon, meanwhile, reinforces his conviction that getting information out of Linda is like pulling teeth.

One of the most important ways you will influence your analytic environment will be by the way you question your analysts. Your analysts will be analyzing your questions for clues as to what you really want or think, especially if you haven't yet elicited their complete trust. Unfortunately, some managers avoid asking tough questions for fear of damaging that trust. You cannot afford to be that passive. As an analytic leader, you need to get deep into a give-and-take over the analyst's evidence and reasoning. To help hone their work and to coach them effectively, you owe them your toughest questions. But be careful what you are really asking. It is easy for the tone of your questioning to convey that you don't trust them, that your aim is to catch them being sloppy, or that you are trying to show you are smarter than them.

Here are examples of questions that can trigger your analyst's worst suspicions, followed by a better way to ask them:

| Question | Hidden Message | A Better Question |
|---|---|---|
| "Why *can't* this violent demonstration be the beginning of the end of this regime?" | "Prove the negative." | "A violent demonstration can be a good opportunity to look afresh at the resilience of the regime. What do you see as recent signs of its security or fragility?" |
| "What is the evidence against your conclusion?" | "Your mind is closed." | "Are there less likely conclusions consistent with the evidence?" |
| "Have you spoken with any experts about this?" | "You are no expert." | "Who have you brought into your discussions about this so far?" |
| "Have you seen *this* bit of evidence . . . and *this* . . . and *this?*" | "You missed something. Gotcha!" | "Here is some material I have that I want to make sure you have. See if anything here affects the picture." |

Remember to communicate clearly what you are trying to accomplish with your questions. Teach your analysts that it is your job to coach them, to hone their case, to explore the issues, and to champion the analysis they produce. You'll do all of this, in part, by questioning them. One of your responsibilities is to fully understand their reasoning on important issues, and you achieve that level of insight through questions. Teach your analysts that you will use questions to help determine whether they are being too bold or too cautious with their conclusions. (With some of my too-cautious analysts, I would tell them it was my job to push them farther out on the analytic limb, and it was their job to tell me when I was pushing too far.) Teach your analysts that one of their responsibilities is not simply to *have* an open mind but to *demonstrate* it to you and the customers. Teach your analysts that you ask who they have talked with because consulting with other experts is a sign of professionalism, not a sign that their own expertise is deficient.

You'll be getting this tricky business right if the analyst leaves your conversation thinking that you just had a dialogue from which both of you learned. You'll have gotten it wrong if, like Linda, the analyst leaves the session feeling there is no way to satisfy you . . . and dreading the next inquisition.

# The Right Question

Of course, asking nicely is not sufficient. You have to ask the *right* question or, at least, *a* right question. In intelligence analysis, a good source of "right" questions is always the customer. This might be a question that the policy maker himself has posed to you. Heaven knows I have heard some dumb questions from policy makers, but the American taxpayer can take heart that these were infrequent. Overwhelmingly, the policy makers' questions, in my experience, were good questions. There is also the unstated but real question from the policy maker: "What do you know that can help me?"

As a leader of analysis, you can help a lot by effectively role-playing your most important customers. Knowing what these customers are trying to do, having a feel for their level of knowledge about your topic, and knowing what keeps them up at night, you can convincingly put yourself in their shoes and ask your analysts good questions on their behalf. You can also teach your analysts to do this on their own.

Another good question is, "What question are you working on?" Notice, I didn't say, "What are you working on?" That will usually elicit a topic and is often too passive. "What *question* are you working on?" conveys your expectation that the analyst generally should be in the more active posture of addressing a question rather than monitoring an issue. "What question are you working on?" also conveys your expectation that, sometimes, the analyst herself should initiate the question. Once you become skilled at asking right questions, it is easy to saturate your analysts with your interrogative stream. It is important to leave some room for them to come up with questions, too. First, you will be amazed what good questions they initiate, questions you didn't think of—often, questions triggered by the source material they are reading. Second, if they have initiated a weak question, you have a wonderful coaching opportunity, launching a dialogue that helps them develop a more suitable question.

Allowing the analyst to initiate *some* of the questions is connected to the critical balance between initiating and reacting that I mentioned in chapter 3. Let me amplify here. Good leaders of analysis so excel at role-playing the customer that they can completely absorb the analyst with questions the customer would ask if she were in the room. This is a top-down approach to intelligence analysis. The customer (or your role-play of the customer) says, "I know what I am trying to do. I need the analyst to provide these answers to help me do it." But generally the analyst is watching a situation or the flow of incoming information. The analyst is searching incoming information, trying to determine what has changed, what it means, and what is worth telling the customer. This is the bottom-up approach. *To be effective, we need both approaches.* For the analytic leader who is a good questioner, it takes a force of will to back off and let the subordinate spend some time with the bottom-up approach.

Take the situation I mentioned before, the buildup of the Iraqi threat to Kuwait in 1990, and let's identify some good questions. Remember, Iraqi forces have massed near the Kuwaiti border, Saddam has made a bellicose speech, and Iraqi diplomats are not appearing very diplomatic.

Clearly, what the president most wants is to know, "What is Saddam intending to do?" As real as that question is, don't let your analysts start there. They often feel a compulsion to "make the big call." This can be a matter of pride or courage or simply an instinct to give the customer what he wants. But prematurely making the big call is really just making the big *guess*. Instead, break the president's question into *framing questions* and *component questions*.

*Framing questions* help frame the issue and the evidence. They help establish working hypotheses. They also help identify potentially relevant evidence (history, characteristic behavior, patterns, missing ingredients) beyond the evidence right in front of you. Here are some useful framing questions in this situation:

- What are the leading possibilities that could explain what we are seeing? (Planning an invasion. Intimidating Kuwait. Any others?)

- What situations like this have we seen before?

- What has been characteristic of Saddam when he assumes a threatening posture?

*Component questions* help break the president's big question into man-ageable bites. They get your team quickly focused on what they know and what they don't know, and they help guide collection. They also help you identify which answers you already have (and can give the president) and which issues you are still just guessing about. *(By the way, depending on the circumstances, especially when the customer must make a decision quickly, you might want to tell your customer your best guess. That can be useful, as long as he understands (1) that a guess is what he is getting, and (2) what your guess is based on.)* There are various useful component questions in this situation:

- How close are the Iraqi forces to being ready for offensive operations?

- If these forces attack, what is the farthest they could push?

- Have we seen anything in previous Iraqi offensives that we are not seeing here?

- What are the Iraqi diplomats demanding?

- How are the Kuwaiti diplomats responding?

- Is the Kuwaiti government asking for help?

- Are there any signs the Iraqi diplomats won't take "yes" for an answer?

- What could the international community do that would influence Saddam's intentions?

You won't be delivering each of these answers one at a time. As a complex issue like this plays out, the policy makers won't have time to stitch a dozen answers together to see what they add up to. (You know yourself how rarely you are willing to read one of those fifty-item lists on some website's overly ambitious "Frequently Asked Questions" page.) Rather, you usually owe the customer a narrative that helps him make sense of the situation. But the combination of answers and analysis your team develops on all these questions will allow your drafters to construct a coherent narrative.

Stepping away from this Iraq crisis, I want to raise another type of question that is often useful, the *provocative question*. I mean the type of question designed to keep ourselves honest, to keep us from getting too comfortable in our mental ruts—the type of question designed to stir an analyst into looking at the issue from a different angle. Three of these can be very powerful:

- Why?

- Why not?

- What if . . .?

These are provocative in a real sense. They can be challenging, perhaps disturbing, to the questionee. They will expose whether your analyst has thought deeply enough about the issue at hand. They will expose lazy thinking. They can force your analyst off his train of thought for at least a moment, which few of us welcome.

But the provocative questions can also be catalysts to fresh insight. They can reveal weaknesses in reasoning that need attention. They can uncover deep thinking that the analyst actually did but had not put into print (and perhaps needs to). They can spark a thought that starts as a tangent but turns into a new analytic path. Innovation literature flags these questions as tools innovative leaders use frequently. As I discussed in the last chapter, that which stimulates creativity or innovation often can also stimulate analytic insight.

Of course, there is a downside with provocative questions. They can, at times, lead nowhere and simply leave your analyst feeling provoked. I worked briefly for a leader who was a font of "what ifs" and "why nots." I felt like he was always taking me on a loop of endless speculation. I also resented what felt like an unfair maneuver on his part; I felt like, no matter how events played out, he could say, "I asked you whether that might happen."

So how do we square this circle? How do we take advantage of the upside of provocative questions without provoking the analysts' gag reflex? First, teach your analysts to ask provocative questions themselves. When you ask one they have already thought about, good things have just happened: their analysis is deeper for having had the thought, and they are glowing with the pride of being a step ahead of you. Second, if you are endlessly imaginative, restrain your wildest flights of fancy. Watch your analysts for that telltale "here-we-go-again" look when you start your questions. They should think of provocative questions as normal but not incessant.

# The Wrong Question

I mentioned that the questions you pose to your analysts are investments— you are spending your most precious currency, their time and focus. You need to think of the concept of "the wrong question" in that context. The wrong question is not a stupid question; you will ask some of those no matter how smart you are. The wrong question is one that predictably wastes your analysts' effort.

Some questions cannot be answered without real evidence. You cannot "reason your way" to some answers. "Do the Iranians have a secret nuclear weapons facility?" I can describe why they might. I can provide a compelling argument that they do not. But the answer to a question like this is "yes" or "no," and it will take real evidence to determine which. Many leaders of analysts will recognize this reality and redirect their analysts to a different question: "*Might* the Iranians have a secret nuclear facility?" That is certainly a question to which an analyst can apply useful reasoning. But it would still be an unproductive investment of an analyst if the customer has no use for such speculation.

Some questions waste the analyst's time even though it feels like evidence is available. In his brilliant *The Black Swan,* Nassim Nicholas Taleb (2007: 40–41) talks about the 1,000-day turkey. This is a turkey which spends his life trying to determine whether the farmer is his friend. Over 999 days he builds a mountain of compelling evidence. The farmer feeds me every day . . . shelters me from the cold . . . lets me hang with my friends. There is no evidence on the other side of the ledger until the 1,000th day, the day before Thanksgiving, and it comes in the form of an ax.

Intelligence analysis has its share of 1,000-day turkey questions. Can the regime in Beijing handle a revolution? What will be the catalyst for political upheaval in the Middle East? It is not that "evidence" related to the question cannot be collected. It is that the evidence is not diagnostic. In the turkey's case, the evidence pointed to the fact that the farmer cared about the turkey's welfare, but it did not help diagnose *why* the farmer cared.

As long as I have you thinking about turkeys, I might as well invite you to think of gorillas too. Another "wrong question" is the one question too many. If all your analysts are *completely* absorbed trying to answer specific questions, they are dealing with at least one question too many.

This is vividly demonstrated in a video made by Christopher Chabris and Daniel J. Simons at the University of Illinois Visual Cognition Lab (http://www.dansimons.com/videos.html) and discussed in their book, *The Invisible Gorilla* (2009). The video shows six players in a loose circle: three in black shirts, three in white. Each team has a basketball, and the video challenges the viewer to count the number of passes the white team makes. The black team is passing their ball, too, and everyone is moving around, so you really have to pay attention. After about a half minute of this, the exercise stops and you are invited to provide your answer. I counted fourteen (off by one, by the way). Then the bombshell is dropped. The video asks whether you saw the gorilla. Excuse me? The video then rewinds and plays back, and in the middle of the exercise, someone in a gorilla suit walks into the circle of players, pounds his chest, and walks out.

No way. Nothing personal, Visual Cognition Lab, but I didn't trust you. My first instinct was that the "replayed" video must be fake (this is the Internet, after all) because I could not have missed such a flagrant event when I never took my eyes off the screen. So I got out of the website and came back to it to start the exercise from scratch—and there was that impossible gorilla. The video is called the *Selective Attention Test*, and it undercut my conviction that I couldn't have missed the gorilla because I was paying close attention. It powerfully demonstrates "inattentional blindness, the failure to notice a fully-visible, but unexpected object because attention was engaged on another task, event, or object" (Simons 2007). I missed the gorilla *because* I was paying close attention—to something else.

This experiment provides lessons in many areas of cognition, but it should scare you if you have every one of your analysts fully focused on specific questions. It feels like good, efficient management to have your whole team fully occupied. As powerful a driver as questions are, as important as they are in keeping your team relevant to your customers, *you cannot afford to leave no space for open-minded observation.* The question you ask that absorbs the last of your team's energy is one question too many—a "wrong question" regardless of how compelling it feels.

So let's step back and see where we are on this tricky but essential business of asking the right question. The right question starts from an attitude of respect for the analyst and for the complexity of the substance being analyzed. Disrespect for the analyst can quickly lead to Waylon's toxic questioning. Disrespect for complexity—by either you or your analyst—closes off thinking when the first answer springs to mind. The right question encourages the analyst to think aloud, sometimes putting thoughts together for the first time. The right question, constructively asked, can provoke new thinking and nudge an analyst out of complacency without driving him into the game of "guess what the boss wants." The right question can be one you ask or one your analyst initiates. The right question *invests* your analysts' attention while stopping short of drawing the last dime from that bank account. The right question can help frame an issue to serve customer needs or help break an issue into digestible components. And sometimes, the right question can be the one you leave unasked because it would be one too many.

Next, we'll turn to the most difficult question an analyst gets: "What is going to happen?"

## KEY THEMES

Analysis starts with a question. Much of your leadership of analysis will consist of the questions you ask. Asking the right questions is the hard part.

Good questions often

- Get to the essence of an issue

- Provoke productive thought

- Advance the discussion

- Help you understand, especially "why" and "why not"

- Come from your customer or from you role-playing your customer

Bad questions often

- Convey distrust

- Sound accusatory

- Play "gotcha"

- Waste the analysts' time with endless "what ifs" or "1000-day turkey" issues

When faced with tough analytic issues, it often helps to break them up into *framing questions* and *component questions*.

- *Framing questions* help frame the issue and the evidence (e.g., Why might Saddam be massing his forces near Kuwait now?). They help establish working hypotheses.

- *Component questions* help break a big question into manageable bites (e.g., If Saddam were to attack Kuwait, what would his forces do first? How would we detect that? Do the forces have everything they need in place?). They get your team quickly focused on what they know and what they don't know and help guide collection.

Finally, beware of saturating your analysts with questions. They need time and freedom to initiate their own. And, as with the "invisible gorilla," they need to be able to see developments in their areas of responsibility that are so unanticipated that nobody has asked a question about them.

# The Hardest Question: What Is Going to Happen?

## Prediction and Warning in Analysis

We have been talking about the leader's need to ask the right question and avoid the "wrong" question. One type of question is in a class by itself for analysts: "What is going to happen?" The whole business of prediction is simply variations of that question. The question stands out as the single most difficult part of the analyst's work. Sometimes this is a "right question"; sometimes it's wrong. When it's "right," it taps into the analyst's expert, considered judgment about what is most likely to occur and how the customer can affect the outcome. When it's "wrong," the question is unanswerable but wastes time and encourages both the customer's and the analyst's delusions about our capabilities. When it is "right," it invites us to shine at least a dim light into the darkness that is tomorrow.

Writing *War and Peace* in the 1860s, Leo Tolstoy noted that even yesterday is dim:

> But all these hints at what happened, both from the French side and the Russian, are advanced only because they fit in with the event. Had that event not occurred these hints would have been forgotten, as we have forgotten the thousands and millions of hints and expectations to the contrary which were current then but now have been forgotten because the event falsified them. (Tolstoy 2010: chap. 1)

Tolstoy was tackling the tendency of historians to build a logical, persuasive narrative of cause and effect that completely misses the reality of chaos in great events. He describes how the Russians beat the French in 1812 despite, not because of, what the Russian generals were trying to do. If *history* is so difficult to get right, imagine how much harder is *forecasting*.

The whole business of prediction is a minefield for analysts. We cannot know the future. We can never know whether we have identified all the variables at play in a complex situation, much less weighed them correctly. We can never know when a wild card might be introduced, a game changer that arrives randomly. Also, prediction elicits the expert analyst's deep bias toward continuity; what has been happening for a long time always appears likely to continue, if you understand the drivers and the drivers are still present. And at best, the analyst can only lay out what is *reasonable*, but we live in a world where the unreasonable, even the ridiculous, happens too frequently. Because of such hazards, our batting average appears low to outsiders. In the bright light of hindsight, our batting can even appear inept.

Because of such hazards, many intelligence leaders whom I respect say flatly, "We don't predict. We don't have a crystal ball." That is true technically—but only technically. We do a range of activities that look forward. We project, we forecast, we warn, we weigh likelihoods, we identify trends. We try hard to figure out what is driving events today in order to anticipate tomorrow. And because our customers think of all this as prediction, we must acknowledge that we are in the prediction business.

What would be nice is clarity as to what is and is not predictable. But no reliable formula is available. And tempting rules of thumb come crashing up against a long list of exceptions. Never predict the outcome of individual battles—but some battles are easy to call. Never predict when more than a dozen variables are at play—except when you can. Never predict an issue when your batting average on that issue is no better than the layperson's—unless your customer asks. So the clarity we need to provide will never amount to a menu we can hand the customer: "Sir, Madam, here is a list of the things we will be able to predict tonight, and might I mention that our election forecast is particularly fresh."

Neither is there a reliable formula for forecasting itself. It is easy to believe that data scientists who have written and tested an algorithm have found just such a formula. That work is enormously valuable, as I discuss in later chapters. But that work finds patterns in the data, and the algorithm presumes the pattern will continue. Saying that "the past pattern will continue" will certainly make any analyst right most of the time, but that rule of thumb leads to failure. Dr. Bruce Bueno de Mesquita (2009) prescribes a game theory approach, identifying the self-interest of each player in a situation and weighing the relative influence of each player, to almost calculate the future. His approach can be applied successfully to some very hard issues but, as he acknowledges, "is right for some problems but not all" (Kindle location 219). My own rule of thumb, which will serve you as well as any, is this: run from anyone who makes forecasting appear formulaic.

Rather, we must analyze each situation to *diagnose what is predictable* and *whether we have something useful to say about the future*. Some situations will require courage to make an unpopular call. Some situations will require us to have the courage to refuse to make a call. All situations will tap our ability to communicate clearly our predictions and their limits. And the test for our work will not be whether we manage to clearly describe an event before it happens. The test will be whether we genuinely help our customer cope with an unknowable future.

# Analyzing Predictability

I know of only a few situations when intelligence analysts are excused from a need to predict. The first year I arrived at CIA, my first boss told me, "Unless we get evidence of a plot, we don't predict assassinations." Three decades and many assassinations later, I never heard a policy customer fault us for this limitation. Prime ministers falling to votes of no confidence in parliamentary governments seem also to be accepted as bolts from the blue. The notion seems to be that if the prime minister, with all his inside knowledge and savvy, was surprised by the event, it would be unreasonable to expect more from us. Nor are we expected to predict the emergence of breakthrough technologies, although we often are expected to project their potential threat applications soon after they emerge.

Most high-stakes situations, however, must be examined more closely to judge predictability. Let's look at one. In September 2012, the Islamic world was ablaze with outrage at an anti-Islam video, *The Innocence of Muslims*, produced in America and posted on the Internet. Was it predictable that jihadists would opportunistically publicize such an offensive video and fan the flames? Absolutely. Was it predictable that more moderate Muslims would be stirred to outrage if they saw the video, even without prodding by the extremists? Yes. Was it predictable that this particular video *could* be a catalyst for violence? You bet.

But was it predictable that it *would* be the catalyst for violence? No. In sorting through possibilities, the difference between *could* and *would* is vast. There is plenty of other anti-Islamic bile on the Internet, posted by racists and other extremists, that gets little attention. Some of it would be considered not simply offensive but blasphemous by pious Muslims. But these other offensive postings did not touch off violence in September 2012. So far, we are unable to predict what goes from obscurity to viral in this context—a problem Internet denizens share in many other contexts. Nor are we able to pick a single catalyst out of a large array of equally possible catalysts for violence. Like the Forest Service does outside my hometown in the summer, we can judge when the fire danger is high, but we cannot predict which spark will touch off the forest fire.

How about predicting elections? One of my most important mentors in leading analysis used to say, "We don't predict elections." Her statement was clear and well-founded but wrong in several situations. I, and the rest of the world, confidently predicted every election Saddam Husayn and Hosni Mubarak ran in through the 1980s and '90s. She'd say, "Well of course, I didn't mean those charades; I meant real elections." But with intensive study and masses of data, Nate Silver (2012) made predictions of stunning accuracy about the US presidential and senatorial elections in 2008 and 2012. He describes his approach in *The Signal and the Noise,* a must-read for anyone in the prediction business. Illustrating just how maddeningly difficult prediction is, Silver could not replicate his US success with the UK general elections in 2010 (Ball 2013). And though Silver did a creditable job of alerting voters to the fact that Donald Trump had a real chance of winning the 2016 presidential election, few observers actually give him credit for a good forecast.[1] Because he did not say a Trump victory was *likely*, shallow observers consider Silver's analysis wrong. This is a cautionary tale for forecasters. If the forecaster says there is a 1 in 4 chance of something happening and it happens one quarter of the time, the forecaster can justifiably claim accuracy, but the customer will look at the forecast in isolation and say, "You were wrong."

Occasionally, we can predict the outcome of wars or battles. When conventional military forces line up against one another, comfortable judgments can be made about the relative numbers of tanks, experience levels, demonstrated capabilities, and the like. When there is a clear imbalance, a strategic call can be made that might be useful to a policy customer. In the 1982 Lebanon war, for example, the imbalance between the Israeli and Syrian air forces was so clear that it would be no challenge to predict decisive Israeli air dominance. In the event, the Syrians lost more than eighty aircraft, compared to two for the Israelis, according to published accounts (see, e.g., Lambeth 1984: 11). Intelligence analysts shouldn't be expected to predict the score in that air contest, but they should be expected to predict a lopsided Israeli win.

We can also help predict the occurrence of specific events *if we have significant evidence*. Before Operation Desert Storm, for example, my analysts were asked to write a paper predicting what Saddam would do in the first two days of the war. I was livid at the time, arguing that we had already written much about Iraqi capabilities but that to predict precise actions was simply a way to be wrong. I underestimated my analysts. Based on what they could see and their deep knowledge of Saddam's war-fighting habits, they confidently judged, for example, that Iraq would launch Scud missiles against Israel and release oil into the Persian Gulf. Operation Desert Storm kicked off January 17, 1991. Iraq fired seven Scuds at Israel that day and released a massive oil slick into the Gulf the next week (National Guard Bureau 2000).

But in both of these last two examples, there were clear limits to our ability to predict. In the 1982 Lebanon war, for example, the ground balance was more even than the mismatch in air forces. Local terrain in ground battles would be critical, but there would be no way to determine precisely where those ground battles would be fought or who would hold the high ground. Certainly tanks could be counted, and certainly Israeli air superiority over the battlefield would matter. But a significant difference between the Israeli and Syrian tolerance for losses would trump such simple arithmetic. In Desert Storm, we could predict that Saddam would send

---

[1] Silver's (2016) *FiveThirtyEight* website showed Trump with a 50.1 percent chance of beating Clinton on July 30, 2016, and a 28.6 percent chance on election day.

Scuds into Israel, but we could not even guess where they would land. Whether one landed in a field or on a hospital was nearly random, given the Scud's technology, but that outcome could dictate the Israeli response.

Even in conventional military conflicts, variables pile up quickly, making some predictions a fool's game. Often troop morale or a commander's creativity—the most human of human factors—will be critical. Now we are not only talking about variables but unmeasurable variables of real, yet indeterminate, impact. Even if you know how forces are arrayed on a battlefield, battles can turn on variables that are simply unknowable in advance. One of my favorite old video games is the complex, detailed, and realistic *Sid Meier's Gettysburg*. Individual units would have their morale and effectiveness drained if the battle swept them into a disadvantageous position. I was endlessly fascinated replaying the scenario of Little Round Top, with a different outcome each time—I knew an enormous amount about each side in the contest, but I still could not reliably predict the outcome.

Move to unconventional warfare and predictions become even more challenging. A fascinating account of the 2006 Lebanon war is presented by Joshua Cooper Ramo (2009) in his *The Age of the Unthinkable*. He shows how "fewer than 500 Hizb'allah fighters had frustrated a 30,000-man Israeli attack, including one of the most extensive air campaigns in Middle East history" (187–90). My own confident but unhelpful prediction at the start of that war—unpublished, since I was not responsible for that area at the time—was, "This is going to be messy." Even years after that war, we can still argue about who won; messy indeed.

Policy makers are desperate for help at least framing their expectations before such contests. We can, indeed, help them somewhat, *depending on their receptivity to informed speculation*. One approach they have found instructive, in my experience, is to game scenarios. We might tell a policy customer, for example, "We have gamed this conflict three times, Blue won twice, and casualties ranged from 10,000 to 50,000." Such a perspective helps them think about possible costs, and often uncovers surprising twists, without claiming a prescience we clearly don't have. And games, of course, can be designed not just for military scenarios, but for diplomatic maneuvers, trade negotiations, energy markets, and zombie apocalypses.

This introduces a key concept in the prediction business: *usefulness*. When weighing possibilities about the future, most attention naturally goes to forecasts and whether a forecast turned out to be right. But a more important metric is whether analysis about the future was *useful* to the customer. Did the analysis "narrow the range of uncertainty" for the decision makers?[2] In the war game example I just used, the game results usually aren't

---

[2] Analytic tradecraft pioneer Jack Davis used this phrase to define the very role of intelligence analysis. He said, "The role of intelligence analysis is to narrow the range of uncertainty for decisions that must be made."

intended to stand as a prediction about the future. The implied forecasts in a game—when Red Commander did X, it prompted Blue Commander to do Y—are far less important than what the actual Blue Commander learns about key dynamics of the situation, the interplay between variables, or the unexpected results of some of his favorite options.

Policy makers frequently ask a question like, "How close is Country X to having a nuclear weapon?" One of my veteran nuclear analysts told me, "Every time I do one of these predictive timelines, the only thing I know for sure is that it's wrong." In the absence of compelling evidence, it would be unreasonable to predict, "Country X will have a nuclear weapon by 2025." That would, indeed, be a prediction and, after 2025, it might be easy to judge whether it was right or wrong. But to be *useful,* we would use a formulation something like, "Based on what we know of their capabilities, the program start date, and the physical realities of enriching uranium, we believe Country X could have everything it needs to assemble a nuclear weapon as early as 2025." With all the proper qualifiers and caveats—all those "weasel words" we must use fearlessly—such assessments help give policy makers a sense of whether they have a year or a decade for their counterproliferation efforts to work. That is useful.

If you look closely at the judgment in the last paragraph, you also see why those senior intelligence officers sometimes are correct when they insist, "We don't predict the future." Look again at the statement, "We believe Country X *could* have *everything it needs* to assemble a nuclear weapon *as early as* 2025." It is a judgment about what is within Country X's reach, not a prediction they will reach it. This far in advance, a judgment about whether Country X *will* reach that goal might amount to informed speculation. If your customer is actively trying to stop Country X's march toward a nuclear weapon, your look forward would not only have to analyze Country X but also consider your customer's counterproliferation effectiveness—including the effectiveness of things your customer has not even decided yet. Speculation would be the best you could offer in this scenario.

Some analogies and categories can help you assess the predictability of the situation your team is examining. For example, you can quickly ask, Is this situation *mechanical?* By that I mean, are major elements of the situation bound by strong if-then relationships? If the price of oil drops by $20 per barrel, then Borostan's annual revenue declines by $4.2 billion. If a small aircraft flying 150 knots disperses 200 gallons of nerve agent X over Washington, DC, and the wind conditions are Y, then this many people would be in the lethal zone. A limiting factor in making such predictions would be whether key variables are known or can be collected. For some customers' purposes, some variables can be reasonably assumed (perhaps the average wind speed and direction over Washington in June is sufficient).

Is the situation like *short-term weather forecasting*? Because we understand weather dynamics very well, and we have excellent evidence about today's weather, some forecasts are easy (the cold front will move in tomorrow morning). Some weather dynamics are chaotic, so I can forecast scattered showers in your area but not how much your particular lawn will receive. Judging likelihoods in some conventional military conflicts has similar elements. The dynamics of some force-on-force contests are well enough understood to confidently predict that one force will prevail. But chaos plays its part in the contest, preventing forecast of casualty rates, especially when battlefields have not even been chosen.

Is the situation like *long-term weather forecasting*? It helps to have a sense of what divides the short term from the long term. For weather forecasting, five days might be the limit of the forecaster's confidence. A forecast looking two weeks out, on the other hand, might be considered long term. That far out, the forecaster won't even be confident whether the temperatures will be in the 40s, as opposed to the 50s, much less which day it will rain. Still, he will know that he is looking at March, so there is little chance temperatures will reach the 80s, and maybe the customer wants to know that. Depending on the customer's needs and how esoteric the topic, framing broad parameters of what is and is not likely in long-term forecasts might be useful.

Is the situation one in which a *pattern prevails*? Patterns are wonderful for forecasters, as long as they hold up. They can be hidden in masses of data. This is a large component of how Nate Silver is able to discern how to convert masses of disparate polling data into a forecast for US presidential and senatorial elections. Or, the pattern might be a correlation of events that experts have noticed in previous situations; perhaps, for example, Waritania's deployment of reconnaissance aircraft to the frontier typically occurs two days before it tests its long-range missiles. This isn't quite mechanical; the aircraft deployment didn't cause the missile test. But anyone closely watching repeated situations will learn to recognize that when X happens, they can expect Y to follow.

Of course, all patterns end eventually. Some day (day?) the sun will not rise. But part of being expert is to (1) learn to recognize patterns and (2) analyze each pattern to determine whether its underpinnings are intact. The first of those comes naturally to experts and can seem effortless. The expert "reads" the situation and, sometimes unconsciously, recognizes something in it and says, "Ah, this again." The second requires more intellectual diligence, and overlooking it is a prime factor at work in many intelligence failures. As leader, you'll need to enforce the diligence. You may be the one requiring your expert to freshly assess whether the key drivers of the pattern remain present in today's situation.

Is the situation one *driven by human characteristics*? This is a particularly challenging arena for forecasting. *Social* sciences are at work and allow much less certainty than any of the other sciences. You often have the chaos of multiple actors interacting independently. But even with human decision making, we often are able to make useful projections. When we are talking about humans at the macro level, characteristics (behavioral patterns) can be highly relevant and predictive. The expected behavior of a culture, sect, or a demographic slice of society might be relatively predictable if you know the variables that matter.

When we are talking about humans as individuals—a leader, for example—some characteristics run deep and have predictive value. As noted, my analysts predicted that Saddam would fire Scud missiles at Israel and dump oil into the Persian Gulf at the start of Desert Storm. These calls, in part, were based on their understanding of Saddam as a warfighter, spotting characteristics he demonstrated over the course of Iraq's war with Iran. But human complexity (complexity that includes whim and caprice) is such that even a well-understood leader will deliver dramatic surprises sometimes. Saddam's hidden dismantlement of his WMD arsenal certainly did not fit his characteristics as we understood them. Tenacious defiance and deception did, which is why many of his own generals believed to the last that Saddam had retained at least some of those weapons.

Holding your situation up to these models and analogies sometimes will disappoint you. You will consider weather forecasting, patterns, and the rest and conclude, "Well, it's not like any of this." For other situations, you will find there are bits of several paradigms that seem to apply. You'll also notice the paradigms overlap. You find patterns, for example, in weather and in human characteristics. Yes, the world is complicated and the business of forecasting does not always divide neatly into a handful of common paradigms. But as you consider and reject, say, the weather analogy, you and your analyst will come up with other analogies that seem more applicable to the situation at hand. Some will be quite current. Does the progress of ISIS in Syria, for example, shed light on what might be predictable about its progress in Afghanistan? Looking backward at the Syria case, can we find forecasting indicators we missed the first time but can use in the Afghan situation?

The point is to get you started at analyzing the predictability of the situations you are watching and then identifying the elements of those situations that are predictable. I will task my analysts to assess when the cold front will move in and whether there will be scattered showers. I will not ask them to forecast how much rain will hit a particular lawn. This analysis is key to focusing the attention of your analysts on productive forecasting, asking them the "right" questions, and not wasting their time on the unpredictable.

This analysis will also help you guide your analysts in the business of forecasting. Keep in mind that you are not doing this analysis of predictability by yourself. You need to do it with your analysts—they usually know the situation better than you do. Work with them to determine whether the situation is mechanistic, fits known patterns, is like weather forecasting, or is influenced by known characteristics. Work with them to determine whether other forecasting parallels apply. In the process, they will develop a sense of what is and is not predictable in the situation at hand. They also will develop clarity on what they need to know to make their predictions. For mechanistic issues, what you need to know is clear, and whether it is obtainable is often clear. And once you have what you need, you can make your projections with high confidence. For the mushier world of human decision making, the range of relevant variables is much broader and often less collectable, so high confidence in forecasts rarely is warranted. All of this might seem a bit "meta" to some of your subordinates. In a way, you are working with them to analyze analyzability. But doing this together with them on real issues will help them become skilled in the more general discipline of forecasting.

Your analysis must not stop with analyzing the situation and identifying its predictable elements. You and your team must also analyze your customers' needs relative to the situation. What is useful to them? What they want to know is whether to water their lawn today. They *want* a simple yes or no, and you know you cannot give it to them. But it will be *useful* to tell them they will see scattered showers tomorrow. It will be even more useful to tell them there is a 70 percent chance their lawn will receive rain. Part of analyzing usefulness is to clearly identify which forecasts are *not* useful even though they are correct. Every leader of analysis sees a remarkable number of these. I still hear from analysts whom I supervised decades ago that they look back fondly on my frequent annotation "N.S." in the margin of their drafts. It was short for "no shit," and would be my way of telling the analyst that they were wasting the reader's time when they said something like, "Prime Minister X will take into account the political repercussions before approving this budget measure."

# When History Pivots

What about predicting history's tipping points? Nassim Nicholas Taleb (2007, 2012, 2013) argues persuasively that we should just quit kidding ourselves. In *The Black Swan* and elsewhere, he makes the case that predicting such events is beyond human capabilities. He describes as "black swans" those high-impact events that fit no pattern and have no compelling precedent. (If all you have seen are white swans, you cannot predict the existence of black swans.) He puts the 9/11 attacks, the rise of Hitler, the precipitous collapse of the Soviet bloc, and the rise of Islamic fundamentalism in this category (2007: xviii). Don't let yourselves be fooled by the fact that evidence existed before these events; before the event, that evidence would not have stood out from the evidence for a myriad of realistic alternatives (Tolstoy's "thousands and millions of hints and expectations to the contrary").

I believe Taleb's insight is sound in several aspects. There are real limits to our ability to predict, and major historical discontinuities exceed the limits of both analyst (to forecast) and audience (to listen). Some big events occur only after virtually random—certainly not *inevitable*—predicates align. Some human decisions, and the dynamic mix of their decisions, cannot be forecast far in advance.

People who expect analysts to provide early forecasts of the pivot points of history sometimes point to a so-called visionary who said something deeply prescient. Usually, those "seers" imagined that something would happen eventually, and—*eventually*—it did. Sometimes, they guess right with stunning accuracy. Each of us has done this once or twice. Sometimes we manage to put our finger on the one overriding truth. But guessing or making a statement of ideological faith is not what we are talking about here. What we are talking about is what is reasonable to expect in the day-to-day business of analysis.

But with acute awareness of our limitations in this arena, let's look at what we can do to be *useful*. Analysts are not helpless in the face of history's tipping points. We can, first, imagine that big change is possible, and second, we can look for whether we have something useful to say. Take, for example, the performance of CIA's intelligence analysts before the collapse of the Soviet Union. They applied their imaginations responsibly, had something useful to say, and said it well before the event.

They did not—*could* not—forecast Soviet collapse ten years before its occurrence. (Others who wish to take credit for identifying the Soviet system of governance as morally bankrupt and economically unsustainable can do so, but who among them in, say, 1985 made a convincing case that it wouldn't at least limp into the twenty-first century?) Gorbachev's profound influence on the collapse of the USSR, and his unique mix of vision and blindness, brilliance and ineptitude, could not be predicted even with his ascendance to power. But CIA's analysts weighed in and, according to their White House customers, mattered.

In his insider's account of the end of the Cold War, *From the Shadows*, Robert Gates (1996) details what CIA said and what the policy customer did about it. Gates, who was then Deputy National Security Advisor, says, "We knew early in the [George H. W.] Bush administration that change was coming fast in the Soviet empire, so fast that we worried about an explosion or widespread instability. Thanks to analysis and warnings from CIA, we at the White House began in the summer of 1989 to think about and prepare for a Soviet collapse" (525). (Remember, the dissolution of the USSR came in December 1991.) In July 1989, crediting "a stream of reporting and assessments I had seen from CIA," Gates recommended to the president that "we should very quietly begin some contingency planning as to possible U.S. responses, actions and policies in the event of leadership or internal policy changes or widespread ethnic violence and repression" (526). The president approved, and a study group of very senior policy makers was discreetly set up that summer. "This group commissioned a number of studies by CIA and used them in reviewing and planning U.S. options" (526). This is a nice example of analytic projections catalyzing policy action—and the dialogue between policy and intelligence officials helping both sides do their work.[3]

In an important lesson for leaders of analysis, some of this influential analysis was published *before CIA analysts reached consensus on likelihoods*. Gates (1996) mentions being struck by a 1989 paper assessing that "Conditions [in the Soviet Union] are likely to lead in the foreseeable future to continuing crises and instability . . . and perhaps even the localized emergence of parallel centers of power. . . . [Instability would] prevent a return to the arsenal state economy that generated the fundamental military threat to the West in the period since World War II" (514). (Talk about a pivot point in history.) Gates notes, "A number of other analysts in the Soviet office disagreed with the paper, saying it was much too pessimistic. And so it carried a caution to readers that it was 'a speculative paper drafted by a senior analyst'" (514). Gates says, "What was important was that the paper was issued. It made a difference" (515).[4] Many leaders of analysis would advise waiting until a more powerful consensus can be delivered to decision makers, especially on such a high-stakes issue. That hesitance would have been a shame in this event.

Of course, the more distant the future, the more speculative our analysis must be. A good example of speculation about what, to intelligence analysts, is the distant future can be found in the National Intelligence Council's (NIC) 2012 paper, *Global Trends 2030: Alternative Worlds*. It highlights what it calls "megatrends . . . which are virtually certain, exist today, but during the next 15–20 years . . . will gain much greater momentum." It forecasts that China's economy will probably grow larger than that of the United States "a few years before 2030" and that

---

[3] Another insightful accounting of what CIA published about the failing Soviet Union is by former CIA DDI Douglas MacEachin (2007).
[4] President Bush (1998) might also have been referring to this paper when he wrote about this period: "I found the CIA experts particularly helpful, if pessimistic. One analysis paper concluded that Gorbachev's economic reforms were doomed to failure, and that his political changes were beginning to cause problems he might not be able to control. . . . Based on those conclusions, some people in the NSC began to speculate that Gorbachev might be headed for a crisis which could force him to crack down in the Soviet Union to maintain order, or might even force him out of power" (154).

"regional players such as Colombia, Indonesia, Nigeria, South Africa, and Turkey will become especially important to the global economy" (iv). These judgments sound supremely confident, but they are balanced by the identification of what the authors label "game changers," which are far less predictable but would have enormous impact. For example, the paper notes, "[M]any countries will be zig-zagging their way through the complicated democratization process during the next 15–20 years. Countries moving from autocracy to democracy have a proven track record of instability" (vii). The paper adds, in this context, "China . . . is slated to pass the threshold of US $15,000 per capita purchasing power parity (PPP) in the next five years, which is often a trigger for democratization" (vii). The net effect leaves the reader with the impression that *here are the forces that will shape the next two decades, here's what you are likely to see, and here's what you might see, and in our increasingly globalized world, brace yourself for major events that cannot be foreseen.*

To further convey that intelligence analysts cannot "see" the future but do have something useful to offer, the NIC authors adopted the unorthodox use of fictional scenarios. They were saying to the reader, in effect, here is some deep thought about the future rather than an intelligence-based assessment of the future. They said, "We have fictionalized the scenario narratives to encourage all of us to think more creatively about the future. We have intentionally built in discontinuities, which will have a huge impact in inflecting otherwise straight linear projections of known trends." They created four scenarios:

- **Stalled Engines**—a scenario in which the risk of interstate conflict rise owing to a new "great game" in Asia . . . illustrating the most plausible "worst case."

- **Fusion** is . . . what we see as the most plausible "best case." This is a world in which the specter of a spreading conflict in South Asia triggers efforts by the US, Europe, and China to intervene and impose a ceasefire. . . .

- **Gini Out-of-the-bottle** . . . is a world of extremes. Within many countries, inequalities dominate—leading to increasing political and social tensions. Between the countries, there are clear-cut winners and losers.

- **Nonstate World.** In this world, nonstate actors— nongovernmental organizations (NGOs), multinational businesses, academic institutions, and wealthy individuals—as well as subnational units (megacities, for example) flourish and take the lead in confronting global challenges. (NIC 2012: xii–xiv)

I see four tests for such a product. First, does the reader understand clearly that this is informed, rigorous thought about *possible* futures and not a forecast of *the* future? Second, is it written with the customer clearly in mind? By that I mean, does it understand the customer's average expertise, prejudices, and concerns? And third, is it worth the customer's time? As a leader of analysis, it is your job to make sure that the product passes the first two tests. Your answer on the third test, however, will be your own best prediction: *Will* this product prove to be worth the time of a very busy policy maker? To me, a product like the NIC's attempt at "Global Trends 2030" would be appreciated by *some* policy makers *between crises*. Most of the policy makers I know would put such a study on their ever-rising stack of papers to be read later. But the few who spend a weekend with it would have been well served.

The fourth test is not aimed at the customer; it is aimed at the analysts: Does this investment of their attentions make them better analysts? For the NIC project, for example, even if few policy customers spend the time to read the paper, the authors' focus on what the year 2030 might be like deepens their own understanding of the strategic forces at work in the world today. That deeper understanding will enrich their own work on many topics, providing a payoff to the customer in other products down the road. In simplest terms, the analyst grows when forced to wrestle with the customer's recurrent question, "What is going to happen?"

## Humility, an Open Mind, and Practice Required

But are we making a fundamental mistake here? A debate has been going on for many years among intelligence professionals. Some argue that we are kidding ourselves and our customers about the usefulness of our forecasts. With so many limits to our ability to look forward, they say, we should simply refuse to look beyond the immediate future. They say this with particular conviction when considering something like the NIC's attempt to consider the year 2030. When none of the over-the-horizon judgments depend on classified information, why use intelligence resources for such a project? Others take an even more stark view, saying we might even be doing harm when projecting so far ahead. Some of our speculation might be flat wrong but still could trigger a policy decision. For us to weigh in on such issues—worse, for us to *initiate* such analysis—is hubris, according to this argument.

To me, the most important word in that argument is *hubris*. Whether forecasting the immediate or distant future, where analysis does disservice is when it forecasts without humility. Overconfidence tainting forecasts is by no means unique to intelligence analysis. Both Nate Silver's (2012) *The Signal and the Noise* and Daniel Kahneman's (2011) *Thinking Fast and Slow* are full of anecdotes about bad predictions confidently made.

Too often, on the journey of crafting their judgments, analysts move from a recalcitrant cry—"How can I possibly know what the future holds?"—to supreme confidence—"I have pierced the darkness!" As Heuer (1999), Kahneman (2011), and many others have shown, analysts are human, prone to delusion about our own capabilities, seduced by our own logic. The human brain is wired to look forward, to anticipate, to develop working models to make sense of what is ahead. When the model explains evidence neatly, it takes a firm grip on the brain. And when the model holds up for an extended period, our faith in it grows. The longer a model holds up, the more time we have to form a compelling narrative supporting it and to describe the future the model predicts. There is no more persuasive forecast than one that comes with a confident, compelling narrative (see Taleb 2007, especially chap. 6). The history of intelligence failures is a history of confident forecasts persuasively argued.

It is your job to teach and enforce analytic humility throughout your products. It is your job—concerning the topics for which you are responsible—to analyze carefully what is and is not predictable in the particular situation you are examining. When your analysts are looking forward, it is your job to make sure they never lose sight of their uncertainty, and that they always convey that uncertainty to the customer. And it will be your job to dial back the confidence of your bolder analysts, changing their "almost certainly" to "probably," and their "will" to "might," when they overreach their evidence.

Nothing teaches humility better than examining our track record on prediction. Part of this is teaching your institution's successes and failures. CIA does this fairly well, especially in mining the lessons of our intelligence *failures*. And I am proud that we routinely do this unflinchingly, well before the finger-wagging outsiders weigh in. For the analysts, the story of every failure carries a huge dose of "That could have happened to me!" Significantly, the story of every intelligence *success* comes with a subtext of how close it came to not happening.

But even more powerful than teaching about *our* history of forecasting is insisting that each analyst keep track of *his own* history. Even though forecasting is the single most difficult thing an analyst does, as individual analysts we all presume we are better at it than we are. Having each analyst periodically go back and score the accuracy of his own predictions will improve his next prediction—at least, it should reinforce the analytic humility I am calling for.

An important recent academic study lends support to my call for analytic humility, while supporting the notion that forecasting is not feckless

(Mellers et al. 2015). A team, largely from the University of Pennsylvania, conducted a two-year forecasting tournament under the sponsorship of Intelligence Advanced Research Projects Activity (IARPA). The tournament focused on geopolitical forecasting, which in my experience is the most challenging arena for prediction, requiring the analyst to untangle the motivations and intentions of interacting collections of humans. Moreover, they used real-world topics, "ranging from whether North Korea would test a nuclear device between January 9, 2012, and April 1, 2012, to whether Moody's would downgrade the sovereign debt rating of Greece between October 3, 2011, and November 30, 2011." Participants were free to choose whether or not to make a forecast, so they were not forced into blind guessing. By the time the tournament was complete, they had a significant body of data, including "150,000 forecasts of 743 participants on 199 events."

The team found that participants did significantly better in their forecasts than random guessing. "We developed a profile of the best forecasters; they were better at inductive reasoning, pattern detection, cognitive flexibility, and open-mindedness. They had greater understanding of geopolitics, training in probabilistic reasoning, and opportunities to succeed in cognitively enriched team environments. Last but not least, they viewed forecasting as a skill that required deliberate practice, sustained effort, and constant monitoring of current affairs" (Mellers et al. 2015).

The team's point about open-mindedness is more than just a call for objectivity. They note, "Actively open-minded thinkers . . . have greater tolerance for ambiguity and weaker need for closure," not feeling compelled to rush to conclusion (Mellers et al. 2015). A good forecaster constantly asks what she might be missing, weighs how she might be wrong. Analytic humility.

The team also strongly endorses the need to track one's predictions, and the tournament facilitated this. Participants made an average of 121 predictions and could see how they were doing over the two years. "These conditions enabled a process of learning-by-doing and help to explain why some forecasters achieved far-better-than-chance accuracy" (Mellers et al. 2015). Both practice at predicting and tracking your success make you better at this tricky business.

One of the authors of the study, Philip Tetlock, tells its story and lays out its lessons in the superb book, *Superforecasting*. In studying the most successful of the forecasters in the tournament, those he refers to as "superforecasters" shared some common attributes. Tetlock shows that "superforecasting demands critical thinking that is open-minded, careful, curious, and—above all—self-critical. It also demands focus. The kind of thinking that produces superior judgment does not come effortlessly" (Tetlock and Gardner 2015: 20).

One of many things Tetlock does well in *Superforecasting* is to clarify the distinction between being expert and being a skilled forecaster.[5] Too many critics give the impression that being expert is actually a handicap in forecasting.[6] Far from considering expertise to be a handicap, Tetlock disowns those who used his earlier research for such a position. He says, "The message became 'all expert forecasts are useless,' which is nonsense. . . . My research became a backstop reference for nihilists who see the future as inherently unpredictable and know-nothing populists who insist on preceding 'expert' with 'so-called'" (Tetlock and Gardner 2015: 4). The issue, as Tetlock demonstrates, is not that expertise is a handicap in forecasting. It helps, especially in near-term forecasting. But expertise in a substantive topic and expertise in the craft of forecasting are two different things. Substantive experts can improve their skill in forecasting with training, practice, and attention to the attributes of Tetlock's "superforecasters."

There are some good reasons why substantive expertise does not automatically come with forecasting strength. One might think that any analyst who has become deeply expert would build up skill in the analytic discipline of forecasting. But I worked with many expert analysts whose knowledge was almost exclusively tapped to diagnose or identify "what is going on," rather than to project "what is going to happen." They could go a year or more without ever being asked to project beyond the immediate. Even analysts who work on inherently turbulent regions like the Middle East might forecast less than you would imagine. The very turbulence means that they are often busy analyzing tactical developments and might make only one or two strategic predictions in a year. That experience often is enough to teach them humility but not enough to build forecasting skill.

## Prediction Is Always a Gamble

For all the examples I have given so far, you'll not find simple rules for when to predict, when to speculate, and when to simply decline. This is one of the areas in which the leader of analysis needs to ply her own best analytic skills. The leader, together with the analysts involved, must examine the situation in all its complexity. She must examine the needs of the customer and whether they have something useful to say. Then the leader of analysis must be willing to gamble.

---

[5] Tetlock had made quite a splash in his 2005 book, *Expert Political Judgment*, noting that many so-called experts did no better than "dart throwing chimps" at forecasting. In describing this more recent tournament to *Harvard Business Review's* Walter Frick (2015), Tetlock said, "The best forecasters are hovering between the chimp and God."

[6] For example, even such usually savvy observers as Chip and Dan Heath (2013), citing Tetlock's earlier research, say "trust experts about base rates [meaning descriptions about the current situation] but not predictions" (Kindle location 2226).

In his book *The Signal and the Noise,* Nate Silver (2012) provides a very useful section on gambling, especially describing the popular poker game Texas Hold'em. The game requires the player to make predictions—judging the prospects for his own hand and judging the skill of his opponents— and to refine predictions as more data (cards and bets) come in. And the game requires the predictor—the gambler—to put his money where his mouth is. Like predictions in intelligence analysis, the game involves both skill and luck. Some professionals are good enough at the game to make six-figure incomes—Silver was one of them for a while. He says, "Skilled poker players are probably better than 99.9 percent of the population at making reasonably good probabilistic judgments under uncertainty" (Kindle location 5200). As a leader of analysis, you are expected to be the "skilled poker player."

Given everything you know about the prediction game you are in, you will be the one deciding when to fold, check, call, or raise. Use your best analytic skills to judge which are the safe bets, good bets, and silly bets. With your analysts, assess what you know in the situation and what you can reasonably infer:

- Judge the odds in this "hand"—that is, judge the trends, precedent, available data, obtainable data, and the degree of order or chaos in this particular situation.

- With your analysts, form a clear-eyed assessment of whether *what you know* has any diagnostic value in determining what lies ahead.

- Don't be seduced by the stakes on the table; they don't influence the odds of the next card being a winner. That is, just because the situation is really, really important—just because your customer is screaming for knowledge about the future—doesn't affect whether you can make a useful prediction.

- Analyze the "players at the table": Are your analysts prone to overconfidence? What biases have they displayed? What might your customer find useful even if it's not the clear prediction he wants?

- Don't let your last bet drive your next bet. New cards are being dealt—this new data might completely change the picture.

- Like the best gamblers, be a devoted student of the uncertainty game (probabilistic reasoning).

- And, like the best gamblers, study yourself—ignoring matters of luck, what does your track record tell you about your own boldness, biases, and wisdom?

Some leaders of analysis will push back at this notion of gambling. They will say, "If you communicate clearly your uncertainty, no gamble is involved." By this they mean, if your forecast says, "The Israeli prime minister *probably will succeed* in his effort to form a unity coalition," you have left room for uncertainty. "Probably will succeed" logically implies that he might not succeed. The weight of your forecast is with success, but if the prime minister fails, your statement was not wrong.

I think this reasoning is at the same time *important* and *misjudges our customers*. It is important because we always must carefully convey the limits of our certainty when communicating our judgments. There is a significant difference between "probably will" and "will," and we must never apologize for obsessing about such nuance. And our most experienced customers learn to appreciate the care we take with our qualifiers. But let's not kid ourselves. Even our most experienced customers will, after the fact, think we were *wrong* if the Israeli prime minister failed to form that unity coalition. The "probably" and its logical implication will only occur to the customer if he goes back to read our careful forecast, which he rarely has the time to do. Instead, he will judge us by his recollection of our forecast. And his recollection will be that we led him to expect a unity coalition.

Finally, our acceptance of the reality that we are gambling helps us connect better to our policymaking customer. The policy maker is always, inescapably, gambling with the decisions he makes. And he frequently, at least in part, is basing that gamble on what we have told him. It is both arrogant and off-putting for us to say to him, in effect, "We know the stakes are high here, and we know you are going to bet on our advice, but even if you are wrong, you'll find *we* were not wrong."

## Prediction Is the *Leader's* Responsibility

Perhaps because of the dangers and difficulty, many analysts shy away from prediction. At the other end of the spectrum are analysts too quick to make too grand a prediction with too little evidence. Both types of analyst—and those in between—have roles to play in prediction. But the responsibility for prediction falls to the leader of analysis.

There are several things the leader needs to do to get it right—or as wise as we can make it when it is guaranteed frequently to fail.

- Make sure analysts at the two ends of the "boldness spectrum" are talking to each other. Their instincts create a useful balance. Their dialogue can help hone everyone's critical thinking.

- Make sure analysts of different disciplines are talking to each other. The most strategic predictions usually cross analytic boundaries. Take perhaps our most important prediction: forecasting war. Too many military analysts will say a leader's decision to go to war is ultimately a political decision, and therefore the responsibility for predicting that decision falls to political analysts. Too many political analysts say they can never predict a leader's decision to go to war without the military analysts' thorough understanding of force capabilities and balance. To some extent, both schools are correct, but they will rarely bridge these positions on their own initiative. The leader of analysis must understand the gifts and hesitance of both types of analyst and draw them together.

- Make sure we are not just analyzing the situation, but also analyzing *predictability* in the situation. With your analysts, identify key variables, weigh the diagnosticity of the evidence at hand, and try hard to identify whether you have something useful to say.

- Make sure your analysts understand what we are asking from them. We are asking analysts to offer something useful about the future. We are asking for the best expertise and critical thinking to be applied to a forecast. We are asking our workforce to be professional gamblers. We are not asking for infallibility.

# What's the Worst that Could Happen? Leading Warning

I called prediction the most difficult part of the analyst's work.

One type of prediction, warning, may be the most *important* thing done in intelligence. The identification of a potential threat before it arrives is the reason the United States launched intelligence organizations in the first place. Protecting Americans from deadly threats—that is why they pay us. This expectation does not just apply to intelligence analysts. Any CEO who has invested in an analytic cadre at least hopes they will warn of developments that threaten the company.

Albeit vital, warning is a tricky business. Sometimes, warning is a prediction, with all the elements that make prediction the most challenging thing analysts do. Sometimes it is not a prediction per se but the identification of a vulnerability inherent in the situation. Beyond the challenge of enlightening a customer, which all analysis strives to do, warning tries to stir the customer to urgent action. And it is a tricky business because it is easy for the diligent and imaginative analyst to get caught in a death spiral of warning about endless threats—threats *conceivable* but *not real*.

Warning is best when analysis is least. By that I mean the most effective warnings come with clear and compelling *evidence*. The evidence often speaks for itself, and it is sometimes the analyst's job simply to get out of its way. Quite appropriately, the intelligence collectors get the credit for this type of warning.

But when the evidence is vague or contradictory, the analyst's challenge is significant. Even when the analyst has put the pieces together brilliantly, and is confident about her assessment, she still needs to convince the policy maker. Understandably, the more vague and contradictory the evidence, the more reluctant the customer will be. In response to a warning, the customer's choices often are to do something expensive—and visible to all critics—or to gamble that you are wrong. You affect that calculus by *earning the customer's trust over time*.

Vague and contradictory evidence comes with another burden to analysts. Knowing that we are seized by the urgency of the threat we have identified, it is powerfully tempting to communicate that threat starkly and unequivocally. Sometimes you just want to grab the policy maker by the collar and shake him. But our responsibility to accurately convey our uncertainty, to acknowledge what we don't know, pertains to all analysis, and no exception can be made for the warning arena. Our responsibility is to enlighten but not manipulate the policy maker in this area, as in all our work. Our credibility depends on this, and nowhere is our credibility more important than when we are warning.

Let me illustrate with an example from the 1990s, when we received evidence of a coming action that would jolt US policies in the Kurdish provinces of Iraq. The evidence ran strongly counter to behavior we had seen for years. I can't provide more detail here, but I can tell you I felt sorry for National Security Advisor Anthony Lake, who was going to have to decide whether to trust us.

My analysts ran to me one morning with some intelligence about an ugly imminent threat in the Kurdish provinces. I got the word up to CIA's seventh-floor leadership, and George Tenet said, "Let's get in the car." We headed to Tony Lake's office in the West Wing, to brief him and Mark Parris, the president's special assistant for Near East and South Asia. I had worked with Lake during my stint at the National Security Council, briefed him and Mark several times since, and have enormous respect for both. We laid out the evidence we had, took great pains to explain why we believed it, and predicted what we thought was likely to happen. We also laid out alternative possibilities, taking time to explain why they were less reasonable. Lake accepted the prediction and, with Parris, quickly formulated a plan of action. As we were walking out of Lake's office, Parris leaned over to me and said, "Ok, we're going ahead, but this is all on you guys." I took this to mean that they were running with our call, gambling that we were right. Our warning was vindicated the next day. Lake's trust in us was also vindicated, and he would likely consider that the next time—but he would never escape the reality that each time is a gamble. I think it helped him in this event that we presented our information and assessment rationally, reasonably, and anticipating his concerns.

It also helped, I believe, that our warning to Lake was not a weekly occurrence. We sounded *this* alarm, but he didn't think of us as alarmists. This would have been a much more difficult gamble for him if he was new to the job and did not have a sense of our abilities. I often wonder whether the Bush administration would have been more receptive to George Tenet's summer 2001 warnings of a major attack by Al Qa'ida had we been another year into the administration (Tenet 2007: chap. 8). They didn't yet have Lake's understanding that when Tenet's hair is on fire, you stop what you are doing and listen carefully.

One of the challenges of warning is that vindication rarely comes as quickly as it did in these examples. Sometimes, if your warning is heeded, vindication never comes at all. There were times, when I was in CTC in 2002 and 2003, when we issued warnings that you heard about because the national threat level publicly was raised. We would brief our evidence and assessment to the policy makers, and they would decide, among other things, whether to adjust the threat level, say from Yellow to Orange. Our warning was based on intelligence that pointed to an imminent attack, but the attack never came. Was our evidence incorrect? Was our analysis bogus? Or was the attack deterred? I drafted some of the public threat announcements myself and, even in retrospect, consider them sound. But to this day I do not know for sure. Eventually, the system of nationwide threat warnings was replaced with warnings more specific to geography or sector. But that wasn't because we were taught to do our jobs differently. Rather, I saw the refined approach as the policy makers' willingness to gamble a bit more that we probably didn't need people in Des Moines to react to a threat we thought might be aimed at Los Angeles.

In these counterterrorism examples, after a time at an elevated threat level, the policy makers would ask whether the threat had passed. This was a completely reasonable question. It was our warning that had triggered the alert, after all. But, as frequently is the case with many types of threat, we had received *evidence of a threat* but, even after weeks, we had no further evidence—certainly *no evidence the threat had gone away*. Ideally, the alert (and the myriad actions triggered by the alert) averted the threat, but how could we know? How could we be confident that the terrorists were not simply waiting for the security forces to stand down? Intelligence owns the alarm bell but rarely owns the all-clear whistle. And the same policy maker who asked whether we are safe now is entitled to wonder whether the threat was real at all. If you install high security locks on your doors and windows because of a rash of burglaries in the neighborhood and you are burglary-free after that, was it because the locks did their job, or did you waste your money? Even without an answer, you leave the locks in place because you already paid for them. In the alert business, however, leaving extra security in place comes at a steep cost, including the tax on public patience.

Both we and our customers would do well to understand that an intelligence community tuned to warn of threats will not be strong at recognizing the expiry of threats. Many analysts were slow to acknowledge the collapse of the Soviet threat. We didn't know that Iraq had secretly destroyed its WMD arsenal. And you can bet we will struggle to declare the ISIS threat dead even if years pass with no attack. Knowing this is an inherent weakness, leaders of analysis should compensate however they can. They might, for example, periodically assign devil's advocate analysts to make the case that a threat has passed, and see how that case looks to fresh eyes.

You should never lose sight of how irritating this can all be for your customer. It is easier for us to warn than it is for him to act, and it is easier for us to stay "on alert" indefinitely because that is our job. Some customers suspect that we often warn simply to cover our asses. "If some unlikely bad thing happens," they complain, "you'll be able to say it wasn't your fault." If you were the one who had to decide whether to cancel shore leave and move the fleet, you'd be cranky, too.

As frustrated as they get being forced to gamble one way or another when they have heard our warnings, they get even more frustrated when we warn repeatedly of something they feel helpless to address. They feel nagged. "I heard you, dammit . . . what do you expect me to do about it?" This is not simply a *cri de coeur;* this is a legitimate question from your customer. We owe it to him to provide our clearest thinking about the minimum level of action that might avert the threat. In the directorate of analysis, we call this "opportunity analysis." It should be a required part of warning.

Finally, a word about threshold. I have referred to the policy makers' gambles once they receive our warning. Again, as the leader of analysis, you must make a gamble as well. You have to decide what threshold to set for warning in the first place. Any good analyst can imagine ten threats that are conceivable-but-remote possibilities. If you hand all ten warnings to your customer, they will tune you out. But the customer doesn't want to be surprised either, so do you pick the most likely two out of the ten? Three? There is no formula for getting this right. You will always be gambling about when to warn and when to just chill.

But I can give you one loud piece of advice and one rule of thumb. The advice is talk to your customer about your warning threshold. If he wants you on a hair trigger for warning, ok. If he wants you to dial it back, fair enough. If he wants you to lean forward on threats to his latest policy initiative but lean backward on another area, you can fine-tune that, too. And check back with him periodically, to make certain you are in touch with his current appetite. But whatever guidance he provides is just that: guidance. His guidance doesn't relieve you of your responsibility to give him the warning he *needs*. You have his back regardless of his appetite. To meet that responsibility, I had success with this rule of thumb: I don't scare easily, but when *I* am scared, I'll do my best to make sure my customer is, too. I won't—I cannot—hype the threat. But I will do my best to communicate the reasons for my concern.

## What Is Reasonable in an Unreasonable World?

Let me end this section with a caution for our customers and ourselves. As hard as we work to peer into the future, as diligent as we can be with both prediction and warning, there is an inherent limit to our success. Analysis can only deliver an assessment of what is reasonable, but the world is not always reasonable. There will always be a degree of randomness in human affairs. There will always be irrational impulses at least tempting— sometimes driving—leaders.

Can we allow for this randomness in our forecasts? Yes and no. No, we cannot write a compelling piece of analysis that requires one or several actors to do something illogical unless there is evidence for it. Yes, we can be humble in making our predictions. We can remind ourselves and our readers that, in the play of events, dynamic interaction often matters more than intent and capability. We can remember that, despite a vast difference in abilities, tonight the worst team in the NBA might beat the best.

When we do look forward with humility and communicate our uncertainty with clarity, I believe we can bring useful insight to the customer about what tomorrow might hold. When weighing the *near* future, when the customer must make decisions, those decisions are likely to be wiser if informed by the best thinking of expert analysts. The farther away the future we are considering, the less expert our analysts are and the more speculative our projection must be. For a distant future, perhaps it would be useful to remind the customer that we are not *forecasting* but *considering* the future, and we are inviting the customer to share our thoughts. On a case-by-case basis, we will have to make hard-nosed decisions about whether to invest analytic resources on issues when informed speculation is the best we can offer. And the customer will make a similar resource decision about whether to invest his time reading it. If he does, the customer will be smarter about the future than he was before.

# KEY THEMES

Forecasting is the analysts' most difficult function. It is also usually the most important. Because our customers can only affect the future, that is where the analysts' interest must be. The future is uncertain, but we work to narrow the range of uncertainty for decision makers.

Run from anyone who makes forecasting sound formulaic. Where forecasting can be easily modeled (Should blackjack players hit on 17?) is not where forecasters struggle. In more complex situations, leaders of analysis must figure out not which formula to use but what we have to say that would be *useful* to our customers.

With your analysts, analyze *predictability* in the situation you are watching. How confident we can be looking forward will depend on the situation:

- Is the situation *mechanical* (meaning there are clear if-then relationships, with strong evidence, and deductive reasoning applies)?

- Is the situation like *short-term weather forecasting* (with well-understood dynamics and abundant evidence)?

- Is the situation like *long-term weather forecasting* (clear historical trends but plenty of exceptions)?

- Is the situation one where *long-term patterns* are evident? Patterns are great and hold up most of the time. But they all end someday.

- Is the situation *dominated by human characteristics*? Humans are complex—individual humans even more so. You may be obliged to forecast what an individual actor is likely to do in a high-stakes situation even before he has decided for himself. Confidence is rarely warranted here, so lower yours and work hard to determine what your analysts can say that is useful.

- Is the situation like none of these? That tells you something.

Humility is required in forecasting.

- Never fall in love with your forecast. Actively look for contrary evidence.

- Restrain your overconfident analysts.

- Work hard to choose the appropriate term of uncertainty ("probably," "may," "a slim chance") and to preserve those terms through the editing process.

- Forecasting is always a gamble (and you won't win them all). The leader of analysis bears the responsibility in this dangerous game.

Warning—flagging threats or vulnerabilities—is arguably the most important type of forecast. ("What do I pay you guys for if you don't warn me of imminent dangers?!"—any CEO who has an analytic unit.) The most effective warning starts with a relationship with your customer:

- It is based on credibility built over time.

- It is sensitive to the customer's appetite for alerts and tolerance for false alarms.

To be effective, warning must be

- Credible

- Actionable

- Heard

# CHAPTER 8

# Ethics in Analysis

I n any business, everyone in the enterprise needs to be sensitive to ethics, especially the leader. In the business of analysis, all the analysts must be "ethically fit," to use a phrase of the late Rush Kidder (1995), one of America's leading experts on the practical application of ethics. But again, the leader's responsibility is even greater. The leader of analysis must wear his values on his sleeve, leading an ongoing conversation about integrity, honesty, responsibility, and—yes—kindness. The leader must show she holds these values deeply, applies them to every aspect of the business, and expects her subordinates to do the same.

There are some good references on the shelves to help intelligence officers think about ethics. And all intelligence officers need to reflect on the apparent contradiction between a business that operates in the dark—stealing secrets, after all—and the universally lauded virtues of honesty and openness. I personally recommend Jim Olson's (2006) *Fair Play* and the ethics chapter of Mark Lowenthal's (2009) *Intelligence: From Secrets to Policy*. Both works have a sophisticated and practical understanding of the thorny issues that confront intelligence officers. Not surprisingly, both are written by intelligence insiders.

Unfortunately, most of the literature in this arena is limited to the ethical dilemmas of intelligence collection and covert action. They tend to skip over dilemmas faced by analysts. Analysts share the ethical challenges inherent in collection and covert action. They also face dilemmas unique to analysis. In fact, although this chapter will focus on intelligence analysis, many of these dilemmas are shared with analysts outside intelligence. Any analyst who has provoked a business leader to make a high-stakes decision and then turned out to have been wrong has felt some of the ethical burden I will examine here.

## What Am I Doing in This Business?

In my years in Navy Intelligence, I am sad to admit I never grappled with the ethics of the business. I should have. Much of what I will talk about in this chapter can apply to the analysis I performed in the Navy. Blame it on my youth—I just didn't have the thought.

But the thought hit me powerfully when I decided to leave the Navy and apply for work as a civilian in the intelligence community. I was tempted to apply to be an analyst in CIA, but could I work for *those* guys? From my work in the Navy, I knew enough to dismiss many of the Hollywood myths about CIA. But there was no escaping the fact that I'd be joining a firm defined by espionage—a business that deceives and manipulates people whose only crime sometimes is that they are foreigners with access to important secrets. Also, this was in 1982, and fresh in my mind were the recent congressional (Church and Pike committees) allegations of CIA excesses. CIA seemed dirty.

But I knew I wanted to be an analyst—not a spy—right? So I wouldn't be joining the dirty part of the business, right? Even my youth didn't tolerate such self-deception. I couldn't escape the fact that I would be working with the spies. In fact, I'd be sending some of them on their missions—in effect, I would be telling them what secrets to go steal.

Here is how I squared the circle. I decided intelligence was a *necessary* business. And I decided, as a man of principles, I could help CIA from the inside—help it to be a more effective force for good and help it avoid the excesses I had heard about. I also committed to just walk away if my calculation was incorrect.

A bit more depth is warranted here. What I'll present now is how I feel about these issues looking back over a full career at CIA. I am proud to say that my calculation in 1982 still feels sound—and does not feel like a rationalization.

Let's start with my assertion that intelligence is a necessary business. Most Americans' urge for intelligence begins with the urge to protect the country from serious foreign threats. So, it should be no surprise that our basic intelligence capabilities grew out of a wartime need. There should be no plainer justification to steal secrets than the need in World War II to thwart and then defeat Hitler's Nazi regime. Few ethicists would regard this as a close call—we were stealing from a wicked regime in pursuit of a clear greater good. Where the enemy is, what the enemy is capable of, and what the enemy intends to do are vital pieces of information in a national emergency. The value of such intelligence proved itself to America in that war, and after the war it became immediately applicable to protecting the country from the perceived Soviet threat.

But once you pin the ethical justification for intelligence to defense from grave threats, the debate is not over. Once you build an intelligence capability to help the country respond to threats, its capabilities become hugely attractive to any decision maker who seeks to advance his agenda. So the president who builds an intelligence capability to protect America from threats quickly finds intelligence is also helpful for advancing American interests. The same capabilities that help the president understand Soviet military intentions toward Europe can help the president understand

Canadian negotiating intentions in an undersea boundary dispute. We have no trouble justifying the ethics of the former, but in the latter, it takes a force of will to revisit the assertion that "intelligence is a necessary business." For the leader of analysis, it takes some courage to tell a senior policy maker, "My analysts will help you to understand the Canadian position in this dispute, but we will not task our collectors to steal Canadian secrets."

It is also relevant in considering ethics to consider this: What is accepted behavior in the community? And in the community of nations, intelligence has long been an accepted element of statecraft. There have been bilateral agreements between two friendly nations to not spy on each other, but there has never been an international negotiation to broadly ban intelligence. Societies have long held that a nation stealing a secret from another nation is not ethically the same as a man stealing from his neighbor. We generally accept this, even though societies have presumed that if we catch one of your spies in our land, we will execute him. Such logic might seem convoluted, but it is widely understood and accepted in the community of nations.

There was an extra ingredient to my judgment that it would be ethically ok for me to work in an intelligence agency. It mattered to me that I viewed—and view—America as a force for good in the world. We can be selfish, misguided, and heavy handed, but in the community of nations, America is an important force for justice, human rights, and democracy, while our opponents stand for the opposite. I believed as an intelligence officer, I could help US policy makers make smarter, more effective decisions and help America be a more effective force for good in the world. Looking back, I am satisfied that I did this. Ethically, my career was sound.

## Leading a Dialogue on Values

So let me turn from an ethical defense of intelligence to the leader's responsibility for guiding ethics in analysis. Much of today's literature on leadership recommends starting from personal values, and that advice could not be more applicable than in this arena. The leader of analysts must be willing to talk—and talk frequently—about his or her personal values. Three things happen. First, the subordinates become convinced that their boss *has* laudable values. This is critical. In their excellent empirical study of the essential ingredients of highly successful leadership, *The Extraordinary Leader,* Jack Zenger and Joseph Folkman (2009: 12–14) discovered that strength in character—consistently acting with integrity—is an absolute prerequisite. And integrity starts with values.

The second thing that happens is that the analysts quickly see that their own personal values are in alignment with those articulated by the leader.

This is not accidental. In his book *How Good People Make Tough Choices,* Rush Kidder (1995: 92) describes a survey he has conducted in countless seminars. He asks participants to list their most cherished moral values. Over and over again, the participants list the same fifty or so values, and of these, they agree that about five are the most important: love, truth, tolerance, responsibility, and fairness. As an ethics instructor, I have used this values exercise dozens of times with intelligence analysts and managers, and their results match Kidder's findings (although "objectivity" often creeps in as a top moral value for them). What this means is that we all tend to share the fundamental ethical values. When the leader talks about his personal ethical values, the analysts are most likely to think, "Yeah, those are my values, too."

Of course, the leader must do more than talk about these values; he must walk the walk. But it is insufficient to just walk the walk—to just consistently behave with integrity—without talking about the values that drive that behavior. Analysts, being analysts, analyze the behavior of the boss. Give them more data—data about your values—and they are more likely to analyze correctly where your behavior comes from.

The third thing that happens when the leader frequently talks about values is that the analysts learn that such discussion is appropriate for their workplace. I had one remarkable boss at CIA who frequently interjected in her staff meetings, "Let's think about what the right thing to do is." That consistently elevated the tenor of the conversation, usually bringing us more quickly to decisions we were happy about. She was not unique among my bosses either. I vividly recall one directorate corporate board meeting where we were considering our policy for paying overtime. We had an extended discussion about what we could afford, potential for abuse, typicality of crises in different offices, and endless additional considerations. Finally our chairman, the DDI, cut off our endless overanalysis with the simple statement, "This is all interesting, but when we tell our analysts to work overtime, we are going to pay them for it because *it's the right thing to do.*" My colleagues and I around the table were indeed moral folks, but it took the boss to move our conversation off application into values, and as soon as we did, our decision was easy—it was embarrassing that none of us had thought of it.

# Climbing Down Off the Analyst's High Horse

Another thing the leader must do is help the analysts with their self-awareness. Individually or corporately, there is no consistently ethical behavior without self-awareness. Analysts typically share many laudable traits I talk about elsewhere. But here I want to talk about the leader's responsibility to help the analysts shed their self-delusions. There are many, but I'll mention three traits to which analysts are particularly prone, traits I have encountered among analysts in the business community as well as in intelligence:

- **Arrogance.** To be an analyst, you have to be demonstrably smart. You don't get in if you don't have a strong academic record. You tend not to be attracted to such an intellectual pursuit as analysis if you don't identify yourself as an intellectual. And as you spend a career competing for promotions with such smart folks, the air gets even more rarefied. From this reality, it is hard for an analyst to resist the following delusion: I am smarter than you; therefore, I am better than you. No ethical behavior flows from the notion that "I am better than you."

- **Self-righteousness.** Because analysts tend to be in the "clean" part of the business, it is tempting to think of ourselves as morally better than our colleagues. In intelligence, the colleagues can be the case officers, who might get their hands dirty in the field. In the business world, the analyst might think of herself as more "pure" than the program manager who will entertain such factors as tactical maneuvering or expedience. This is not as extreme a problem as it was when I joined the agency in 1983. Back then, the separation between the analytic and operational directorates was stark. I don't think I even met a case officer my first year. Today, the partnership between analysts and collectors is much more intimate, with analysts integrated into many operations. But the problem has not disappeared completely. As deputy director of the Counterterrorist Center, in the Operations Directorate, I worked directly with many of the operators. In a quiet minute I occasionally would ask them whether the analysts still seem self-righteous. "Don't get me started!" was their consistent reaction. And it is not only the "ops guys" who feel our self-righteousness. Ask any policy maker who regularly interacts with analysts. Every senior director at the NSC (National Security Council) can tell you how frequently they detect an analyst's suspicion that they have set aside their values—that they care only about politics and foreign policy expedience. Or any assistant secretary of state can tell you of the analyst who audibly sniffed when he made an unsavory choice, when the only alternative was worse.

- **Cynicism.** This is the analysts' disease. We are trained to be skeptics. We are trained to warn of pending disaster. We are professionally embarrassed when we miss the call. This combination makes us quick to identify bad things that might happen and tell our customers of them. We become masters at the game "Find what is wrong with this picture." It takes a force of will for analysts to allow that sometimes good things happen in the world, too, or that this US foreign policy or that military operation might succeed. What has this to do with ethics? Can you think of any of history's ethical paragons who were cynics? Indeed, aren't most of them extraordinary optimists? Our role in national security policymaking requires us to be skeptics—we cannot share the optimism of those paragons—but cynicism is ethically toxic.

Not all analysts suffer from these traits, of course. But they are so common that they tend to define us when we interact with others. On top of these unattractive traits, add one more. We know we have them, but *we think they don't show*. Ouch.

# Driving Collection

There are other ethical challenges in driving collection besides our tendency to think of collectors as lesser mortals. The issue of intelligence collection drips ethical ramifications—how far should we go to get the information we want?

This is more important than ever because the intelligence community leadership accepts that analysis must drive collection.[1] The notion is not new. For decades it has been apparent to many intelligence leaders that within the intelligence community, the all-source analyst is best positioned to dispassionately evaluate what is known on a topic, what is knowable, and what is most important to discover to serve our national policy customers. But they have moved from the sentiment that analysts must have an input into collection to the conviction that they must *drive* collection. When the DDI John Gannon began aggressively trying to sell the notion in the mid-1990s, it resonated intellectually with some seniors but offended many collectors. One of my case officer friends referred to the policy as "analysis driving collection—crazy!" But now the partnership is much closer, and many more collection leaders are likely to solicit analyst input.

This puts a greater ethical burden on analysts. Whereas in the past, analysts could simply list what they wanted to know, now they are more likely to have to consider which form of collection should be sent after which question. Ethically, might it be ok to steal from a friendly nation to gain an

---

[1] See, for example, Hayden (2007), where he says, "Painstaking, all-source analysis is crucial to supporting and driving operations." Also, the concept is embedded in the nature of the intelligence cycle itself, where analysis and collection inform and prompt each other (see Central Intelligence Agency 2009: 26).

advantage over that nation? Recall my point above about the temptation to steal the Canadian negotiating plan in a boundary dispute. The analyst may have to decide to limit himself to what is available in open sources on such an issue. Or consider the ethics of sending a spy in harm's way. The analyst may have to consider, Is what I want to know worth risking an asset's life?

Again, the ethical burden of driving collection is not unique to just *intelligence* analysts. Researchers in the pharmaceutical industry are acutely aware of the ethical challenges inherent in collecting data through testing human and animal subjects. Any journalist on a high-stakes story may face the temptation to elicit facts from a reluctant source by manipulation or even deceit. And a data analyst will know the weaknesses of the data he relies on but may be tempted to gloss over those weaknesses when presenting his findings.

# Resisting Politicization

One point of pride among analysts is that we "speak truth to power." Analysts must tell the customer what we think and know without demur, even when we know the customer does not like the message. We have to tell it straight, or what good are we?

And in my experience, this is no hollow claim. In fact, we tend to love it. Part of our identity, part of our self-respect, depends on a cold-eyed willingness to face the truth and then to pass that truth on to the policy makers we serve. I have seen countless examples of analysts holding their ground against the pressure of policy makers who tried to bully them into changing or burying an inconvenient conclusion. The most mild-mannered analyst tends to set his jaw and clench his fists when he thinks he is being told to cave under political pressure.

But that bullying policy maker, as an ethical challenge, concerns me less than you might think. He concerns me if he turns the relationship with the analysts into an adversarial one—it is dysfunctional if the customer we are trying to serve will simply not listen. But that is a mission concern rather than an ethical concern. As far as the threat the bully poses to our ethics, he is such a clear and overt source of attempted politicization that he is easily recognized and guarded against. Rather, what concerns me more from an ethics perspective is the subtle source of politicization—an urge inside an analyst, or inside the analyst's organization, that prompts us to shade the truth rather than anger a customer. Let me amplify.

At its essence, politicization can be simply stated. This is how I have explained it to hundreds of analysts and their managers: If you change a presentation to suit a customer, that is customer service. If you change a *conclusion* to suit a customer, that is politicization. But several things complicate the issue and frequently make politicization hard to diagnose:

- First, on important issues, analysts live in a politically charged environment. They often know what a customer believes on the issue. They certainly can know what a customer—often a politician—has said publicly. The analysts also are smart enough to sense what the customer wishes were true. Beyond this, an analyst occasionally will like or dislike the customer, hoping for or against his or her reelection. We tell our analysts—and our leaders of analysis—that they must close their minds to all such factors, letting no customer preferences taint the analytic process. And for the most part, we can be proud of our success, but to bat a thousand would be inhuman.

- Analysts, and their leaders, have a strong sense of customer service. We genuinely want our customers to be happy. We bend over backward to win their attention. We spend enormous energy trying to provide products that are useful, user friendly, digestible, and timely. We try to answer even their most unreasonable questions. And when a customer expresses displeasure with us, we often flog ourselves into a frenzy of tormented self-examination. Does this urge to make the customer happy ever subtly nudge our analysis? It must.

- Analysts and their leaders also need to retain access to their customers. A policy maker who won't read your papers, won't take your briefings, won't meet with you . . . won't let us do our job. So when we are delivering analysis that we know will irritate the customer, we try to avoid triggering an angry "Get out and don't come back!!" Does this instinct mean we occasionally soft-sell an unwelcome analytic message or delay delivering it? It must.

- Connected to the urge to retain access is an urge to not simply and endlessly repeat an analytic line the customer has already rejected. This instinct has gotten me crosswise with a subordinate more than once. When an analyst is told that the policy maker was not convinced by an argument, the analyst's first instinct is to try again, to make the argument more clearly, to pile on even more evidence, or to make the same point a different way. This is laudable. But I have occasionally had to tell an analyst, in essence, "Look, you made your best case three times and this customer just doesn't believe it. Making the case a fourth time isn't going to convince him, but it will make him mad. We are going to wait until we have more compelling evidence before we take another run at this customer on this topic." The analyst's first instinct is to tell me I am politicizing the analysis. To which I respond, "So . . . how many times do *you* think we should tell the customer the same thing?" The right balance, I believe, is to tell the customer enough times that you are confident he knows (1) what we believe and why and (2) that we *still* believe it but not so often that the customer feels like we are gratuitously poking a thumb in his eye.

- Sometimes, the customer is *right*. What an unwelcome complication that is. Sometimes when a customer rejects a piece of analysis, she explains her position and provides new information or a new angle worth considering. An analyst must weigh the new information or argument with an open mind and adjust the conclusion if appropriate. What makes this complicated? Sometimes the analyst discounts the new input. The challenge for the leader of analysts is to determine whether the analyst is simply being stubborn.

- Finally, sometimes changing the presentation *does* change the conclusion. To get the attention of a difficult customer, I might ask an analyst to begin a presentation with something the customer agrees with, saving the controversial element until later in the piece. That approach might elicit a more open mind from the customer than to jump right into the controversy without preamble. But am I really asking the analyst to bury the controversy? Both my intent and the actual impact on the customer will matter here.

With all this subtlety and complexity at play, it is not surprising that politicization can creep into the analytic process without being diagnosed. It is not surprising either that analysts sometimes suspect their bosses have caved to political pressure. When the accusation is pointed enough to provoke an investigation—not a rarity in our business—the charge is usually judged to be unworthy; no actual evidence of politicization is found. My concern, however, is that sometimes the issue is so subtle that the only real evidence lies in the heart. Did I shade the analysis to make a customer happy? Sometimes even *I* might not know. Indeed, veteran intelligence officer Paul Pillar (2011: chap. 6), in his *Intelligence and US Foreign Policy,* makes a compelling case that the notion of caving to politicization is so abhorrent to us that I would refuse even to admit to myself that it swayed me.

So what is required to produce analysis consistently free of political influence? First, it requires acute sensitivity on the part of leaders of analysis that "if I let my guard down, I *will* politicize." The human urge to please an audience is that strong. It is not a problem to be solved; it is a condition that comes with the territory. When the only evidence of the presence or absence of politicization sometimes lies in your own heart, you must search your heart frequently. Am *I* allowing politics, or my urge to make readers happy, or my conflict-avoiding nature to influence my analytic leadership? Like so much with ethics, just reflecting on the ethics of a situation—just asking, "Is this politicization?"—will positively influence our behavior.

Second, leaders of analysis must communicate on the issue of politicization. Talk to analysts about what politicization is and what it's not. Educate them to be sensitive to the subtleties of politicization, as well as the subtleties of effective customer service. And build an environment where they feel comfortable speaking up when they suspect you are letting political pressure affect your decisions. Also, talk to your most important customers about the issue. The customers most likely to bully the analysts won't have the patience for this conversation, but others can be reached. Tell them, "We expect you to challenge our analysis, and we want you to ask us hard questions, but also tell us what you know that we might not, so we can factor it into our analysis."

Third, make sure your analysts' reasoning is explicit in every piece—written and oral. In exposing the underpinnings of our logic, suspicions of politicization sometimes are replaced with clarity about evidence and inference.

Now let us widen the aperture again beyond intelligence analysis. The very word *politicization* seems to pertain to intelligence analysts letting politics threaten objectivity (remember, I said earlier that intelligence analysts often list "objectivity" as one of their top moral values). And in our system of government, the decision maker is frequently a *politician*, with a *political ideology* and *political agenda*, raising the specter of *politicization*. But many sense-makers outside intelligence face similar pressures. Surely climate scientists inside the EPA and deficit experts in the Government Accounting Office can identify with the subtle and overt pressures I have been talking about.

But the dynamic also is in play far outside of the political arena. Any time an analyst has a key customer with an ideology or agenda, the analyst can get crosswise with either. Any time an analyst must deliver bad news—and that is inevitable—the analyst's credibility may be challenged. "Our data shows your program is not succeeding." "Our analysis suggests that your key strategic assumption has been rendered moot by the declining price of oil." "We are reporting to the CEO that your division's quarterly earnings will be 25 percent below our previous projection." It is human nature for that customer to argue the conclusion. It is human nature for the customer to vent his anger and assail the analysts' competence. And it is human nature for the analysts—and their leaders—to soften the message to make it more palatable to that customer. Politicization without politics? It happens to analysts in every arena where the customer has power.

# Are We Responsible for Consequences?

Much of ethics deals with the weighing of consequences and determining the "greater good." Occasionally, in good conscience I can do a generally bad thing—lie—if by lying I am protecting the innocent from the wicked. So I lie to the Gestapo if they ask where Anne Frank is hidden. I can engage in espionage if the consequence is to defend our nation from real threats. Kidder (1995) describes such consequentialism (or "utilitarianism") as one of the time-honored approaches for making ethical decisions.[2]

But is the analyst to consider the consequences of the action she provokes? This is a serious dilemma. Feelings run strong but the answer is not easy. As with so much in ethics, a lot depends on the actual details. If an investment analyst recommends buying stock in a company that then suffers an unforeseeable catastrophe—almost a lightning strike—he may feel bad but not responsible. But if the head of an investigating team finds they have gotten an innocent suspect convicted, she is likely to be moved to take remedial action.

I remember one time when I was a Near East analyst in the 1980s, crafting a piece for our current intelligence publication called the *National Intelligence Daily* (NID). The NID was a community pub, so I needed to coordinate the text with my counterparts outside CIA. The process went smoothly until I heard from my friend—call him "Tom"—from State Department's Intelligence and Research Bureau.

"I can't coordinate on this," he said.

I replied with surprise, "But we've talked about this before, Tom, and you agree with me."

Then he shocked me. "I do agree, but if my assistant secretary reads this, he'll go nuts. I know what he is itching to do in the region, and this will provide just the ammunition he needs. People will suffer." This violated what I thought was a universal ethic for analysts: *we* provide insight, the

---

[2] Even the other two, a rules-based approach and a care-based approach, have a consequentialist component. In arguing for a rules-based approach, Immanuel Kant said that we are notoriously weak at determining consequences, so consequentialism is a poor foundation for ethics. Better, he claims, to think deeply about rules to live by, and then follow those rules regardless of apparent near-term consequences. But even Kant is considering a significant consequence, saying, in effect, we'll all be better off if we follow my approach. With a care-based approach, the Golden Rule has us consider the consequences from the other guy's perspective.

*policy maker* decides action; to manipulate policy is to usurp their proper role. How can that be ethical?

But Tom's perspective was different. "How can you ignore the consequences of your analysis? How is *that* ethical?"

But . . . but . . . hmm . . . he had a point. Then and now I consider Tom to be an ethical intelligence professional, and his stance on this issue is ethical, I believe. But I disagree with him, for the most part. To understand why requires a framework.

First, in ethics, *role* can matter. It is ethical for a defense attorney to do his best in support of a defendant he suspects is guilty. His role—and our system of justice—requires this. His best effort is necessary if there is to be something balancing the best case made by the prosecutor. For the defense attorney to take any other approach would be unethical. Similarly, it is ethical for an ambassador to deliver a demarche that he personally disagrees with. He is speaking for the president and must keep a straight face in carrying the president's message.

And for CIA analysts, our role is to inform the policy maker but not to cross the line into policymaking ourselves. This role is explicit and is clear to both the analysts and the policy makers. The policy maker can invite us across the line—I have had many policy makers ask, "Ok, so what would you do if you were me?" But unless the invitation is explicit, the understood role prevails. My job is to provide the best intelligence analysis to help the policy maker make the decision. And the policy maker is responsible for the decision and its consequences.

But my role does not excuse me from paying attention to consequences. Quite simply, the more dire the potential consequences, the more effort I must put into providing analysis to the policy maker. Each analyst tries to do his or her best on each product, but not all products are equal. If my analysis might result in someone being killed, for example, I need to triple-check my sources and second-guess my reasoning. As a leader of analysts, on such high-stakes issues I am going to assign my best analysts and probably more of them—perhaps assign someone to conduct alternative analysis and take extra trouble to make sure the policy maker understands the issue in all its nuances. Serious consequences require me to provide more *support* to the policy maker but do not allow me to make the decision for her.

Are there limits to this? Are there consequences so dire that the intelligence analyst must do everything he can to prevent them, even casting aside the role that he has willingly accepted? There must be. Ethicists love to spin hypothetical situations of soul-grinding choices where something bad happens either way. But extremes are necessarily rare. If you find yourself in such an extreme situation, you will know it when you see it. And if you are "ethically fit," to use Kidder's phrase, you are more likely to ask yourself, "What am I really doing here," and do the thing that is ethically right for you.

# Impact of Covert Action

One area of intelligence that many analysts touch at some time in a CIA career is covert action. It comes with a special set of ethical ramifications, only in part because of the high potential for serious consequences I spoke of above.

What is covert action? The National Security Act of 1947, Sec. 503 [50 U.S.C. 413b] says,

> The term "covert action" means an activity or activities of the United States Government to influence political, economic, or military conditions abroad, where it is intended that the role of the United States Government will not be apparent or acknowledged publicly.

One of my functions when I worked on the National Security Council was to help administer the White House's oversight of covert action. My colleagues at the NSC taught me a much simpler, but fully functional, definition of covert action: When CIA *intentionally changes reality abroad*, that should be considered covert action.[3] And CIA would only be *allowed* to intentionally change reality abroad as part of a *presidentially directed and approved covert action program*.

In changing reality abroad, we are necessarily affecting people's lives, sometimes intentionally and sometimes as a matter of collateral impact. It frequently is a more immediate and direct impact than with the more routine exercise of US foreign policy. That carries a serious ethical burden.

What has this to do with analysis, beyond what I have already addressed? First, analysts are increasingly integrated into the support of covert action programs. Many analysts, including me, have served as deputy to a covert action program manager. Some have been program managers themselves. From my desk at the NSC during the Clinton administration, I had access to every covert action being conducted at the time, and it was very apparent which of those programs had analysts integrated into their planning. Quite simply, when analysts were completely involved, the programs were much more likely to be coherent, consistent, and measured—and much less prone to wishful thinking. (Interestingly, I didn't find analysts to be better *managers* of covert action than their ops counterparts. The analysts' habit of overthinking things can be a real drawback when you are trying to get difficult things done in the field.)

---

[3] An explicit exception to this would be when CIA changes reality abroad as a collateral effect of its collection operations. You are naturally changing reality to some extent every time you recruit a source, but that is not considered "covert action" in the way the National Security Act means.

Second, in many covert action programs, the team approach is so active that the line between analysts and operators fades. We do what we're trained to do, and what we're best at, so we usually don't lose our identity as analysts or operators. But lines are crossed more casually. In one covert action meeting with DCI John Deutch, after a deep and involved conversation, the DCI remarked that I sounded like an ops guy and my ops counterpart sounded like an analyst. I quipped, "Sir, you have just managed to offend us both!"

Third, in covert action the line between analysis and policymaking also fades. The policy maker is certainly involved. Covert action programs are all "the president's programs" in a very real way. He signs the Finding that orders the program to be established. Before he signs, there is real scrutiny and debate by senior policy makers. And the conduct of the program is monitored by them and frequently adjusted. But in the conduct of the program itself, as long as it is operating within defined parameters, intelligence officers decide what to do and how to do it. If not quite making policy, we frequently become active advocates. We are executing the policy. We are making things happen abroad. The ethical distance from consequences that I described above disappears.

By now in this section, some of you might be thinking that, at last, I have found an arena that is unique to intelligence analysis. Covert action, at least the way I have defined it here, is clearly an intelligence activity. Well, not so fast. Many analytic units in corporate America operate in an environment similar to what I have described in covert action. Start with the fact that the line between analysis and decision making is rarely as sacred in business as it is in intelligence. As with analysts inside a covert action program, many analysts in the business world feel they are inside the business team, not simply supporting it. The customer for analysis may even be the analyst's boss. The line between analysis and decision fades.

So, how should the analysts—or leader of analysts—respond to the ethical burdens of this situation? They must work even harder than usual to make certain that their analysis is objective. This is extremely difficult when you are personally involved in trying to make the program succeed. Analysts can help by thinking through two questions: What is *success* here? and How will we recognize it? What milestones or metrics should be apparent if we are succeeding? What achievements are necessary and on what schedule? What achievements are linchpins? By that I mean all covert action and business programs will produce some successes, but not all successes are equal—certain successes, the linchpins, are required for the others to matter.

The leader of analysis must ensure that, beyond all these cold-eyed assessments of success, the most rigorous analytic tradecraft is going into analyzing the entire situation. The leader should be repeatedly asking, "What are our assumptions, which are key, and what has changed that might affect them?" She should also work to ensure that some analysts not involved in the program are independently assessing it. Perhaps more challenging, she should ensure that those analysts are listened to when they disagree with the analysts inside the program. It is powerfully tempting for officers inside the program to dismiss the outsiders, saying, "You don't know what we know, so why should we listen to you?"

Beyond working extra hard to maintain the integrity of the analysis, there is an ethical requirement to keep an eye on cost. What is this covert action program costing, from a moral perspective, and is the cost appropriate for what we are trying to achieve? This certainly includes the cost of collateral damage. Even if we are not talking about military collateral damage, we need to be asking how we are harming innocents. Is every tactic we are considering worth its potential cost? We know we are trying to do something worthwhile, perhaps something morally righteous, but that would not excuse every behavior that advances our cause.

This latter requirement does not belong to the analysts alone. Everyone involved in the covert action program must be sensitive to the moral question, "Is *this* worth *that*?" And many, many times, I have seen operations officers show an admirable moral sensitivity. I have seen them reject both tactics and strategies solely because of the potential of harm to innocent bystanders—or in some programs because of the risk of undue harm even to the guilty. But in my experience, it is harder for an analyst to be the lone voice in the room to raise this issue. If you work a desk and are not out in the field directly facing risk and reality, it takes courage to stand up and say, "We cannot do *that* because it would not be ethical." This is where the leader of analysts needs to aggressively set the standard, inviting the analyst to raise moral concerns and making sure he is listened to when he does.

Finally, let me address a fear I have heard dozens of analysts raise. They all have said something like, "I could not be part of a covert action program because the risk is too high and I would be asked to do something I consider immoral." Although the fear is real, and therefore must be respected, I find the underlying judgments to be flawed.

- First, if you are part of an organization like the CIA that conducts such programs, you are "involved," even if not actively.

- Second, don't presume covert action is immoral or that it uses immoral tactics. The standards and oversight are different now than they were in the days when CIA (at White House direction) tried to assassinate Castro (see, e.g., Lowenthal 2009). Covert action frequently is a middle option between war and diplomacy, and it need not be less moral than either of those. That it is *covert* doesn't imply that it is *shameful*—it is covert because secrecy is a necessary ingredient to its success.

- Third, if you are so ethically sensitive, we need you in the program. Its chances of being conducted ethically are greater if it is populated by ethical individuals. And from my experience in many covert action programs, once you are inside you will find you are not alone.

- Last, if once inside the program, you encounter a reality you cannot live with or change, you can walk away. This is a choice the soldier doesn't have, a choice protected by CIA leaders.

## In Closing

Looking back over an intelligence career, I am proud that I was among ethical professionals. The intelligence officers I worked with wanted to make a meaningful contribution to their country's security. The analysts I worked with considered themselves, at bottom, to be searchers for the truth, an excellent ethical starting point.

Yes, intelligence professionals—like any human population—include a few who forgot or set aside their ethics. I personally know three who were sent to jail for their misdeeds. But they stand out as anomalies in a population as noble as any I have ever seen.

Maintaining high ethical standards—indeed, raising them even higher—requires constant diligence among intelligence leaders. In my career, I saw oversight by Congress increase. But no amount of oversight by outsiders will be sufficient. We routinely operate in the shadows. Whether we behave honorably in those shadows will always depend most on what we require of ourselves.

The leaders of analysis must set the tone, not just behaving ethically themselves but being an active voice for ethics in the organization as a whole. They must introduce the words *ethical* and *moral* and *right* into decision meetings. They must hold themselves, their subordinates, and yes, their seniors, to a high ethical standard.

## KEY THEMES

As a leader, you are responsible for ethics: your own and those of your organization. Decisions are driven by values. And don't think it's sufficient to walk the walk—you must learn to talk the talk. That is, you must get comfortable speaking about ethics with your subordinates, giving them enough information about your values that they can both trust you and apply those values to their decisions.

The business of analysis comes with particular ethical challenges the leader must help navigate. Some come with a pronounced set of tendencies among many analysts.

- Arrogance. Analysts are frequently the smartest people in the room and this breeds arrogance. No ethical behavior stems from arrogance.

- Self-righteousness. Analysts can delude themselves that they bear no responsibility for decisions made by the customer or actions taken by those collecting their evidence.

- Cynicism. We are paid to be skeptics, but there's a fine line between skepticism and cynicism. No ethical behavior stems from cynicism.

Other ethical challenges come with the work of analysis.

- If we are impactful, we are impacting peoples' lives. We must feel the ethical burden of that.

- If we are impactful, customers often will enlist us to be partners in their programs. This can be healthy, but it requires that you take extra measures to maintain objectivity.

- If we are impactful, customers will press us to reach conclusions that fit their agenda. (In the national security arena, we call it politicization.) Standing up to those powerful decision makers without losing them as customers is tricky and frequently an ethical challenge. You can help navigate these challenges by

  o Vigilance. If you lose sight of the threat of politicization, you will find yourself succumbing to the drive to make the customer happy— making you the problem.

  o Communicating to your subordinates on the issue. Teach them what is and what is not acceptable pressure from the customer. And teach them to speak up when they think *you* are politicizing.

  o Making sure your analyst's reasoning is explicit in every piece. The best defense for an unpopular analytic conclusion is clarity about how we reached that conclusion. (Note I said *we*.)

# 9 Analysis as a Business

I'd been at CIA just a few weeks when I knew I'd found my home as an analyst. I was the new Libyan military analyst, having watched that country for Navy Intelligence for the previous few years. I was sitting at my desk, and Martha, my supervisor, brought me a command from Bob Gates, who was then CIA's Deputy Director for Intelligence. He had been impressed by a piece of freshly collected intelligence in my area and sent it to our team with something like this scribbled on it: "This could be important. We need a piece on it in the NID." The *National Intelligence Daily* (NID) was our widely distributed current intelligence publication back then. Martha told me, "You're up!" Great! A chance to publish! A chance to impress my boss's boss's boss's boss!

Then, deflation. I read the report and realized I had seen it already—and had dismissed it. The report was squarely in my area of expertise, and I knew it was simply wrong. I explained this to Martha, laying out my reasoning for disregarding the report. I convinced her and she said, "Just tell Bob that in a Blue Note." Huh? She explained that a "Blue Note" was a little slip of paper, 4 inches on a side, which we used to send simple communications to the Directorate front office. (Yes, children, there was life before e-mail.) I was to write a few sentences about why this was a bad report, staple it to the report, and send it back up to Bob. Huh? Nothing in my Navy experience told me such a thing was possible. My Navy experience taught me that, at my level, the admiral is a burning bush; he instructs and I obey. Now, I can tell the equivalent of a full admiral that he is mistaken in an informal note, and that is the end of it. So I did. I even addressed it to "Bob," and that was that!

As an analyst, that event convinced me I had found a loving home. And I said to my young self, "This is what it is like to work for analysts. Analysts (Martha and Bob both were veteran analysts) know how to run the analysis business."

Well, I was naïve. *Martha* and *Bob* knew how to run the analysis business, but I eventually met many analysts who did not. Sadly, I watched more than a few who could lead *analysis,* but they couldn't lead the *business.* It was yet another lesson that leading analysis is different than doing analysis. There are things about analysis that make it a unique business—else I would not have written this book. But there are also things about it that are common to any enterprise. It is these things that too many leaders of analysis recognize too late in their tenure, when the enterprise is faltering.

This is an issue because, overwhelmingly, analytic organizations are led by *analysts*. On balance, this is a strength. Someone who has mastered the craft of analysis is going to have some advantages in leading that craft. She is going to have a sense of what it takes to produce quality. She will have an instinct for when confidence is warranted in judgments and when confidence is inappropriate. She is going to have a flair for asking the right question and knowing which questions honest analysts will never be able to answer. She will have an empathy for the workforce that makes everything about leading them easier.

I have seen this tested many times. In my experience in Navy Intelligence, I frequently saw analysis being led by nonanalysts, officers who had a background in operations or a background in other intelligence disciplines, who by rank and circumstance found themselves responsible for an analytic unit. I fondly recall an analytic debate I had with one captain—a former submarine commander—leading an analytic unit with which I had to coordinate. He complained to my own boss about my nerve, as a lieutenant commander at the time, "arguing" analytic conclusions with a senior officer (him).

Similarly, in the urgent establishment of post-9/11 organizations such as the National Counterterrorism Center and Department of Homeland Security, intelligence professionals with no analytic background would occasionally be in charge of analysts. A few had a flair for the business of leading analysis, showing all the right instincts, but many did not. In many cases, these otherwise-competent professionals would struggle. Some would lead with too heavy a hand, saying, "How hard can it be? Let's just get the product out the door." Some would judge production by volume but had little sense of quality. Others recognized quality when they saw it but had no sense of how to teach it or enhance it. Some would put themselves in the editorial chain but, with their editorial "fixes," would introduce basic errors in analytic tradecraft.

But the analyst's advantages in leading analysis only carry so far. At some point, leading the business of analysis requires the same skills as leading the manufacture of plumbing fittings. Understanding such issues as supply, delivery, budget, and production logjams is essential. In my interviews of dozens of analyst-executives, office directors of large analytic units, these things regularly came up when I asked, "What do you wish you had known before you started the job?" And when I interviewed *their* bosses, more senior executives, many found a way to express their frustration that they were having to attend to basic business fundamentals because their office-director subordinates ignored them.

In some cases, the office directors even failed because of this weakness. They were masters of analysis and superb at asking the right question, bringing useful insight, and advancing an issue. I recall two cases where the leaders were not only good analysts but stood out as *brilliant*—a label analysts rarely give anyone. But their organizations foundered. They ignored basic business essentials, and they just couldn't get the job done.

## The *Business* Part of the Business

So what part of the business of analysis is not the *doing* of analysis? I ask that any business professionals who are reading here please look away. I am going to cover things so basic that you will not be able to accept that some of the smartest people in the world need to be told about them. Bitter experience—including my own—tells me we do.

If you are selling analysis or plumbing fittings, you need to be constantly tending three broad areas:

- The production cycle. This involves everything required to get a product into the hands of the customer.

- Brand loyalty. This involves convincing the customers that yours is the best product "for the money" and that they can rely on you to deliver it consistently.

- Support from the front office. This involves convincing your seniors that your unit has its act together. In some cases this will earn you more resources. In some cases, more abstract but just as important, it will earn you the *benefit of the doubt* in a business riddled with doubt.

Lead these things—all three areas—as a *business*. What do I mean by that? Start with a dictum from a highly successful business leader who also wrote one of the most profound books on leadership, Max De Pree. Max was the CEO of Herman Miller, the office furniture manufacturers who made Aeron chairs an object of lust for office workers around the world. Later he wrote *Leadership Is an Art,* a transformative book on how to think of yourself as a leader. De Pree's (1989: 11) dictum is as follows:

The first responsibility of a leader is to define reality. The last is to say thank you. In between the two, the leader must become a servant and a debtor.

Apply De Pree's "first responsibility" to your enterprise. Define reality. Find the real answer to the essential questions:

- How do my customers get our product (analysis)?
- What makes my customer want more of our product? And what turns them off?

- What do we provide that is recognized as better than the competition?

- Is the competitive landscape changing? (The answer, by the way, is always YES!)

- What is my unit's reputation with the front office? What do we do that earns or loses their respect?

A hidden reality in any such vital area could be the one that kills your business. Some of you in the government sector are saying here, "Wait a minute. What can really kill an analytic unit inside government? They don't depend on profit so they won't go bankrupt and close!" But any leader that allows his analytic unit—inside or outside government—to repeatedly fail in its mission of bringing insight to decision makers has killed that unit. It might walk around in its zombie daze, but it is dead. Its talent will flee and its resource base will wither, even if its name still exists on an org chart.

A significant hidden reality for me in one unit was that I mistakenly presumed that a handful of key customers were getting our published analysis. We were writing for certain decision makers at State and Defense Departments and publishing the analysis in products I knew were sent to both places. But when I talked to them, they clearly weren't reading the material. Chasing down the log jam involved detective work in both places. One assistant secretary could only read our classified material if he went to a vault in a different part of the building. Another would see the material only after a slow internal routing system allowed one reader to hold it for two weeks before passing it to the next. The reality was that I had a breakdown in the delivery of our product. What could be more mundane? What could be more removed from analysis? The most junior manager at Domino's Pizza knows how to recognize and deal with delivery problems, but it caught me flatfooted. The work-around was that I had to put analysts with locking briefcases in cars to hand carry our most important pieces to these customers until something less burdensome could be arranged. Staying oblivious to such realities—or simply saying that *delivery* was not my unit's responsibility—would have meant mission failure for us.

To uncover critical realities, you can start by listing everything you can think of that your unit requires to accomplish its mission. The list gets long very quickly. Any business leader in the for-profit world will quickly think in terms of supply, personnel, delivery, support, brand loyalty, and R&D, for example. All of these apply to the business of analysis as well. For one of my analytic offices, even an abbreviated list included the following:

- Analytic tradecraft training for my new analysts

- Computers, desks, paper, file cabinets, safes

- Easy access to food and water . . . and coffee!

- Transport for briefers

- A reliable supply of the best source material (raw intelligence reporting and open source reporting)

- A reliable supply of replacement analysts

- Knowledge of customer needs

All these things—and many, many more—are *needs*. Neglecting a single need can cripple the enterprise. As the leader of the enterprise, I must pay attention to each need. Some can be simple and no burden. At CIA, it was someone else's job to provide access to food and water to the workforce. That person (organization, actually) knew it was their function and performed very well. So for most of my tenure as a leader, I didn't need to spend time on food and water.

Other needs masquerade as someone else's responsibility, but you at least share them. For example, my new analysts need training. There are broadly two types of training for analysts: analytic craft and substance. At CIA, each analytic office would provide the training in substance through a mix of on-the-job training and specialized classes. But it was the responsibility of the Sherman Kent School in CIA University to provide new analysts with training in their craft. They do an amazing job at it. So could I simply check this need off my list? No. It turns out (we learned this the hard way) that the Kent School can only succeed if office directors like me send some of our best officers there to be teachers. It is an expensive but indispensable investment if I am to receive the quality service I need. So in this (and in many other ways) I shared the Kent School's responsibility to train my analysts in their craft.

Other needs are purely my own responsibility. On my short list above, I included "knowledge of customer needs." Any business leader can tell you this is no simple question. Instead it is a complex and dynamic reality. It needs constant attention from the leader. First, the leader of analysis must *identify* primary and secondary customers. The primary customers are those you need to be in frequent dialogue with, those your analysts will have in mind when they are crafting a piece. The secondary customers generally are those who might read your published pieces, but do not frequently interact with you. Other secondary customers may be those who tune in to a situation only when it is hot; some of these might, depending on their responsibilities, jump up to primary customer status in a crisis.

Once the leader has identified her primary customers, she must spend time with each, getting to know their needs for analysis. What do they know? What are they trying to do? On what schedule? In talking to these customers, I recommend what in intelligence training circles has come to be known as "Hazlewood's Law." Leo Hazlewood was a long-time CIA and NGA (National Geospatial-Intelligence Agency) executive and a keen observer of our business. Leo said, "Whatever you do, you must frequently talk to your customers—and you must dismiss *half* of what they say." What he was getting at is that policy makers generally are not good at telling intelligence analysts what they need from them. Rather, they are only good at identifying what they *want*. They talk about their appetite rather than their nutrition. They think of their uncertainty in comfortably making a decision and invite intelligence to erase that uncertainty. They seem to be saying, "If I don't know something, and need to know it, it is your job to provide it." But generally they do not know—and should not be expected to know—what is reasonable for intelligence to collect or analyze, to figure out or predict, in time to help the policy maker make the tough decision. So in talking to such a policy maker, the leader of analysis is listening for the precious *half* that helps her figure out how her analysts can most help this customer.

## Ensuring Brand Loyalty (Getting Your Customers Hooked on Your Service)

While we are on the subject of customers, consider an inherent challenge in the business of providing analysis. A solid business dictum is, "Keep your customer happy." But in this business, part of the job is to deliver bad news. You will frequently be delivering analysis that angers the customer. This can be the case for any number of reasons. Sometimes the analysis will be revealing a reality that does not match the customer's worldview. Sometimes the analysis will be revealing an inconvenient complexity or closing off the customer's preferred levers of influence. Sometimes the analysis will ignore a crucial fact that the customer—an insider in the situation—knows but the analyst doesn't.

Fortunately, most mature policy makers and business leaders do not expect analysis to always make them happy. They expect analysis to be useful, to help them make sense of a complex and challenging world. They do not expect all news to be good. As one senior PDB[1] briefer once expressed it, "Our job is to put together a nourishing meal. The reader wants steak and dessert, but our job is to make sure he gets the broccoli, too." My experience with several PDB recipients is that they all understand this. That they occasionally vent when they are reading something that angers them does not matter if they come back to us tomorrow.

---

[1] The PDB is the President's Daily Brief. It is written for the president and distributed also to a small group of his most senior advisers.

So, if "Keep your customer happy" does not serve as a useful dictum, what can help us in the business of analysis? In their remarkable book, *First, Break All the Rules,* Marcus Buckingham and Curt Coffman (1999) of the Gallup organization provide some truths derived from empirical evidence. The Gallup folks reached out to more than a billion customers over twenty years to try to "identify what customers really want." Despite a wide variation in what customers talk about, "four customer expectations remain remarkably consistent across various types of businesses and types of people" (128–132):

1. **Accuracy.** In plumbing supply, this means a 1/8″ copper tube is always, precisely 1/8″. In analysis, this means when you state a fact, you always get it right.

2. **Availability.** In plumbing supply, it means your organization can always be counted on to provide enough 1/8″ copper tubes for my organization to build its prefabricated vanity cabinets without slowing us down. I can trust your firm to be part of my firm's production process. In analysis, I know that I will have your input in time to help with my decision, and I will be able to read it quickly and understand what it says.

3. **Partnership.** If my firm builds vanity cabinets, is your plumbing supply firm willing to cut your 1/8″ copper tubes to the 10-inch length we need and bend them to the needed shape before delivery? If so, your supply firm can become a true partner in my enterprise, tailoring your work to meet my needs. If I am a decision maker, will your analysts anticipate my questions? Will they decide what to analyze by wrapping their minds around my program? Will they reliably warn if my plans are going off track? Will they consistently provide insights that help me be more effective?

4. **Advice.** Let my plumbing supply firm teach your vanity assemblers how to bend copper tubing themselves, so they don't have to worry about grabbing the right shape in advance. More, tell us what you are thinking of in next year's line of vanities, and my firm will help identify plumbing solutions that can provide you higher quality at a lower price. In analysis, advice might mean flagging opportunities for the policy maker or business leader to advance a key program.

The sequence of these four expectations matters. You have to provide accuracy before your customer will even care about availability. If your product is not consistently available, the question of partnering with you does not even come up. If you haven't earned my trust as a partner, if I am not confident that you are interested in my success, I'm not likely to seek your advice.

Where leaders of intelligence analysis often balk is on the issue of *advice*. In the United States, intelligence analysts are taught that they must not prescribe policy. *You* provide the insight; *they* make the decision. You must not withhold information to stack the deck in favor of the policy you like. (See chapter 8 on ethics for more discussion of this.) Don't get caught up in the policy maker's optimism to have a particular program succeed. Very simply, don't cross the line between intelligence and policy. These things are drilled into the heads of analysts, and they are important for retaining the policy makers' trust.

As I described in chapter 8, the line between analyst and decision maker can be blurrier in the business world than in intelligence. But this reluctance to advise the decision maker often exists there, too. Data analysts often will say, "These are my findings, but the decision is yours." Perhaps the data analyst is acknowledging that the data don't address all the considerations relevant to the decision. Investment analysts, sensitive to the accusation that they are playing with someone else's money, may stress that their role is to present opportunities, not to make the decision for the customer. And any analyst who has advised a manager of business operations has heard some version of, "But you're just an analyst! I have years of experience doing this stuff." There is nothing like being bluntly put in your place to breed reluctance to be too prescriptive in one's analysis.

But at some level of customer service, even the line between policy and intelligence becomes less rigid. At a certain level of the relationship, when the customer's trust is high, we will occasionally be invited to cross the line. Take, for example, Bob Joseph, the Bush administration's senior policy maker for nonproliferation. He was one of our most important customers when I led WINPAC, CIA's office for the analysis of weapons, proliferation, and arms control. Dr. Joseph has a clear understanding of the line between intelligence and policy. In one committee meeting he was chairing, where he was weighing policy options, I strongly advocated one course over another. I recall him gently reminding me, "That's not your role here." He was correct. In a different conversation on a different topic, I recall him asking me, "Bruce, tell me what you would do here if you were me." The difference between the two incidents was his invitation. He trusted us enough that we had a standing invitation to alert him to opportunities to advance his nonproliferation agenda. But to advocate one policy over another was something I could only do at his explicit invitation—and in a way that made it clear that I was stepping out of my role as Director WINPAC.

Meet all four customer desires—consistently deliver accuracy, availability, partnership, and advice—and you will have a devoted customer. When he was CIA's Director of Intelligence, Michael Morell (2008) published this vision statement:

> To be so good at what we do that our customers seek our analytic views before making major decisions.

To me, that gets it right. It works at winning devoted customers. Devoted customers but not *satisfied* customers. In analysis, there is no such thing as a completely satisfied customer. First, consider what analysis does. Analysis deals with the unknown. Analysis takes two known things and builds a picture of what might reasonably link them. Is that reasonable picture correct? Not 100 percent of the time and not 100 percent correct even one time. Are the two known things even linked? Perhaps not. Analysis helps a decision maker navigate the darkness, but analysis can never remove the darkness. Once the light comes on, you don't need analysis. Decision makers, to some extent, accept that they must traverse this darkness and accept that the world contains uncertainty. But they will never be *satisfied* that analysis is sufficient; they will never be completely confident that the analysis is correct.

Second, as Buckingham and Coffman (1999: 128) point out, "There are no steps leading to customer satisfaction. Required steps only prevent dissatisfaction." What they are getting at is that the customer appetite is insatiable—whatever you give them, they want more. Don't chase the Holy Grail of the truly satisfied customer. Instead, provide a level of customer service that exceeds anything available from the competition. Work to reduce inaccuracy or unavailability to a level your competition can only dream about. Consistently provide value in your partnership. And provide insight, maturity, and empathy when you are invited to provide advice to the customer. Attend to these things and you will have customers not satisfied, but addicted to what you provide. You will have developed something precious in the business community . . . *brand loyalty*.

## Prioritize Your Customers

In business, the more customers, the better. In the business of analysis, this is not always the case. I suspect a company like Oxford Analytica, an international consulting firm, sees expanding the customer base for its analyses as key to growth and revenue. But many leaders of analysis, including analytic units inside corporations I have visited, work in an environment where customers don't *purchase* their services. In the government, the customers demand service, but providing that service does not translate into a profit that can be rolled into growth. Few business leaders would sympathize with my oft-stated quip as a leader of analysis: "The only problem with our business is that we have too many customers." For my offices, providing better and better service often translated into saying "no" to more and more potential clients.

How do you cope with this reality? The key is to prioritize customers. All successful businesses prioritize their customers to some extent. Some customers are vital to a firm's health, whereas some come and go unnoticed. The heaviest purchasers and the market opinion shapers will always draw the greatest energy from a firm's front office. Best Buy sent me their "Premier Silver" card, a sign that I had purchased enough to move up a notch in their priority ranking.

There are many ways to prioritize customers, and you can find the mix that suits your situation. The key is to consciously *decide*. Too many leaders of analysis let momentum, or the ringing phone, decide which customers are most important. In the intelligence community, there are so many legitimate customers—decision makers who are paid by your taxes to do a job that would benefit from intelligence analysis—that you cannot even know them all, much less serve each at the *partnership* level or *advice* level.

Start with identifying your most important customer or, at least, the top tier. In the 1990s, in one of several strategic programs that I was involved in to overhaul the PDB, we began referring to the president as "the First Customer." Whatever else our directorate did, we were going to make this daily product the best we could imagine. You must be careful with such strategic choices because they have a ripple effect throughout the business. This program did, indeed, raise the quality and relevance of the PDB, and many PDB articles would be disseminated to a broader customer base, so other customers were benefiting. But my own feeling is that we also became so obsessed with the First Customer that two things happened. First, parts of our analytic corps who did not write for the president felt marginalized. Despite what was said by the leadership of the directorate, these analysts *heard*, "You don't write for the president, so your work is not important." Second, the assistant secretary–level of the national security establishment—a critical cadre of decision makers and implementers—felt ignored. Their agendas were getting less attention from us than they felt they needed.

For the top customer tier, the attitude should be, "*We will do all we can (within the bounds of ethics, of course) to help them.*" The aspiration for serving these customers should be for the top leaders of your organization to get to the top levels of customer service: *partnership* and, when requested, *advice*. For this level of customer, your service should not be defined by the competition. It is not enough to say we will work to provide our top customer with the best service they can get anywhere. Rather, you must commit yourself to providing the best service you can envision.

For the second tier of customers—say, the assistant secretary–level if you are serving the federal government—combine three approaches:

1. Aspire to the *partnership* level of service.

2. Assign someone in your organization, and perhaps some unit of your organization, to treat those specific customers as their *most important*. One of your subordinates must make that customer feel as special as the president. (This, by the way, is a powerful business strategy and extends beyond the second tier of customers. It should mean that most of your subordinates—your junior managers and the analysts themselves—will routinely be directly in contact with some level of customers. Directly serving a fourth-tier customer will make even the newest analyst better at his job.)

3. Be ever watchful to root out the behaviors that drive these customers away. Maintain a quality standard that says, "We will never knowingly tolerate inaccuracy (*slop*) in our product." And rigorously attend to the issue of *availability*. Double check to make sure the assistant secretary is receiving the product you think you are delivering—"receiving" in the sense of physically getting the product and "receiving" in the sense of taking in a helpful message from the product.

Lower tiers of customers for analysis are likely to be anonymous to you—and even to most of your subordinates. They legitimately receive—or can ask to receive—your products, but the products are rarely written with their specific agenda in mind. For these customers, your organization should stand out as better than the competition. These customers should know that, from your organization, they will get *accuracy* and clarity. And they will find a level of expert insight that keeps them coming back for more.

## Tend Your Organization's Reputation with the Front Office

In many enterprises, and certainly in the business of analysis, it is not enough to attend to your reputation with customers. You must also nurture a positive reputation with more senior levels of the organization. When you get the benefit of the doubt from your senior bosses, resources and latitude flow to you. When the bosses begin to lose trust in you, a friction arises that your whole organization feels.

Why is this an issue? I have seen leaders of analysis who were dedicated to excellent customer service but were tone deaf to the top leaders of their own organization. They did not survive. Further, at the upper echelons of the organization, the top bosses are usually not analysts. Even if they are analysts, they may not be expert in the substance your unit covers. They may not recognize just how superb your unit's products are—they may not have time to read them. And they may never happen to talk to the customers who love your products. Instead, they may judge you by, say, how quickly and thoughtfully you responded to their last request for budget data.

I am referring here to both your personal reputation and the reputation of the unit you lead. For some issues, they are one and the same. Especially for leaders who have been in place a long time, the person and the unit might be regarded as one entity, one organism. But only when a leader is new can the reputation of the leader be positive when the reputation of the unit is negative. That is a honeymoon period when the new leader is given some time to "fix" things. I have been that leader several times; the honeymoon is remarkably short.

I was once assigned to lead an office that was notorious for sloppy staff work. The truth was we were drowning in it. This unit had the highest number of required staff reports of any office I led, especially congressionally required reports connected to arms control. I quickly decided that we needed to double the size of the staff that was cranking out such routine staff reports. My only choice was to take several analysts from substantive accounts and put them on short rotations in this admin staff. My line managers were outraged. How dare I put such staff work ahead of the "real" work of our experts? My response was this: "Look, we have staffs all over the building and on Capitol Hill angry at our office for being tardy. Those staffs complain about us to people who control our resources. People consider us unprofessional, and they don't assume we suddenly become professional on the substantive stuff that matters most. Right now, we need to stop the bleeding." It worked, and the next year I got the additional personnel resources to give those managers their analysts back.

The higher you go in an organization, the more *your* reputation matters. You cannot escape the fact that you will need things from seniors who know you slightly or not at all. I have had decision makers and budget breakers make multimillion-dollar choices based on whether they thought they could trust me. And in the high-stakes arena of national security, in the politically charged environment of Washington, D.C., their trust can be very fragile. It is very sobering to hear a senior say the words, "I have lost confidence in . . ." followed by the name of some previously respected officer.

To some extent, we are taught to ignore reputation. "Let your work speak for itself." "If you consistently produce quality and act with integrity, the respect of others will be yours." This is indeed laudable, and I think you should be paying *most* attention to these things. They matter more than reputation and are essential to building a positive reputation. But they are insufficient.

The central reality to deal with here is *time*. The most senior people in a large organization often simply don't have the time to get to know the real you. (This applies to some of your important customers as well.) You might get only snippets of time from these busy people. Over time, repeated exposure to the seniors can add those snippets together, building genuine respect. Sometimes you may be able to engineer that repeated exposure (for yourself or a subordinate) to win respect. It is pejoratively called "face time." But chances to personally build rapport and respect are limited, and you will inevitably encounter "deciders" who have never spent time with you.

Part of good situational awareness is to consider what reputation you might be walking into a meeting with. If the reputation is negative, you must adjust your approach accordingly. Homework on the underpinnings of that reputation will help you identify the elephant in the room. Sometimes you will know that you have no personal reputation with the seniors, and you will carry the reputation of your unit by default. In my working life, the senior deciders who could affect my resources often were congressional committees who didn't know me personally. Sometimes—not always—I got the impression that they expected me to be "the company man," just a guy in a suit putting a rosy gloss on reality but withholding anything that might make us look bad. I always tried to be honest with any audience, but I made an effort to be especially frank with those committees, making warts-and-all presentations. When I got more senior, I made an active effort to win the respect of the congressional committees—and their staffs—so I wouldn't have to fight a natural skepticism when I needed their help. I was in front of the Senate Select Committee for Intelligence so much that I once got a question that stands out as my favorite over three decades of working with Congress. Senator Evan Bayh, in the midst of an otherwise somber and substantive briefing, lightened the mood by asking me, "So, Mr. Pease, . . . why did you shave off your mustache?"

Let me conclude this section on reputation with your seniors with a warning: *While paying attention to reputation is essential, fixation on reputation will backfire.* You cannot let reputation become—or seem—more important than performance. When I discussed the issue of reputation with one director of intelligence, he confided that he and his CIA seniors recoil from officers who seem to exhibit "me-centric" behavior. Such behavior is quickly labeled "obsession with advancement." It is a career killer—and should be. A reputation of thinking of yourself first is as negative as any other reputation you need to avoid. Being a leader who is servant to all, putting yourself last, and at the same time paying attention to your reputation is one of the difficult contradictions you will have to conquer. This isn't about taking cosmetic steps to improve your image. You improve your reputation by sustained, actual, positive behavior and by rooting out the negative behaviors that mean something to your audience.

# Align Your Enterprise

Another basic business concept is aligning the enterprise. Alignment in business is intended to generate organizational movement on a few clear priorities. All large organizations are trying to do many things and have many subenterprises, each with a unique set of challenges and priorities. But when the entire organization needs to produce strategic movement or progress on a vital initiative, steps must be taken to align the organization.

For example, in the 1980s, when Ford was challenged by a growing impression in the market that Japanese imports were simply better built, it desperately needed to produce a companywide improvement in quality. It would mean nothing to design and build reliable power trains if a windshield wiper motor was jittery or there was a rattle in the door. They launched their "Quality Is Job 1" campaign. This was not simply an ad campaign; everyone working for Ford understood it was important to find ways to reduce flaws and improve quality. Ford aligned itself around this priority.

In their classic, *Built to Last,* James Collins and Jerry Porras (2002: 221) discuss how important aligning the enterprise has been to visionary companies. "Alignment brings the vision to life, translating it from good intentions to concrete reality." They also offer an important corollary: beyond creating alignment, a company must obliterate misalignment with core ideology (238). Let's examine both concepts as they apply to an analytic enterprise.

One large analytic enterprise was CIA's Directorate of Intelligence (DI), recently renamed the Directorate of Analysis (DA). When it became clear in 2004 that the DI had been fundamentally wrong on its judgments about Iraq's WMD arsenal, there were wide repercussions. Coming so soon after the perceived analytic failure of 9/11, our customers and the public lost faith in our competence. This was not simply an accusation that a few Iraq weapons analysts got it wrong. Rather, there was a palpable challenge to our analysis across the entire spectrum of key issues. I would lead briefings to key customers on various issues and get this skepticism: "If you were so wrong for so long on such an important issue [Iraq WMD], why should we believe you now?"

In response, the leader of the DI at the time, Jami Miscik, launched an enterprise-wide campaign to visibly improve our analytic tradecraft. She launched a serious investigation of what really went wrong in Iraq WMD analysis. We had outsiders already loudly prescribing surgery for us, but we needed to find facts about what we did wrong and what we did right. After that was done, she imposed mandatory tradecraft refresher training on the entire analytic workforce. (I was one of the trainers, addressing several auditoriums-full of analysts.) All the papers we were drafting got extra scrutiny for two things: (1) Was the tradecraft sound? and (2) Was it on display? The meaning of the second was that, like a sixth-grader doing arithmetic homework, we had to show our work. We had to explicitly show the reader more about the reliability of our sources than ever before. We had to show the reader our key assumptions and how we had reached our conclusions. All this provoked resentment from some of the analysts, who cried, "But I didn't touch the Iraq WMD issue! Why are you doing this to *me*?" Part of Miscik's burden was to show them that the flaws in the Iraq analysis could have occurred on any topic, and that some new flaw—in, say, analysis of Cuba—might convince customers that we "just don't get it."

And during this period, Miscik put me in charge of WINPAC, the office most blamed for the Iraq WMD failure. My part of this enterprise alignment around tradecraft was to win back credibility with WINPAC's customers. High on our customers' agenda were the nuclear programs of Iran and North Korea. We made certain that our tradecraft on these issues was visible and meticulous, and our customers noticed. Even members and senior staffers of the Senate Select Committee on Intelligence (SSCI), which had judged WINPAC harshly for the Iraq failure, noticed and complimented our efforts.

Miscik got right several essentials to aligning an enterprise. She *reached the entire organization*. Everyone in the directorate knew tradecraft was being improved and that no product would be exempted. All analysts and managers got the message that we would be unprecedentedly explicit with customers about what we knew, what we didn't know, the strength of our sourcing, and our confidence in our judgments. *Her message was clear, it was reinforced at all opportunities, and she followed up quickly anytime the new standards were violated.*

Not every effort to align the enterprise requires the "no exemptions" approach of Miscik's tradecraft program or Ford's "Quality Is Job 1" campaign. Collins and Porras (2002: chap. 7) note that visionary companies try many things and keep what works. That conscious experimentation will often produce parts of an analytic organization that feel different from the mainstream and can be intentionally exempted from a strategic initiative. For example, I may run an office in which budget realities require my units to be very conservative with their spending this year, while I am allowing one unit to gamble on a particularly promising data-crunching technology that could revolutionize their mission. There are two keys here. First, my exemption of that unit from the general alignment must be *intentional*. If any part of my office is not complying with my strategic initiative—budget conservatism this year—it must be with my active collusion. Accidental exemptions, or exemptions unnoticed by me, will be noticed by others and taken as a sign that my strategic priority is not really serious. Second, exemptions must not undercut the broader strategic alignment initiative. If it does that, it creates misalignment that must be obliterated.

So, what about the notion to "obliterate misalignment"? Aren't you doing this when you are actively aligning the enterprise? This part gets tricky but is important to understand. A business leader (including a leader of the business of analysis) can get into trouble if an effort to align the enterprise is done with too light or too heavy a hand. Too light, and the enterprise won't take the program seriously. Too heavy, and the costs of collateral damage can become unacceptable. "Obliterate" implies a heavy hand. It implies more than corrective action to tweak or reinforce alignment. Alignment is constructive. Obliterating misalignment is destructive. It should be reserved for extreme cases.

Collins and Porras (2002) recommend obliterating misalignment with "core ideology." Misalignment with top priorities should be examined. Is this a misalignment I should allow, for example, because it serves another top priority? Or is it a misalignment that I need to correct? Is this sheep straying and I need to send my border collie to head it toward the same pen as the rest of the sheep? But misalignment with an organization's *core ideology* is not just a straying sheep; it is a wolf that threatens the rest of the herd.

"Core ideology" in analysis? It sounds like an oxymoron. We teach analysts—like scientists—to let no ideology interfere with search for the truth. But in the business of analysis, core ideology can be thought of as our core sense of purpose. Why are we here? I have seen many try to define what analysis *is* or try to articulate the mission of an analytic organization. But the best description I have seen of our core purpose comes from Jack Davis, a pioneer of analytic tradecraft and observer of the business from the inside for more than five decades. He said this:

> The role of intelligence analysis is to narrow the range of uncertainty for decisions that must be made. Its purpose is not to be right. Its purpose is not to "tell it like it is." The role of intelligence analysis is to provide clarity of thought to those who must decide.

Is it important to be right? Of course. Must we "tell it like it is"? Yes. But we have not achieved our purpose if we stop at these two things. Our purpose is to *help someone else make a decision* when the unknowns are significant.

What types of things might threaten our core purpose that, as a leader of analysis, I must obliterate? First, remember we are talking about things I can control. There may be external factors that interfere with our purpose that I must adjust to but cannot simply obliterate: the snowstorm that keeps my analysts at home for three days; the arrest of a key intelligence source. But here are some examples of threats within my span of control that I would need to *obliterate*:

- An analyst who tries to use his position to manipulate policy, threatening the trust on which our access to the policy maker depends.

- A mid-grade manager trying to politicize his group's product.

- A promotion system that drives analysts out of their area of expertise when we need that expertise.

- An assignment system that encourages mediocre performers to become trainers.

- A unit disregarding security controls on their information, threatening sources on which our insights depend.

# Business Is Too Good—I'm Swamped!

One challenge every business hopes for, but is a challenge nonetheless, is success. I've already discussed that one result of success, growth, is often not available to analytic units the way it might be to for-profit enterprises. The mechanisms of supply and demand are relevant to leaders of analysis, but the dynamic is mushier. A different result of success is as important to leaders of analysis as leaders of any business: you're busier!

In 2008, I spoke with dozens of leaders of analysis at CIA, looking for what makes for success and failure in the business. I asked them all, "What frustrates you the most?" They used different words but all had the same answer: *I need more time!!* There is a widespread sense that the pace of the business of analysis has increased dramatically in the last three decades, and the leaders of analysis feel this powerfully. (I'll discuss several aspects of this in chapter 11, "Analysis at the Speed of Information.") They all have a list of things they want to do, things that can truly matter to their organizations. But the press of business daily pulls their attention from the list of things *they want to do* to the list of things *they feel they must do now*.

To some extent, this is inevitable in any successful business. Every successful boss knows what it feels like to have her plans for the week bulldozed by a series of customer demands or front office demands that come out of the blue. And every boss knows the feeling of having to put everything aside to deal with a crisis. If you are leading analysis, you *are* going to be hit with a crisis in your substantive area. Specializing in threat, my career was an endless parade of no-kidding, real-world crises.

But I've seen too many leaders of analysis allow themselves to be victims of the pace of their business. They blame the pace for their inability to get important things done. These are bosses whose "normal" routine is so frenetic that it seems like a crisis. These are bosses who are in effect saying, "There simply isn't time for good leadership!" This is the road to failure.

This is a call for *ruthlessness*. Do not tolerate a routine that marches you to failure. Recall Max De Pree's first responsibility of a leader: *Define Reality!* The leader of analysis must unflinchingly define and confront reality. Is the pace of business right now normal or just a short surge? Am I letting the ringing phone, the e-mail in-box, and the daily meetings run *me*? If I am repeatedly setting aside my priorities, are they really priorities? If my routine feels like a crisis, how can I deal with a crisis when it comes? Am I simply trying to do too much myself because I don't trust anyone to help me carry this load? Am I spending so much time keeping my boss happy that I know I am not being a good boss myself?

Whatever *reality* is in the situation will be the key to the solution. As a leader of front-burner, high-stakes components, I cannot claim that I was always successful at dealing with the reality of the pace of business. But here are some things that worked for me, things that protected my time from the crisis du jour:

- Schedule time to *think*. Every leader's daily calendar fills up by itself. Every leader, to some extent, feels like a mother with eight kids—seven of them are constantly saying, "Mommy? Mommy?" One of them is quiet in another part of the house getting in trouble. For me, it helped to put time to think on my calendar. It was like a meeting with myself. Like any good meeting, it helped to have at least a loose agenda, to focus on just one issue, and to keep "minutes"—a few notes on my most important thoughts.

- Schedule *action* time. For all those routine things that need your signature, your answer, your acknowledgment, your endorsement, many are tempted to jump right on them and get them out of the way. But this can be a momentum killer. These things may be inescapable, but it often will be more effective if you set them aside for an hour you reserve for just these trivialities. You will never be free from interruptions, but some interruptions can be at least corralled and wrangled at *your* convenience.

- Determine *how* you think best. For my most difficult intellectual challenges, I write my way through the issue. Honing ideas into useful prose is my most effective way of arriving at answers that stand the test of time.

- Determine *when* you think best. I learned as a first line leader of analysts that I edit long papers best in the morning. So when I had a difficult draft on my desk, I would delegate the morning meeting to one of my senior analysts, lock myself in my office, and go to it. I could overhaul a messy draft paper in a few hours rather than a few afternoons. When I was more senior, I learned that I think most *creatively* in the afternoon. My mind is more disciplined in the morning, but that discipline tends to shut down creativity. For me, 2 o'clock in the afternoon is also "drowsy time." (Sadly, one of my senior subordinates named it that.) But being actively creative wakes me right up.

- Lead a "task force." For one particularly intractable problem when I was a mid-grade leader, I led a task force to develop a strategy. I announced to my subordinates that I would be "gone" for two months to lead this effort. I was still in the building but out of my office most of the time, and I delegated nearly all decisions to my deputy. That it was a task force rather than a "study group," and that I was personally leading it, meant to everyone that real decisions and real action would come out of it. The result was the most coherent strategy I have ever worked with, one that guided our work for years.

- Appoint an "executive assistant." This is a person who would filter my in-box for me. He or she would look at my e-mail and incoming paperwork and determine what I needed to see first, what I didn't need to see at all, what I would find interesting on a slow day, and what should be held up to my face now. Very quickly, my best EAs got to know me so well that they could answer some requests on my behalf. They also were activists—in collaboration with my secretary—in protecting time for my top priorities.

- Take a trip. Simply getting out of the office for days or weeks frees the mind. Your head is still back in your office, but it's not absorbed by the trivialities. As a leader of analysis, you are expected to occasionally be "in the field," getting the pulse of reality and seeking the perspective of others who are grappling with the same substantive issues. At CIA, we called this "TDY," for temporary duty, and we genuinely regarded it as a duty. Embrace this as a chance to think, a chance to "go deep" on your most important priorities. And whatever you do, don't waste the trip by trying to run your unit by remote control.

- Take a virtual trip. The culture that expects you to occasionally travel for your job also establishes the fact that you don't always have to be at your desk. One of my most productive trips as an office director was to my own office. When I was new to WINPAC, I was having trouble getting my arms around the sprawling range of issues we dealt with. So I told my office and my bosses, "Every morning for the next two weeks, I will be TDY to WINPAC." Every day from 8 a.m. until noon, I visited a different analyst in a different component of WINPAC and sat watching them work at their desk. "Just show me what you do on a normal day. What tools do you use? Where do you get your best information? What frustrates you the most?" The analysts generally started puzzled and defensive, but they would open up gradually and really got into the discussion. Inevitably, the analysts in neighboring cubicles would also eventually chime in. I learned more about important realities in my office in those two weeks than I had in the previous six months. And I started hearing from my mid-grade managers, "The analysts are saying you turned out to be just a guy!" Best feedback I ever got!

I can hear some of you now. You are saying, "Well, this might all have worked for you, but my boss won't let me work this way. My boss expects me to be on top of every detail and yells if something slips by me." Ok. For a couple of you, this is true because, yes, there are some bad bosses in the analytic workplace, like every other. If you happen to have one of those, that may be the reality you must define and deal with as best you can.

But I have had a broad cross-section of bosses, from visionaries to micromanagers, and even one our ship's doctor labeled a sociopath. And all of them allowed me the latitude to manage my time the way I have described above. Whenever I was doing something a bit unorthodox, like the TDY to WINPAC, I made a point of telling my boss ahead of time that I planned to "try this experiment." Even the most conservative of them tolerated experimentation if it was labeled that, and some got instantly enthusiastic, recognizing the need for creative leadership in their workplace. I had a couple of bosses who were not only enthusiastic but would raise my experiment at their next staff meeting, so I could squirm while they told my colleagues, "Bruce is doing this neat thing that some of you might want to try. Go ahead and describe it, Bruce." (Always awkward.) No senior boss thinks things are going so well in his organization that all routines are sacred. They all will tolerate efforts to try something different if you pick your timing well and recruit them in advance.

Yes, if you are successful at this, your unit will be better led and more successful, and both you and your organization will be rewarded with more work. But you are not more important than the president, who somehow manages to not work twenty-four hours a day. Some days, even months, you will have to work heroically. But in simple terms, *if your routine feels like a crisis, you are doing it wrong.*

# Change Is Reality

Last, the leader of analysis must embrace what the survivors of the business world have long accepted: change is constant; complacency is failure.

Please don't take this as yet another frustrated appeal to wake up to your imminent doom. I get tired of the endless stream of exposés by intelligence professionals who say, in effect, "Now that I am leaving the business, I need to tell you it's on the brink of disaster!" I address elsewhere the important changes in the field of intelligence analysis as well as my prognosis for what will and won't change in the coming years. It is serious stuff, but it's not meant to be a desperate alarm bell.

Rather, I think the most effective leaders of analysis look at change with an attitude of opportunism. But this attitude does not come naturally—it must be a conscious choice.

There are several reasons the attitude does not come naturally. First, our job is to study subjects that are themselves changing at a breathtaking pace, leaving little time for the study of anything else. Whether your subject is the Middle East or energy technology, it is easy to spend all your intellectual energy trying to understand and anticipate the change you are witnessing. It takes a force of will to reserve some of that energy for the study of change in your own business.

Second, it is easy to become inured to the promises of the technologists. As I describe elsewhere, the pile of tools that have been offered to analysts is huge—tools that were to "revolutionize" the business. The pile of tools analysts actually found useful remains small (albeit vital). It is powerfully tempting for the busy leader of analysis to simply say, "Neither I nor my analysts have time to sort through the bogus tools to find the few useful ones."

Third, as I describe elsewhere, analysts—and by extension, most leaders of analysis—are trained skeptics. When offered a proposal to change, they are masters at quickly finding "What's wrong with this picture?" They instantly and accurately identify flaws, weaknesses, or at least uncertainties in any proposal, making "NO THANKS!" their default answer.

With such restraints, it is a wonder that change occurs at all in this business. But it does occur, largely thanks to leaders who—like good business leaders—keep an eye on at least three things:

- What is the competition doing? In this business, "the competition" is anyone repeatedly providing useful insight to your customers. It might be CNN. It might be a think tank like Rand or Brookings. It might be Wikipedia. It might be Google searches. Your job is to be more available and more useful than that moving competition. When regarding the competition, I recommend a *posture of productive paranoia*.

- What is emerging that we can take advantage of? What tools can help us better find answers, or better communicate with each other, or better communicate with the customers, or simply save us time? What are we learning about the way humans think that can help us be right more often, or overcome our own or our customer's misconceptions? What sources of information might be available today that were not yesterday? I recommend an *attitude of active opportunism*. (Don't worry about going off the deep end. Your and your colleagues' deep-seated skepticism will prevent that.)

- What experimentation is going on in my own organization? They are a minority, but you have creative people on your workforce who want to try new things. Is your leadership actively nurturing them? Actively encouraging reasonable gambles? Tolerant of occasional—even frequent—failure among their initiatives? *If you can find no experimentation in your unit, you are doing it wrong.*

## It Doesn't Take an MBA

None of the business principles I've discussed should feel like dramatic revelations to a leader of analysis. Success doesn't require years of immersion in the for-profit business arena. And applying good business principles should not feel unnatural in the analytic arena. It's just good business.

Too many leaders of analysis fail because they don't step back from the analytic substance and ask, "How's business?" Too many leaders of analysis, especially at the junior and middle ranks, suffer from the prejudice that "this business is unique." Get over it; *all* businesses are unique. Read the best business literature and you will find tips and insights you can immediately apply in your own leadership. Think of yourself as a CEO—even if your organization only has ten people—and you'll find yourself tending to essentials you were ignoring before.

## KEY THEMES

There is more to leading analysis than leading *analysis*. Many executives with deep analytic expertise struggle with the business side of leading an enterprise. Unlike any successful business CEO, many are oblivious to such issues as supply, delivery, IT support, recruitment and retention, building the brand, and more. Failure in any of these areas can kill your enterprise.

Every leader of an analytic enterprise needs to attend to such business questions as

- Who are the top-tier customers who need my personal attention?
- Who in my enterprise is talking to customers from the lower tiers?
- How do my customers get our product (analysis)?
- What makes my customer want more of our product? And what turns them off?
- What do we provide that is recognized as better than the competition?
- How is the competitive landscape changing?
- What is my unit's reputation with the front office?

Align your enterprise around clear, articulated priorities.

- Identify the two or three things that require focus and emphasis across nearly the entire organization.
- Make certain each unit understands what it can do locally to advance those priorities.
- Allow exemptions only if (1) they make sense *and* (2) they don't impede the larger enterprise. (In aligning your enterprise, not everything has to fit, but nothing can get in the way.)
- Tolerate nothing that prevents fulfillment of the core purpose of your enterprise, which is *to narrow the range of uncertainty for decisions your customers must make.*

Because change is constant, accept that you will have to adjust your business practices. Keep an eye on at least these three indicators:

- What is your competition doing? (Be productively paranoid.)
- What is emerging (tools, information, HR practices, anything) that we can take advantage of? (Be an opportunist.)
- What experimentation is going on in my own organization? (Champion your pioneers.)

# 10

# The Tools of Twenty-First-Century Analysis

W elcome to the future. You are on the bridge of the starship *Enterprise* in the twenty-third century. A human commands the ship, and humans are doing tasks that I recognize from my shipboard days. There's a helmsman, a communicator, a weapons officer, a navigator. Now look at the tools they are using. The captain's log exists but is nowhere to be seen. Captain Kirk speaks at it and some machine hears and stores the information. The navigator is at a console, but the console seems to be doing all the real navigation. There is no sign of a navigation chart, much less a compass or sextant. There is no window on the bridge; there is a giant screen displaying whatever the captain needs to see. A medical emergency occurs—the guy in the red shirt has collapsed—and Dr. McCoy shows up with a medical tricorder, a gadget that assesses just what's wrong.

When *Star Trek* debuted in 1966, these tools made the twenty-third century look dazzling to me. Now, many of the tools look like no stretch at all—some even exist today. Some of the tools simply make a person's job easier (the captain's log), while others do what had always been a person's job (the tricorder and the nav-computer). *Some* of the people who were with me on the bridge in my Navy days already have been replaced by technology. But the people on Starship *Enterprise* are doing the *interesting* stuff. And, critically for the purposes of this book, Captain Kirk turns to a human (ok, half-human), and says, "Spock, analysis!"

Here in the teens of the twenty-first century, analysts are living the relationship with IT tools captured by *Star Trek*. Three levels of information technology are changing our work.

- *First-level tools: Make routine aspects of your work much easier.* This is the mundane information technology. A word-processing program is an example.

- *Second-level tools: This IT is replacing functions that used to be the sole domain of humans.* This is far more interesting and changes the user's work much more profoundly than first-level aids. Your GPS is an example.

- *Third-level tools: These are tools, mainly algorithms, which are making some analysis possible for the first time in human history.* An example would be algorithms using Twitter to conduct nearly instant polling of the concerns of millions of people.

Individual tools will, of course, shift categories as they become old hat. As a third-level tool becomes incorporated into the business of analysis, as its use becomes routine, we are no longer talking about analysis that is possible for the first time in human history. Massive instant polling, my example of a third-level tool, is becoming routine. As refinements are introduced to automate some of its processing, replacing some of the hands-on work analysts have been doing to make the polling results useful, the tool becomes second level. What was cutting edge becomes mundane.

With IT tools at these three levels, the balance between what analysts do and what their machines do is shifting at an awesome rate. The balance is also changing between what is analytically feasible and what is not. As a leader of analysis, you will need to preside over this ever-shifting balance. You will need to be a master of assessing the tools, incorporating them into your enterprise, and letting the tools take over any function they can.

# Judging Tools for Analysis

Judging the usefulness of many IT tools is easier than you might think, even when you don't understand the technology that goes into them. *Tools come and go, but what makes for a useful tool is more constant.*

Let me try to capture what I mean by that last phrase. When I worked as a military analyst, one of my most-used tools was a simple set of dividers. If you have never seen dividers, they look like a compass for drawing circles, except there is a pin at both ends. You use dividers to measure distance on a chart (map). I learned to use them with nautical charts in the Navy. On display in my CIA cubicle was another set of dividers. This pair was used by great-great-grandfather Phineas Pease in the Civil War—his dividers were my sentimental reminder of a link between us. The technology hadn't really changed in 130 years (see Figure 10.1).

The pair of items, divider and chart, were powerful information tools. I could determine distances nearly instantly. And more, the chart put other useful information in front of my face. Say Libya was going to move bombers from Tripoli to the Chadian border; I used the dividers to gauge how far they must go. But in looking at the chart, I notice Sabha, another airfield south of Tripoli from which the aircraft could stage. I make a mental note to check the latest imagery of that base. The chart had *the information I sought*—the airfield in Tripoli and the one on Chad's border. But the chart *also put in front of my face useful information I hadn't thought about*—Sabha. Here are the elements of fine first-level information technology: (1) fast; (2) easy to use; (3) the information I seek is there; and, (4) without distracting me, without having to wade through it, other information I could use—but didn't think to seek—is also there for me. Terrific!

Figure 10.1 Dividers

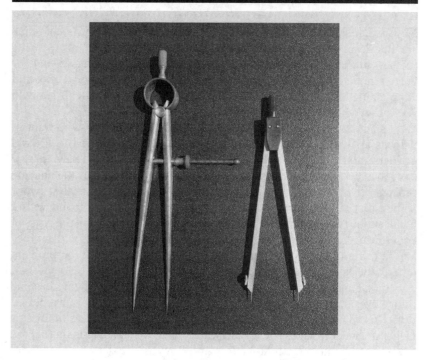

Phineas Pease's dividers on the left measured marching distances during the Civil War. My dividers on the right measured threat radii in the Middle East.

I haven't used my dividers and chart since I loaded Google Earth on my desktop. The same four features that make the dividers and chart useful make Google Earth useful. But for me to set aside the former, the latter had to be *more* useful in ways I could readily notice. Fast—a tie. Easy to use—tie. The airfields presented—the two that I wanted and the third one that was relevant—tie. Two things win the competition for Google Earth. First, the chart I used all the time, the one on my wall, was the one of Libya. But what if I wanted to know the distance from Libya to Lebanon? I'd have to dig for a different chart. Google Earth has that information ready for me with a twitch of my mouse. Second, remember what I said about the value of information in front of your face? Google Earth allowed me to take the chart off my wall and display some other information there. Google Earth is in front of my face (on my screen) *only* when I want it.

# First- and Second-Level IT Tools to Help All Analysts

Now, let's look at some classes of tools that are in every analyst's kit. Some are first-level and some are second-level tools. It is your job to make the best in each class available to your analysts—and, in some cases, convince a reluctant analyst to lay down a comfortable but obsolete tool and adopt something better. But how do you know what is "better"? How do you know which tools are helping the analysts the most?

I spend a lot of time with IT tool builders—engineers—who want to help us analysts. Oddly, my story of Google Earth compared to my old dividers and chart leaves them flat. They swear they can help analysts more than that if I just tell them how analysts work. "Just explain the analytic process," they ask. I always answer that I will tell them how analysts work if they first tell me how engineers work. To which they respond with a blank stare. There are at least as many types of analysis as there are types of engineering, and, like engineering, the "process" usually starts with a problem, a thing to be figured out. Different analysts will attack the problem differently. No two will follow precisely the same path.

But *all* analysts, following whatever thought path suits them, do some things over and over again. It is not the analytic process but our repeated functions where the tool builders often can help us most, at least until artificial intelligence makes some giant leaps. What do all analysts do that the latest tools can help them do better? And how, as a leader of analysts, can you judge these tools? You can start by examining six things all analysts do: search for evidence, search for knowledge, identify and display relationships, share information, write, and shift between tools.

## All Analysts Search for Evidence

Analysts are looking for material relevant to the topic they are working on. The IT tools most relevant to this are search engines. There is a hot competition among search engines going on out there. You know your personal favorite from your use of the Internet at home. If your analytic workplace has its own holdings of information separate from the Internet, you will also be familiar with how successfully your analysts find what they are looking for in that domain. Are they finding the most relevant and best pieces of evidence among your holdings? Are they spending too much time simply sifting for the best tidbits of evidence? *Anything that dumps a giant load of information on your desktop, and requires you to sift through it, is a loser.* Anything that frequently misses the pivotal piece of evidence is problematic. *Any search tool that saves analysts time or makes them more effective at gathering evidence is a winner.*

The first-level search tools that are out there now are wonderful at finding digital documents containing the words you specify. You type search terms "Vladimir Putin" and "KGB" and the search tool will find digital documents that contain both terms, perhaps ranking the documents based on how close the terms were to each other.

Second-level search tools are starting to deliver what you *want*, not simply what you asked for. Google made a strong start with this by paying attention to and delivering the web pages that most people valued when searching on a particular topic. Others are working to determine what you *want* by understanding language beyond keywords—in short, understanding synonyms. Say you asked for "Vladimir Putin" and "KGB." A second-level search engine *also* looks for documents that contain equivalent words—say, "Russian president" and "Soviet intelligence." Productively searching for synonyms is a huge technological challenge, thanks in large part to the fuzziness of our language. Sometimes "contract" means to shrink; sometimes it means an agreement. Another daunting challenge is that, by broadening the search to include such synonyms, it is easy for the search to return vastly more documents, including more irrelevant documents. Again, what you want in a second-level search tool is one that consistently returns what you want (beyond the key words you specifically asked for) without dumping a big pile of documents on your analyst to sift through.

## All Analysts Search for Knowledge

Often your analysts need simply to retrieve something that is already known—a fact. This is different from searching for evidence, the material that can help them figure out the right answer; this is searching for the answer itself. If the search for evidence is *gathering,* this is *hunting.* Computers started out as tools for providing answers—calculations—faster than a human. Going from computing a mathematical equation to reliably retrieving a fact is a long and tortuous journey for info technologists. As a consultant with IBM on one such tool, Watson, I have been involved in mind-bending conversations about "what is a fact," and "how can a machine recognize one?" In a world of exploding *knowledge,* your analysts need to retrieve knowledge as quickly as possible. A first-level tool will find knowledge quickly. But analysts need more than this; it must be knowledge they can trust as accurate. This usually means asking the tool to "show me your work, or show me where you got this answer from." *A second-level tool delivers the fact—the bit of knowledge—along with the fact's source.*

## All Analysts Identify and Display Relationships

Discovering relationships in evidence is a big part of any analytic process. Connections between individuals, correlations (*co-relations*) between data, cause-and-effect cascades—all are a part of understanding how this world we analyze actually works.

There is an explosion of IT tools for identifying and displaying relationships. Some of the first-level tools are chronologies (X happened *before* Y). Some are "link charts" (terrorists Ferdinand and Hans both called the same phone number the day before the attack). More advanced are second-level tools that can at least suggest such things as hierarchy, relative importance, or proximity.

Display is a major challenge with many relationship tools. The value of display tools is putting information in front of your face—allowing you to *see* a relationship—but it is easy to put so much there that it becomes impenetrable. In the Counterterrorism Center more than a decade ago, to take advantage of our link-analysis tools, we had to buy printers that could turn out pages the size of bed sheets.

A more recent example of what I would consider a second-level relationship display is the illustration of tweets and re-tweets on Twitter. Figure 10.2 is SocialFlow's visualization of the network graph concerning tweets anticipating President Obama's announcement of the death of

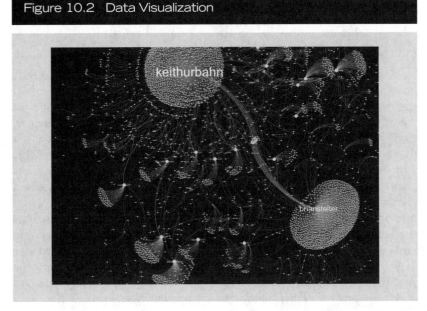

Figure 10.2   Data Visualization

*Source:* Gilad Lotan (2011) http://www.socialflow.com/breaking-bin-laden-visualizing-the-power-of-a-single/.

A good visualization of data draws the analyst's eye—in this case showing that Urbahn's and Stelter's tweets got more traction than anyone else's in the competition to predict what President Obama Was about to announce.

Usama Bin Laden. According to Gilad Lotan (2011), Twitter carried many rumors of what the president was about to announce the evening of May 1, 2011. Several people tweeted predictions that Bin Laden's demise would be announced. But while most of those predictions fell flat, one by former DOD official Keith Urbahn exploded across the Twitterverse. Brian Stelter, *New York Times* media reporter, was among the recipients of Urbahn's tweet, according to Gilad Lotan's reconstruction. In this display, Urbahn's and Stelter's tweets resonated where others fizzled—and you can instantly *see* it. There is no understanding the subtleties—and predictive value—of social media without such sophisticated display tools.

One amazing second-level IT tool for helping the analyst see relationships is data-driven animation. This still requires identifying relationships between data—most typically the relationship of data to time. But the IT tool animates the data for you. Take a few minutes to watch Dr. Hans Rosling's (2006) TED talk, "The Best Stats You've Ever Seen." Using UN data on fertility rates and longevity in different countries over time, he identifies countries that have enjoyed the most rapid progress in life expectancy in the last fifty years. His display allows him to literally set the data in motion, showing things like the incredible rise of life expectancy in South Korea compared to Brazil.

Traditionally, an analyst working reams of spreadsheet data would hypothesize one or two factors to track and then laboriously plot out the track to check the hypothesis. By setting data in motion, as Rosling does, the display enables your brain's special attraction to movement (a superb survival attribute) to notice which data have the greatest rate of change and are therefore perhaps more interesting than the rest. Anne Milley (2010), Senior Director of Analytic Strategy, Worldwide Product Marketing, SAS, notes that visualization particularly helps during the discovery phase. "When you are wallowing in the data . . . and trying to understand 'what do I need to pay attention to?' . . . you need a paradigm that is more visual." She also speaks of "data movies" as a way of making data intelligible to strategic decision makers.

## All Analysts Share Information

At one primal level, *all* analysts share information, in the sense that they provide their findings to their customer. Certainly, the technology for doing so is evolving rapidly. More and more customers of intelligence analysis receive theirs electronically on something that looks like a website. And I'm going to guess that the proportion who prefer receiving the analysis digitally rather than on paper is similar to the proportion of them who prefer to read their morning news online. *What you have to pay attention to here is the rapidly evolving appetite of your customers.* Three questions you and your analysts need to repeatedly ask your most important customers are, How do you want it? Did you get it? and Did you *read* it? (That last question addresses the fact that they get a lot of stuff, but sometimes the customer will only read a particular product if you draw her attention to it or if it is in a format she considers digestible.)

A different challenge, for you as leader, is that not all of your analysts share well *with each other*. You may have one curmudgeon who says, in effect, "I'll share what I know if they come and talk to me." You also probably have an analyst who spends long hours answering the simplest e-mail query with an interminable reply, filled with evidence, links, and argumentation. And you have other analysts who share effortlessly and productively, building networks of expert contacts and acquiring relevant information along the way. Whatever their personalities, I'd invite you to pay attention to two things in this arena, one attitudinal and one technological.

The first point is that you need to pay attention to your subordinates' attitude toward sharing. Your enterprise cannot afford the arrogance of that curmudgeon. In part, he is intimidating analysts he should be training. In part, he is hoarding information you cannot afford to have walk out the door the day he retires. In the analytic world, it isn't just the old veteran who is like this. Any analyst who knows more on a topic than every colleague in the room has felt the seductive question, "Why am I wasting my time in this room?" Your organization cannot afford that attitude. Bran Ferren (2008) points to "viscosity of knowledge" as one of the biggest things today's organizations must get right or they will fail. Viscosity of knowledge refers to how long it takes for an idea to flow in an organization. Aggressive sharing among colleagues—and broadening their definition of "colleagues"—needs to occur for the sake of the enterprise.

The technological point is actually easier to deal with. What IT sharing tools do your analysts feel comfortable using? They probably will develop that comfort outside the workplace. If they share mostly by e-mail at home, chances are that is what they'll prefer at work. Instant messaging? Twitter? Blogging? The same. I consider all of these first-level IT tools—they make the analyst's job of sharing easier—but the challenge lies in the fact new ones are coming along constantly. Regardless of your attraction to any of these, *you need to let your subordinates share via the technological medium they prefer*. When a new mode comes along, do your best to add it in your workplace.

One veteran leader of analysts rolled his eyes when he heard me make this last point. "Let your subordinates share via the technological medium they prefer" is easy to say, but we are dealing with multiple generations of analysts in the same workplace. We know they are far from unified in their preferences for which medium to use when sharing. Within reach, but not here yet, is a technological bridge between generations to make sharing easier. How would that look? Each person would define how he or she likes to *receive* information, regardless of how it is *sent* by others, and the tool delivers it in that medium. In the meantime, as a leader, you will need to attend to the social dynamics of whether your analysts are sharing with each other effectively.

## All Analysts Write

When most analysts think of tools that help with writing, they think of their favorite word-processing programs. Those are powerfully important—they certainly changed the way I compose—but this chapter is about *twenty-first*-century analysis. The word-processing programs that became widespread at the end of the twentieth century are excellent first-level tools and still the norm for most analysts.

For a chapter on tools in the twenty-first century, think instead about tools that write *for* you. This is a tool doing what only humans used to do—a second-level tool. Not transcribing your speech into text like Captain Kirk's log but writing prose without human involvement. Consider this excerpt:

> Friona fell 10–8 to Boys Ranch in five innings on Monday at Friona despite racking up seven hits and eight runs. Friona was led by a flawless day at the dish by Hunter Sundre, who went 2–2 against Boys Ranch pitching. Sundre singled in the third inning and tripled in the fourth inning. . . . Friona piled up the steals, swiping eight bags in all. (Levy 2012)

With his finger ever on the pulse of technology, Steven Levy (2012) quotes this snippet, written by one of Narrative Science's computers. Narrative Science is a small firm in Chicago that has developed algorithms to teach computers to write narrative in a distinctly human voice. One of the firm's cofounders predicted that "more than 90 percent" of the news will be written by computers within 15 years. Well . . . shoot. It's not enough that computers will identify and analyze patterns humans can't even find, at speeds no human can match—are computers even going to write the story of that discovery?

It is important to understand what is really going on with the computer "writing" the story of a Little League game. This is not a parlor trick, but it is not analysis. The computer is programmed to take data (the details of the game) and instantly use them to generate a "story." This is more than Mad Libs—more than filling in some blanks in a cleverly constructed narrative. The algorithm is sophisticated enough to recognize that the final score is of overriding importance—the story's lead—and that eight steals is an unusually high achievement, more worth noting than, perhaps, the number of double plays in this game. But if the shortstop made the most incredible catch ever seen in Little League history, that feature would not be captured on a score sheet or by the machine unless a human intervened. This is writing by formula.

That sounds more negative, more dismissive, than I intend. I look back at my career as an analyst and wish I had such a tool at my disposal. In my early days in Navy Intelligence, I did my share of writing reports—inevitably in the middle of the night—that were just as formulaic. "The TU-95 Bear aircraft departed Soviet airspace at 2245Z, rounding the Kola Peninsula to enter the Norwegian Sea 350 nautical miles northeast of Jan Mayen Island." This writing was always a tedious chore, and the computers are welcome to it.

Less formulaic is an approach to writing used by an Israeli firm, Articoolo. Asked to write on a topic other than an oft-repeated event like the Little League game above, its algorithms seem to compile a reasonably lucid string of thoughts or ideas from available content. One reporter challenged Articoolo to produce advice on "how to be happy." It responded with this: "Don't dwell on negative ideas, kick them out and gradually encourage yourself instead. Give yourself permission to grin or laugh out loud as you recall. Do something to make another person feel good, it'll brighten your day overly" (Lomas 2016). Not bad for a machine. Not only is this not formulaic, Articoolo's CEO claims, "Even if you ask for the same topic 100 times. You will get 100 different articles."

In your working lifetime, these writing machines will grow more and more sophisticated. They will handle routine news stories, and they will write narrative so beautifully as to pass not simply for human but for a novelist. And, of course, they will write porn. They will handle—handle very well—routine stories in which the only things that change are the particulars. And they might synthesize or compile some information. These tools can help analysts on occasion, but they don't replace the analyst's eye for what is important.

## All Analysts Shift between Tools

Keep in mind another point about tools that will help analysts: *IT tools that cross boundaries are especially valuable*. Your analysts all search for evidence, search for answers, identify relationships, share information, and write. Especially valuable for them will be tools that do several of these things or, at least, make for easy switching between them. Technologists today are acutely aware of this and they are "mashing" tools together all the time. This is not about the IT tools that have 150 capabilities, 140 of which are never used (like my word-processing program). This is about, for example, search tools that allow the analyst to effortlessly share the search results with colleagues or relationship displays that can be quickly captured and embedded in a written product. It is about link charts that incorporate geographic display and chronological sequence. It is about maps that, when you zoom in to a military base, show the order of battle routinely housed there and alert you to anomalies.

## Third-Level Tools: Big Data, Data Science, and Predictive Analytics

••••••••••••••••••••••••••••••••••••••••••••••••••••••••••••••

Recall my definition of the third level of IT tools: tools that are making some analysis possible for the first time in human history. This is the rapidly emerging world of big data. What I have discussed so far are the tools that help *all* analysts. But these third-level tools only apply to *some* analysts, *some* types of analysis, and *some* analytic questions. Where they apply, these tools are powerful—so powerful that it's worth building teams around them. Where they apply, they break new ground in what is *knowable*.

Judging these tools is much more challenging than what I described before. Terms like *fast, easy to use*, or *timesaver* tend not to apply. "Try it for a few days and see if you like it" probably won't get you far. In fact, even trying these analytic tools requires resisting our reflexive judgments that they are too different, too complex, too niche, or too opaque. They also typically require a significant level of investment up front—time, money, and experimentation often will be required before you actually know one of these tools will be worth it.

So what do I mean by big data? I like the definition Foster Provost and Tom Fawcett (2013) use in their excellent primer, *Data Science for Business*: "*Big data* essentially means datasets that are too large for traditional data processing systems, and therefore require new processing technologies" (Kindle location 401). Hadoop, HBase, and MongolDB are three popular such technologies today. Provost and Fawcett describe *data science* as the "set of fundamental principles that guide the extraction of knowledge from data" and *data mining* as the extraction itself (Kindle location 274). With increasingly sophisticated tools, patterns, correlations, and trends are often discovered in the data, some of which have predictive value, giving rise to the term *predictive analytics*.

With their responsibility to forecast, as discussed in chapter 7, leaders of intelligence analysis should want to master this new field. But it comes hard to many. Foundational in data science, for example, are such equations as these: "$p(AB) = p(A) \cdot p(B|A)$" (Bayes's rule for calculating joint probability) and "entropy $= -p_1\log(p_1) -p_2\log(p_2) - \ldots$" (a measure of disorder that can be applied to a set of data). For analysts who have spent their career predicting a foreign leader's actions based on behavior characteristics they have observed for decades, this is a whole different place to start thinking about a forecasting problem. Nevertheless, if predictive analytics is the source of some useful forecasts, if data mining reveals some useful insights, leaders of *all-source* intelligence analysis cannot ignore *this* source.

A useful way of thinking about this new field was provided by MIT's Erik Brynjolfsson. He calls data measurement the modern equivalent of the invention of the microscope (Lohr 2012). Nearly four centuries ago, the microscope enabled us to see things we simply could not before, confirm some theories and disprove others, and discover some things that had simply been unimagined. The microscope was revolutionary in medicine and biology. And like the microscope, data science is an essential tool for some things and irrelevant for others. Leaders of analysis must quickly learn which is which.

The big data revolution is being driven by businesses interested in things like marketing, fraud detection, and customer satisfaction. In the computer age, data are flowing to companies who are learning how to exploit them. Every credit card purchase, every Google search, every click on an Amazon web page is data. And every day data scientists are presenting business leaders with lucrative insights.

My first conscious interaction with a business application of data analytics was a decade ago. On the Internet, I found my wife's next Christmas present, a karaoke machine. (She sings like an angel.) I tried to order the machine online using my credit card, but nothing happened. I tried again, and again the order failed to go through. Seconds later, my phone rang, and it was my credit card company telling me there was some "unusual activity" on my card, with "someone trying to use it in South Korea." That is how I learned that this karaoke machine was made and sold in South Korea. I explained what I was trying to do, and they freed my card to make the purchase (a hit with my wife, by the way). What I had encountered was a data algorithm that was designed to spot credit card use outside of my established habits. The analytic algorithm established a pattern for my credit card use, spotted a purchase outside my pattern, and "warned" that my card might have been stolen. (Recall from chapter 7 that warning is a form of prediction.)

Each of you has encountered more recent business applications of data science. Any user of Google, Amazon, or Netflix services has taken advantage of (and fed) their data sophistication. Pandora Internet Radio is masterful at aligning their music suggestions to my tastes. If I like the musical poetry of rough-throated Leonard Cohen, might I like to try something by Tom Waits? Yes, please. And its assessment of my tastes grows more accurate with every song I endorse (click that thumbs-up!) or reject. For Pandora, these data-driven actions are also self-correcting. If I skip over some Tom Waits songs, their sense of me gets a little smarter and their profile of me adjusts itself.

The fact that the most visible applications of the big data revolution are business-oriented trips up some leaders of intelligence analysis. Their first reflex might be, "How do any of these data applications apply to the issues I am responsible for?" Or they might say, "Relevant data flow to Amazon and Pandora as a normal part of their business model. For me to get masses of data would require a huge investment (at least of time and attention), and that investment would have to be made up front, way before I am confident it would pay off." Perhaps an even more powerful temptation to dismiss big data is the instinct to say, "If Target or Pandora get it wrong, they have wasted a coupon or a suggestion, but we deal in the high-stakes arena of national security."

But to these reflexive skeptics, I say again, broaden your gaze. Businesses are discovering new applications of data science all the time— be on the lookout for ones that might parallel your needs. Further, data scientists are finding information in data that would not even have been called data a decade ago—you have messy repositories that new tools might be able to treat as "data" for the first time.

And broaden your definition of your responsibilities. You might be narrowly weighing this: "Which of my customer's questions can be answered through data science?" Instead, entertain the possibility that, in sifting through now-available data about your area of responsibility, your team might discover things that your customer would love to know but doesn't know to ask for.

## Two Keys: Volume and Repetition
••••••••••••••••••••••••••••••••••••••••••••••••••••••••••••••

Let me offer a tentative rule of thumb concerning where data science can help you. Of the many issues for which your team is responsible, where do you have both volume of information and repetition of events? Data science can often help you if you are dealing with events that recur. And data science thrives when there is a large amount of relevant data. Neither concept is as simple as it sounds. By "recur" I don't simply mean when that particular thing might happen repeatedly (another earthquake and tsunami damaging the nuclear reactor at Fukushima) but when something *similar* might happen. We might want to look for similarly vulnerable reactors worldwide or look for other industries where something like the Fukushima disaster could rock a ruling regime. And remember that I have called this a *tentative rule of thumb*. Data science, computing power, artificial intelligence, and machine learning are developing so quickly that what counts as volume and what counts as repetition might be redefined in your working lifetime.

Target provides an excellent example of volume and repetition coming together to identify patterns of predictive value. Andrew Pole (2010), Senior Manager of Media and Database Marketing at Target, presented the store's approach at the Predictive Analytics World 2010 conference. He described Target's effort to more effectively "capture guests," sending tailored advertising and coupons to customers who fit patterns. For example, "We develop a model to predict if a [specific] woman is likely to be pregnant with child. . . . We found that prenatal mothers start nesting. They start buying things in preparation for their child." Contributing to Target's data are such things as customers' online browsing behavior and in-store purchases combined with a chronology of this behavior. Apparently, expectant mothers frequently exhibit a telltale pattern of product purchases well before they are ready to buy such clear predictors as a crib. Target's data are so rich they often are able even to predict an estimated due date—triggering when to send coupons for diapers as opposed to prenatal vitamins.

Read more of Target's data effort, and those of many such enterprises, in *Predictive Analytics: The Power to Predict Who Will Click, Buy, Lie, or Die* by Eric Siegel (2013), the founder of Predictive Analytics World. He offers that analytics will very soon be able to help you with your morning drive to work, "predicting" your traffic, entertainment desire, breakfast appetite, car maintenance need, and driver attention at a certain point. It also enabled the drive by determining such things as your qualification for a car loan and your insurance risk. The data flows from your—and everyone else's—digital transactions (volume), and the patterns emerge from your habits (repetition).

This, indeed, is *prediction*—and useful as such. Beyond the volume and repetition, this type of analytics often also requires prediction about what needs to be predicted. Your music entertainment preferences are tracked—and an algorithm tailored for you—because someone thinks you would like "your car" to anticipate what you'd like to listen to on the way to work.

The task for the leader of analysis is to evaluate which areas of his responsibility can be helped by such analytics. Siegel (2013) points to some data-analytic insights that have already been revealed and appear relevant to intelligence analysis. For example, a study done by a large British bank suggests that suicide bombers do not buy life insurance. The African telecom firm CellTel found that "impending massacres in the Congo are presaged by spikes in prepaid phone cards."

In analyzing world events, much of what you are responsible for won't fit this approach. There are no masses of data and frequent repetition to tell whether the next leader of, say, Venezuela will cling to his or her predecessor's foreign policy line. But the data might be there—or be gathered—to identify certain Venezuelan diplomatic habits that are triggered when, say, the price of oil drops $20 per barrel. Is there a correlation between Venezuelan diplomacy and oil prices? Data science can confirm or refute the correlation. And if a correlation exists, data science can tell you its strength and particulars and identify a pattern that you can use the next time the price of oil drops.

*Volume* and *repetition* are both needed. Without sufficient *data*, the model doesn't have enough to chew on. Two points always make a line, but what are the chances that the line will parallel the aggregate of one thousand points? Equally, without *repetition*, there is no trend to reasonably project into the future.

Now, let me illustrate a case of trying to do too much with what appeared to be both abundant data and repetition. This anecdote also is intended to illustrate that the concept of data algorithms was not invented just yesterday. In the months before the first Iraq war, an outside analytic modeler approached my team at CIA, claiming to have a forecasting algorithm of predictive value. There was much interest at the time in the potential cost—in terms of casualties—of the coming war to evict Saddam's forces from Kuwait. He said he could help. He had examined numerous military contests, looking in detail at the military data on each side. He would weigh relative equipment strengths on each side as well as combat experience, training, fortifications, and the like. He would then run his model to predict casualty figures on both sides. He certainly had generous amounts of relevant data. What he lacked, however, was sufficient *repetition* for the issue he was trying to forecast. Each new military contest is unique in significant ways. He was not simply trying to predict the winner of the game or even the likely point spread. He was trying to predict the precise final score. When the battle for Kuwait was over and his model had failed, he explained that, looking back at the fighting, he could now add certain factors he had not included in the model, so that the casualties would be more predictable *next* time. I may be doing him an injustice—he may indeed have been ahead of his time—but it seemed to me his model would only ever be able to "predict" the casualty levels of the *previous* war.

Short of predicting the casualty figures in the Iraq war, it seemed to me that this analyst's model did a reasonable job in predicting the lopsided winner. Certainly, his figures showed a huge imbalance between likely coalition and Iraqi casualties, an imbalance clearly in our favor. But that model did not take the prediction any farther than my team could already go using our traditional approach to analyzing the balance of forces. The international coalition was going to prevail and it wouldn't be a close call. So was his model useless? No. I considered it a potentially helpful check on our own predictions. Had his model picked a different winner than my analysts did, it would have been a warning to my team to look again.

Now, more than two decades later, predictive analytic tools not only can take advantage of vastly increased amounts of available data, they also are stretching the bounds of what we consider "data." A collection of written products—newspaper articles, books, intelligence cables, whatever—traditionally has been looked at as a library of knowledge. But is it "data"? Your first guess is that perhaps it can be turned into data if the knowledge is curated into specific topics and judgments. This might allow you to say, for example, 80 percent of experts predict that ISIS will fragment within the next decade. But data scientists are turning masses of written products into data at an even more elemental level. Provost and Fawcett (2013) describe data science's "bag of words," in which each document is a collection of individual words and the order of those words, at least at first, can be ignored. Let me illustrate how such a seemingly abstract approach can go from data science to analytic insight.

My first supervisor at CIA, Martha Kessler, once impressed me with this advice: "If you want an early predictor of revolutions, watch the poets." I remember thinking that this was a profound insight—and useless. I could envision myself, as a new analyst, putting in countless hours to judge the mood of hundreds of, say, Tunisian poets, and then trying to convince a policy maker that the country was tipping toward revolution. It would have been a short career for this analyst.

Fast-forward to today, and a "bag of words" starts you on a path to insight. An important stride starting with a bag of words is described in a fascinating research article, "The Expression of Emotions in 20th Century Books," by Alberto Acerbi, Vasileios Lampos, Philip Garnett, and R. Alexander Bentley (2013). This team takes advantage of Google's digitization of several million books and the Google Books "Ngram Viewer," combined with the text analysis tool, "WordNet Affect." They looked in twentieth-century Google book data for words that convey mood in six categories: anger, disgust, fear, joy, sadness, and surprise. They convincingly show "that moods tracked broad historical trends, including a 'sad' peak corresponding to Second World War, and two 'happy' peaks, one in the 1920s and the other in the 1960s." They also show "the mood of Fear, which declined throughout most of the early century, has increased markedly since the 1970s." The surprise here isn't that people were sad in World War II but that such sterile and unstructured data could so clearly track emotion.

More pointedly using such techniques to gauge stability in a specific country is work done by Kalev Leeatru (2011) on the 2011 Tunisian revolution. Leetaru is Assistant Director for Text and Digital Media Analytics at the University of Illinois. He does what he calls "sentiment mining" on the global news coverage of Tunisia, as captured by the Summary of World Broadcasts (see Figure 10.3). Leeatru says, "Measuring the tone of news coverage about a single geography over time, a fundamentally new approach to conflict early warning is developed that 'passively crowd-sources' the global mood about each country in the world. This is found to offer highly accurate short-term forecasts of national stability." He writes, "[T]he two-week period prior to Tunisian President Ben Ali's [January 14, 2011] resignation was the sixth most negative period in the last 30 years, coming after a decade-long plunge towards increasing negativity."

Are such data predictive? Are such analyses sound? Leetaru (2011) is appropriately cautious; the Tunisian example was done *after* the 2011 revolution. Certainly the quantitative information doesn't stand by itself. A shallow analyst using such data could easily cry wolf every time sentiment dips, say, below −2. But used with other sources of information, used with broader analysis, this sentiment-data might be useful. It might, for example,

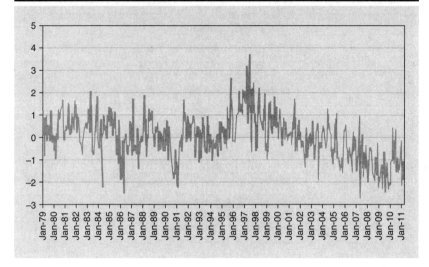

Figure 10.3 Tone of Country-Level Coverage Mentioning Tunisia, *Summary of World Broadcasts*, January 1979–March 2011 (December 2010 is 1–17 December). Y–axis is Z–scores (Standard Deviations from Mean)

*Source:* Kalev Leetaru (2011) http://firstmonday.org/ojs/index.php/fm/article/view/3663/3040.

help judge whether a Tunisian stability is relatively fragile or resilient today. It might also help explain why a catalyst such as the self-immolation of a street vendor set off widespread protests in Tunisia when something similar might fizzle in Turkey. Using Leetaru's model *instead* of analysis would be dangerous—and he doesn't seem to advocate it. Using the model to draw your attention, to invite you to weigh what might be going on, could be helpful.

Leetaru now has a website, *The GDELT Project,* that claims to monitor "print, broadcast, and web news media in over 100 languages from across every country in the world to keep continually updated on breaking developments anywhere on the planet. Its historical archives stretch back to January 1, 1979 and update daily (soon to be every 15 minutes)" (see http://gdeltproject.org/#intro). In the business of analysis, it shows how the bounds are being pushed of the question, "What is knowable?" The analyst responsible to judge, in this case, political stability needs to keep an open mind as to whether important new tools are available to her. Secondarily, she needs to have an informed answer ready should the policy maker say to her, "I just saw Indonesia light up on GDELT. What do you think?" The leader of such analysis needs to judge when it makes sense to launch a team to employ such tools and techniques. For the first time, Martha Kessler's insight, "Watch the poets," might be both actionable and testable.

## The Dreaded—but Inevitable—Black Box
••••••••••••••••••••••••••••••••••••••••••••••••••••••••••••

Information tool developers regularly hear a repeated refrain from analysts: "Don't give us a Black Box!" By this the analysts mean we don't want a tool that gives us information if we don't know how that information was derived. We won't trust the answer it spits out if we don't understand how that answer was developed. "Show us your work." This is what we leaders of analysis insist on when we are reviewing the papers our analysts produce. It is what the analysts want from their tools.

This is not an issue with programs that are what I would call *service* tools, mostly first-level tools. Word processors, calculators, e-mail and instant messaging systems, and the like provide services we rely on. We don't really care how they work; we simply expect them to, and we know when they don't.

But we raise the "Black Box" concern when we are considering *substance* tools. When the product is information—about patterns, correlations, linkages, answers to questions, material retrieved from an archive, or material gleaned from the Internet—we are dealing with the air analysts breathe. We fear such tools introducing error into our analysis, and we insist: *NO BLACK BOXES!*

But this is increasingly unrealistic. We are rapidly moving into an era when the information tools—especially the second-level and third-level tools—are impenetrably complex. The most important and sophisticated information tools are the products of many hands. Teams of engineers work on them, refine them, improve them. They may contain a million lines of code. The algorithms they use are tweaked and retweaked over time, with lines of code added—often anonymously. Beyond this, machine learning increasingly is involved. The machine itself refines its operation to produce the desired outcome. The machine may alter the weight of a predictive variable if the previous weight produced a wrong answer. Then tests are done to determine whether the machine performs better. Over time, with all this human and machine intervention, the tool *evolves*. The box becomes blacker and blacker.

So, if we are stuck with Black Boxes, how do we productively channel our concern that they might introduce error into our analysis? We must shift our focus. Rather than worrying about *how* they work, we must constantly test *that* they work.

Tools that retrieve information or answers must be frequently checked. Did the tool find the document that you know is in the archive? Did it find what you consider to be not only relevant information, but the best information? Analysts will do these kinds of checks until they trust the tool. As a leader of analysis, you must enforce continued spot-checks of their favorite tools routinely, even after the tool has earned their trust, because behind the scenes, their tools evolve.

Predictive analytics tools (algorithms) must also be spot-checked occasionally. Algorithm developers know not to fall blindly in love with their models. In the early stages of building a predictive model, for example, they are aware that, as Eric Siegel (2013) notes, a constant hazard is machine "overlearning." The machine (the predictive model) so completely learns the data—both its signal and its noise—that it looks for a pattern that precisely matches *that* data. But it doesn't recognize a pattern that is meaningfully *similar* because it is looking for a pattern that is nearly *identical* to the first batch of data. In short, the model doesn't generalize well. It would be like a weather model that says it will only rain tomorrow if the barometer is dropping, the temperature falls three degrees, there is a band of cumulus clouds in the west, and the Nationals beat the Dodgers 5 to 2 because those were the conditions in the data set it was fed. Siegel advises that the art of producing a more useful predictive model requires "architecting a [machine] learning process that strikes the balance between learning too much and too little." To help achieve this, he says, "Hold aside some data to test the model. Randomly select a test set . . . and quarantine it" (Kindle location 3446). Even after the model is well developed and tested over time, because it evolves it needs to be retested against data it has never seen to determine that it remains trustworthy.

Testing our tools, although essential, will not completely prevent mistakes when using second-level and third-level tools. Rather, we must expect that substantive information tools will be fallible. We expect this in humans; as the intelligence of IT tools comes closer to rivaling that of humans, why would we expect they would be inhuman in this respect? However brilliant the model, whatever revelations it has delivered in the past, it remains a product of design choices, assumptions, trade-offs, and short cuts made by humans—or it might have evolved via the machine's own learning. And even a time-tested brilliant model will fail when the underpinning reality shifts. Consider the example I pointed to earlier: the data shows that suicide bombers do not buy life insurance. That behavior surely would change if prospective suicide bombers learned that the indicator was being used against them. However reliable your power tool, don't close your eyes when you use it.

# The Analyst Is Not About to Be Replaced

So with the increasing sophistication of the information tools we are seeing, with the arrival of machine learning, with the increasing applications of big data, are we on our way to making the analyst obsolete? Some of my colleagues fear it is so. A few fear HAL, the computer in *2001: A Space Odyssey*, who is smarter than them. More fear that the instant answers provided by Google and Wikipedia will be good enough for customers in a hurry.

Still others fear what former analytic executive Carmen Medina (2008) described in her brilliant essay, "The New Analysis." She says, "In this new era of analysis, prose prepared by so-called subject matter experts, which still accounts for the overwhelming majority of analytic product, increasingly will be viewed as not analysis at all but just a form of commentary not unlike that which can be found in *The Economist,* the *New York Times,* or web-log spaces" (Kindle location 3790). She forecasts, "The analysis of the future will increasingly and by necessity be digital. Analysts will be processing huge amounts of data and will be picking up potentially relevant tidbits from any number of sources, both secret and open" (Kindle location 3820). While conceding that Medina's forecast may be valid, many analysts hope it doesn't happen during their careers. I have heard more than one seasoned analyst confide, "The last thing I want to do is become someone's data monkey."

So, yes, the arrival of second-level IT tools (which replace the human in some functions) and third-level tools (which enable new types of insights) can feel daunting to some analysts. It is particularly daunting for my friends who feel, like John Henry, they must compete with the technology. Remember the legend of John Henry, the steel-driving railroad man, who competed with a steam-powered hammer, winning the race but then dying when his heart gave out? John Henry was on the cusp of being surpassed by the technology. We can see many functions in which the same is happening to analysts. But there are other critical analytic functions in which we humans have advantages that will not disappear in our lifetime.

I offer a simple rule of thumb for the analytic functions that will be taken over by sophisticated tools: **If the analysis can be reduced to an if-then logic tree, let a tool (algorithm) do it.** I look back to my work as a military analyst in the 1980s and recall many such functions. Many I&W (Indications and Warning) lists of potentially dangerous military developments to watch for were that formulaic. Some military activity patterns were that mechanistic. Don't get me wrong; the if-then logic tree is not restricted to simple problems. Self-driving cars use them and are quickly becoming safer drivers than humans, even in tremendously complex traffic snarls.

When if-then logic can apply, the only question for the leader of analysis is a resource investment one. Does this particular issue happen frequently enough to make it worth the effort of building an algorithm to take over the function from an analyst? And remember, the tool will deliver its findings *to the analyst.* The analyst will then assess the findings, their context, and their implications and decide whether they are meaningful.

Which brings us to the human advantages in analysis, advantages I believe will keep analysts employed through this century. First, the analyst is needed to decide which question is important and which tools to apply. What counts as an insight for our customers? Can a tool deliver insight on this question or help in any way? What data are already available, and are the data diagnostic for this question? No information technology is on the horizon that can make such choices.

Second, the analysts *doubt*. Doubt is a critical facility in analysis, and no machine has it. No engineer knows how to build it into a tool. Yes, there are self-checking and self-correcting features with some IT tools, but this is not the same. Analytical doubt is much more than ensuring that your output remains within some narrowly defined parameters. Analytical doubt is the constant nagging notion that "I could be wrong here; this just doesn't make sense." We know what happens when analytic doubt is missing—the post mortems of nearly every famous intelligence failure tell us. The closest any IT tools come to addressing the importance of doubt is to present several possible answers to the user. As attractive as this is in such tools, it still is the tool designer's way of saying to the human user, "Over to you to decide which answer is right."

Third, analysts sometimes can discern something important from what is missing. They are Sherlock Holmes noticing the dog that didn't bark. Machines do not do this. Big data algorithms and machine learning tools focus on what they find. They tend to ignore what they did not find because it *is not there*. I am not referring here to anomaly detection—or detecting change in a pattern—at which AI is getting pretty good. I am referring to conceptualizing that something should be present when it is not. It takes a human analyst to say, "Wait a minute . . . something's missing here." It drives us to broaden the context, to dig deeper, to remain unsatisfied until we discover the tidbit that allows us to say, "Ahh . . . now it makes sense."

Finally, we humans have a fourth advantage, one that really matters: We are infinitely better than machines at providing an answer to the question, "Why?" Machines can be brilliant in finding correlation—that is how Walmart discovered that the sale of strawberry Pop-Tarts leaps prior to hurricanes (Provost and Fawcett 2013). And in low-stakes decisions, sometimes correlation is all that matters; if I am in charge of Walmart warehousing, I will use that data to pack in extra cases of strawberry Pop-Tarts before the storm without caring why it is true. But for high-stakes decisions, *why* matters enormously.

Our customers, the decision makers, exhibit the strong human need to understand *"Why?"* "Why?" is the most important question in the analytic function of sense-making. Until we can explain causality—explain *why* something just happened or is likely to happen—analysts cannot credibly claim to understand it. Until we can clearly communicate causality to the decision maker, she will not be comfortable taking a high-stakes action.

Will a machine be built that competently answers "Why?" I am not prepared to dismiss that possibility. The data scientists are acutely aware that spurious correlation is a huge hazard in their work, and making progress on causality could reduce spurious correlation. They also are aware that, in predictive analytics, customers often ask "Why?" when a forecast is surprising. But of all the advances we are seeing in machine intelligence, a breakthrough on "Why?" appears farthest away.

So the analyst's job looks secure. This doesn't mean it won't continue to change because of increasingly smart tools. Fast-forward maybe ten years. We didn't have the tools or skills to alert policy makers to a coming Arab Spring back in 2011, but imagine a cadre of analysts whose work is more akin to what we expect from weather forecasters. A typical report in 2025 might be something like this:

> Our models for impending disorder are generally quiet globally, but one center of activity we are monitoring is in Indonesia. Several social media sentiment trackers are showing a sharp drop in Indonesia. Passions run highest on the topics of local corruption and banking practices. Recent government attempts to address the concerns have had no impact. Our projection algorithms suggest that widespread anti-government violence is one Category III trigger away. (The Tunisian self-immolation triggering the Arab Spring was Category III.) The Indonesian government is considering requesting US food aid, but our economists suggest that targeted banking reform and a surge of micro-lending would have more impact.

To get to this seamless integration of analyst and technology, the critical variable is the leader's attitude. The leader of analysis who sees increasingly smart machines as competition will be left behind. The leader who is an active opportunist, who sees second-level and third-level tools as a rich and dynamic chance to discover and deliver new insights, can thrive.

The leader of analysis will have to avoid the extremes of the debate about analytic tools and smart machines. Ignore those who say that big data analytics change everything. Ignore also those who cannot spell "algorithm." Waste no time yearning for a return to the days when analysis was simpler or fearing a day when artificial intelligence will push us aside. Rather, to thrive as a leader of analysis now, embrace an attitude that says,

- Analytics ≠ Analysis, but can help us

- Data ≠ Information, but can contain useful information

- Information ≠ Knowledge, but is a prerequisite for knowledge

- Artificial Intelligence ≠ Intelligence, but can free my analysts from mental drudgery

- Good information tools save time. Time is precious.

- The tool is a means, not an end. Delivering insight is the end.

# KEY THEMES

Three levels of information technology are changing the work of analysts.

- *First-level tools: Make routine aspects of their work much easier.* This is the mundane information technology. A word-processing program is an example.

- *Second-level tools: This IT is replacing functions that used to be the sole domain of humans.* Your GPS is an example.

- *Third-level tools: These are tools, mainly algorithms, which are making some analysis possible for the first time in human history.* Think of Twitter, with the ability to instantly track the concerns of millions.

As a leader of analysis, you will have to preside over an ever-shifting balance between the work done by the tools and the work that can only be done by human analysts. You will have to decide what new tools to invest in, as well as how much time your analysts will need to put into learning or experimenting with the latest thing.

Some information technology is easy to judge: (1) fast? (2) easy to use? (3) the information I seek is there? and often, (4) without distracting me, other information I could use—but didn't think to seek—is also there for me. Your analysts won't need to be prodded to adopt these tools. Just do your best to keep up with current versions. For more advanced tools, expect most analysts to resist investing serious time in experimenting with them—but you need them to learn that in twenty-first-century analysis, that is part of their job.

Here are things that can help you judge first- and second-level tools that all analysts use:

- All analysts search for evidence. Anything that dumps a giant load of information on the desktop and requires analysts to sift through it is a loser. Anything that frequently misses the pivotal piece of evidence is problematic. Any search tool that saves them time or makes them more effective at gathering evidence is a winner.

- All analysts search for knowledge (something already known, like a fact). A good first-level tool usually finds the fact quickly. A second-level tool will deliver both the fact and its source.

- All analysts display relationships (e.g., chronologies, links between actors, cause and effect, flow charts). Many second-level tools display data in motion, drawing the eye to relationships that might otherwise be missed.

- All analysts write. Some second-level tools are producing at least simple first drafts for the analyst to approve or revise. This technology is developing rapidly.

- All analysts share information. They tend to like the info-sharing tools they have at home. You will have to determine whether your analysts are sharing effectively across platforms with each other and with their customers.

The era of big data, data science, and predictive analytics—third-level tools—is expanding what analysis can discover. Some of these tools are so complex it takes years to learn them, and employers are hiring for those skills. But all analysts need to learn what sort of problems can benefit from these tools and methods. In general, when there is both *volume* (more data than an analyst can deal with) and *repetition* (events occur in patterns), think of employing these tools.

With all these tools, and with the rapid advance of machine learning and artificial intelligence, analysis can do more than it ever has. Welcome that you will be able to offload much of the drudge that consumed analysts' time. Any of their work that can be reduced to an if-then logic tree can be done by an algorithm. But the analysts are not about to be replaced. For now, the analysts have distinct advantages over the tools:

- Analysts can adjust to the new and novel. Humans are better at deciding which tools to apply to which new problems.

- Analysts doubt. This is indispensable to analysis and does not yet apply to machines.

- Analysts can discern something from what is missing—Sherlock Holmes's dog that didn't bark.

- Analysts wrestle with the question, "Why?"

Remember, in this changing landscape, *you* play an essential role. To get seamless integration of analyst and technology, the critical variable is the leader's attitude. Investing money in a new technology may be your decision. Investing your analysts' precious time in experimenting with a tool that might be worth a try will usually be your initiative.

# 11

# Analysis at the Speed of Information

There is a final challenge to be addressed for leaders of analysis, a distinctly twenty-first-century challenge: We are sailing in an information hurricane. We needn't feel special about this. Industry after industry is feeling it. They all struggle for the competitive advantage that comes from making more effective use of available information. Companies steeped in retail or manufacture—Walmart and GE, for example—are learning to be information enterprises. They see assembling and analyzing information as essential to their success. But they are daunted by just how much information there is. They worry how much is blowing right past them that might contain the seeds of some competitor's success. Business after business sees both opportunity and danger in the information hurricane, and to many business leaders it feels like a crisis. That absolutely describes the pressure felt by leaders of intelligence analysis. They tell me, "Sure, we used to have crises, but crisis is constant now!"

Analysts have always been strong at dealing with information in volume. We triage the incoming information, using our substantive experience to sort it by quality, relevance, and impact. Part of becoming expert is to grow skilled at assessing information in just seconds. We separate the likely from the conceivable in an instant. We develop and hone a set of assumptions to guide our focus, and we use tested techniques for revalidating assumptions over time. We also are able to see information that others overlook, like the diving coach reading a splash to diagnose flawed form. But none of these strengths is sufficient for today's information volume.

IT tools were supposed to compensate for our human insufficiency. The builders of the search tools engineered the ability to scour billions of digital documents in moments, delivering the results in an order that usually makes sense. Powerful digital forensics can find almost anything on the Internet. But analysts complain that often these tools deliver mountains of low-grade ore which still must be sifted for the few nuggets that matter. And some analysts are quick to say the IT tools are making matters worse: "I can't keep up with the information that crosses my desk as it is, and now some clown with an algorithm tells me he has uncovered some correlation that changes everything, so I have to stop and figure out what the hell he is talking about!"

The IT tools also deliver a reality that many analysts regard as a curse. If a key bit of information can be found *after* the event—and IT tools can find everything digital eventually—the analysts feel they are held responsible to find it *before* the event. Before the surprise or intelligence failure, the analyst feels she is expected to find, weigh, and make sense of every bit of relevant information that is available. Her inner congressional inquest screams, "It was *available*, right? Why didn't you *avail* yourself of it?"

James Gleick (2011) captures our dilemma well in his masterful *The Information: A History, a Theory, a Flood*: "We have information fatigue, anxiety, and glut. We have the Devil of Information Overload and his impish underlings, the computer virus, the busy signal, and the PowerPoint presentation" (11). Gleick also put his finger on the greatest challenge of today's analyst: "When information is cheap, attention becomes expensive" (410).[1]

The challenge to analysts is not simply the volume of information out there—it's also the impact of information. The information age is dramatically changing the world we are trying to analyze. Would there be an Arab Spring without Al Jazeera, YouTube, and Twitter? Will China's state managers survive a population that can communicate with itself at a volume that legions of censors cannot control? What does the explosion in smartphones across Africa mean economically and politically? To address such issues, analysts need to understand such information phenomena and then need to assess whether the states they study "get it" or will be overwhelmed by it. And to deepen the challenge, some analysts who study those states are having to wrap their minds around the possibility that, in the information age, *states* may no longer be the engines of history. It all leaves many veteran analysts and their leaders feeling overwhelmed.

This is not pressure that analysts feel alone—their customers, the policy makers, feel it intensely. If a new development *seems* important, the policy maker is on the hook to react *now*. To wait to understand an issue is to be accused of dithering. America's foreign policy apparatus has been screamed at to place bets on the Arab Spring, to pick winners and losers in a game we have never seen before. More than one senior policy maker has confided to me that he desperately wants analytic help but cannot afford to wait for it. Veteran analytic leaders tell me that they have never felt so much pressure from the customers to deliver analysis that is both *right* and *right now!*

To deal with this pressure, analysts have developed a variety of coping mechanisms. To deal with the volume of information, they pay close attention to where the best information *usually* comes from, and they

---

[1] Gleick might have been inspired by Nobel laureate Herbert Simon, who said in the 1970s, "[A] wealth of information creates a poverty of attention and a need to allocate that attention efficiently among the overabundance of information sources that might consume it" ("Herbert A. Simon" 2018).

drink from that well every day. This is highly practical. If the "good stuff" usually comes from this source, that's where I will invest my attention. In intelligence analysis, it might mean spending most time on the classified information, where trained intelligence collectors have responded to your requests, where satellites have collected the images you tasked, where you have some influence on which intercepted communications get processed. In the world of data analysis, it might mean watching the variables that historically have had the greatest impact, or the data streams that are most consistently available, or the curated data you have worked so hard to gather and format. Whatever the domain, the analyst copes by attending to the information stream that has served him best so far, knowing that he risks missing some vital tidbit from an esoteric source.

To deal with the pressure for instant analysis, a coping mechanism is to "go tactical." You simply provide analysis in smaller bites, on smaller topics, answering smaller questions. Your customer is desperate for your prediction, so you predict what will happen tomorrow. In fact, there is a strong temptation to make the safest prediction about what will happen tomorrow, reducing the chances of being embarrassingly wrong. Part of this is very natural: your harried customer is making mostly tactical decisions and is likely asking you tactical questions. When will you get around to doing that vital strategic analysis—the analysis that might even obviate your tactical work? When you get some time . . . sigh.

So how does one lead analysis in this maelstrom? How do we take advantage of the information hurricane—how do we actually *thrive* in it—rather than whining about it? There are several things you can do to help, starting with attitude.

# Get Your Mind Right and Theirs

First, shed unrealistic expectations. *Your analysts will never be able to take full advantage of all the available information.* There is already too much, and it's increasing. In the information hurricane, important information *will* be missed.

Further, there is no such thing as perfect analysts or perfect analysis. No analyst, no team of analysts, and no analytic approach will always be right. Analysis is a powerful aid to decision making when it narrows the range of uncertainty. Analysis is not—and never will be—a guarantee of success. Analysis will prevent many surprises, but analysis will never preclude surprise. It will not identify every threat or every opportunity in time to act wisely. Analysis at its most insightful will not always overcome a customer's reticence to act. And when it all works beautifully—the analysis is brilliant and persuasive, the customer acts on it, and a wonderful outcome results—it will be the rare customer who gives the analysis significant credit.

Next, help your customer shed unrealistic expectations. Analysis is the art of sense making, but people do not always act sensibly. Experts know better than anyone else what characteristically happens in simple and complex situations, but what characteristically happens is not what *always* happens. Analysis will appropriately predict something as "almost certain"—90 percent likely—which still means there is a distinct possibility it won't happen. Your customer demands, "No surprises!" Your response should be, "First, there *will certainly be surprises*. Second, let's talk about where to put our warning setting and your tolerance for false alarms."

It is vital to shed one other attitude: that of victim. Too many leaders of analysis complain to me that they are forced to work at a breakneck pace, deluged by information, for insatiable customers. Some claim that they are forced to deliver less than the best analysis because there simply isn't time. Over and over I hear some variant of the complaint, "The only kind of deadlines we are handed are ones that don't allow deep thought!" A victim may say the status quo is forcing failure. A leader adjusts to external realities and helps shape a new status quo.

Part of feeling like a victim of the situation is to focus on realities that affect you but you cannot influence. Some of these are real, like the sheer volume of information coming at you. But some of these realities masquerade as binary choices that trap you between two unattractive outcomes. Here are two false binary choices:

- Meet unrealistic deadlines or be irrelevant. Unrealistic deadlines from a customer are a sign that you and your customer don't know each other well enough. They should trigger dialogue. What is behind the question you asked us or the deadline you gave us? (Perhaps we can at least partly address that need because we don't have the time to fully answer your question.) What can I provide in time to help you? Will a conversation with our analysts help you, given that we don't have time to write a formal assessment? Where is your agenda headed, so we can better anticipate your questions? Most customers welcome this type of dialogue—they certainly like it better than a rushed analytic product short on insights.

- Master all the information or miss a vital piece. This is not actually a choice, any more than it would be for generals to think they must plan for everything or lose soldiers in the battle. They cannot plan for everything, and they will lose soldiers. In today's information environment, your analysts will never master all the available information. And yes, there will be occasions when your analysts miss a vital piece of information. Accept those unattractive realities, and focus on doing the best you can.

And of course, leading will always involve shaping the attitudes of your subordinates, the analysts. Among them, you will find these counterproductive prejudices related to doing analysis in today's information hurricane:

- *I'm too busy to try new tools.* Analysts who are overwhelmed by the task of sifting masses of information can be loath to touch an unfamiliar tool, but tools that can help them sift are coming along every year. The analysts often express two sources of reluctance. First, they fear a new sifting tool will miss something. Yes, it will. But the analyst stuck in a one-potato-two-potato slog through a pile of potential source material is already missing something. Second, they have been disappointed before. That is, they wasted time trying tools which just didn't deliver. Your answer must be, "Yes, and you will be disappointed again, but hang in there. There is no method of coping with the information hurricane that does not involve new tools." (Of course, just telling them this will be insufficient. As I'll discuss later in this chapter, you also must deliver your part of this business need: you must carve out the time they need to experiment with these tools.)

- *Don't bother me with information I can't trust.* At some level, every veteran analyst knows this prejudice is inappropriate. Each has had the experience of a key truth coming from a dubious source. The source might be a person who has exaggerated in the past. It might be an extremist's blog. It might be messy data of unknown pedigree. But at another level, every skilled analyst also knows he could waste all day chasing such rabbits—a completely open mind is an unproductive mind. So what attitude should you encourage? Expect that a good analyst will spend *most,* but never all, of her time with sources that have been useful before. Require her to demonstrate an open mind, to spend some time scanning for new sources or taking a fresh look at sources that have earned her skepticism in the past.

- *Trust me, I've been doing this successfully a long time; my old approach is working just fine.* Such complacency should set off your alarm bells. Because analysis is so hard, because it can never be perfect, because there is more useful information than can be used, no analyst it entitled to be complacent. To be a master analyst today is to live with a nagging inner voice saying, "What am I missing here? What might work that I haven't tried?"

# Build an Information Strategy

A leader in any industry will keep an eye on supply, and your business is no exception. Your analysts' most vital supply is the flow of information they can use. In an environment of information glut, it is easy to take this supply for granted, but this is a mistake. Analytic enterprises are (unrealistically) held responsible to take advantage of all the available information. To deal with this reality, you and your analysts must develop a strategy for dealing with the available information as best you can, even knowing you cannot master it all.

Here is what happens with many analytic teams. Say I'm an analyst on a team studying Borostan's stability. I arrive in the morning and start my routine for determining what information has come in on the topic since yesterday. I look first at "the good stuff"—whatever source of information that has been most helpful in the past. Perhaps that is the intercepted communications of Borostani leaders. Maybe I'll also do a quick check of the satellite imagery of the Borostani security forces' key garrisons. And then I'll scan what passes for an opposition press in Borostan.

Oops, it's time for our team's morning meeting. I have only looked at 20 percent of the information available to me, but I feel pretty good because I know that 95 percent of the stuff worth reading is routinely found in that 20 percent. In the meeting, we start talking about the interesting tidbits we have gleaned. It is a rich conversation because we all agree that one specific report was by far the most important piece that we saw: those intercepted communications captured something that fascinated several of us. We offer varying interpretations of the implications of that piece, and we have an excellent discussion of what to do next to determine which interpretation is correct.

The leader of that team is in a position to notice something the analysts did not. Before the meeting, everybody on the team found and read that fascinating intercept. In fact, most of the time, everybody on the team reads the same 20 percent of the take. After all, that 20 percent is "the good stuff," and nobody wants to be left out of that conversation in the morning meeting. *But 80 percent of the available material went unexamined by anybody on the team.*

An information strategy—developed in consultation with your analysts—can address this vulnerability. For my Borostan stability team, I might want two people looking first at the freshly intercepted communications (the single most valuable source we have on this topic). Another analyst will check the satellite imagery and another the opposition press. I'll have another reading the political blogs of Borostani expatriates and someone else checking Twitter (which this morning might reflect yesterday's student rally in the capital). And I'll have my last analyst surf the Internet for anything new on Borostan that did not fit in one of the previous categories. The iron-clad rule that I will enforce is that, as soon as anyone finds an interesting item (and there will be a low threshold for what is "interesting"), they must share it with the rest of the team. This strategic approach to sifting the available information does not provide 100 percent coverage—the Internet simply is too vast. But it does wisely allocate the energies of your team, takes advantage of much more than the 20 percent you had been redundantly sifting before, and reduces your chances of missing something important.

Some team leaders among you are saying, "It must be nice to have seven analysts all working a topic like Borostani stability! But I have ten analysts each working a different topic, so your strategy doesn't apply." You are correct: *my* strategy wouldn't apply. You need to craft your own strategy. As I did in the Borostan case, **you need to develop a strategic sense of the universe of information relevant to your area of responsibility and judge how best to invest the attention of your analysts**. Perhaps you manage the *only* analyst working on Borostan's stability. In discussion with him, you develop a rhythm in which he reads the intercepts and looks at satellite photos every day, the opposition press every third day, and the expatriate blogs once a week. And perhaps you engineer an arrangement with your organization's Twitter expert, who agrees to push interesting material on Borostani stability to your analyst when it comes in.

Even a team of highly experienced analysts can use your help strategically investing their attention. In fact, many experienced analysts fall prey to several bad habits in this arena. Some say, "I can't have colleagues sifting the sources for me; they might miss subtleties I would catch." This reveals that they are not communicating those subtleties to their colleagues. Another problem might be that some made their judgments about the most lucrative sources of insight years ago, and because they are busy, they haven't gotten around to taking a fresh look. Some simply are dismissive of the "new" sources of insight, from big data to blogs. Or they think that Googling something is enough of a nod to the Internet's vast resources. One particularly creative analytic leader I know would kick his veteran analysts out of the office at least once a year. "I want you to get out of the office for a week," he'd say, "and I want you to visit information you don't pay attention to here." Any source would do, as long as it was one the analyst was ignoring before. To a person, they came back impressed with "how much useful stuff is out there!"

# Can We Analyze Faster?

Any engineer would look at the information overload challenge from another perspective. He or she would at least consider the possibility that maybe the problem isn't that the information is coming in too fast—maybe your analysis is too slow.

I must acknowledge that in the next decade science might deliver real ways to think faster. Already on the market are controversial pills and machines that claim to increase focus, attention, clarity, and recall. Nootropics ("brain-enhancing" drugs and dietary supplements) and low-voltage machines that offer transcranial direct current stimulation are available now, and their claims are the subject of serious research. I'm certainly not ready to touch, much less advocate, such products. I want many more years of testing for side effects before I am willing to intentionally mess with my brain chemistry. I find the risks daunting now, but in your careers as leaders of analysis you might see them go mainstream.

For now, I see three low-risk ways to speed up analysis: invest in strategic analysis, carve out time for tools, and accelerate the process of growing experts. Let's examine each of these.

## Make Time for Strategic Analysis

Earlier in this chapter, I described that the speed of information and the demand for instant analysis is driving us toward the tactical. I mentioned that strategic analysis might even obviate some of the tactical analysis you are spinning your wheels on. But there is a more subtle dynamic at work as well: *an analyst who has done the strategic thinking can work faster than he did before.* Incoming information is more quickly sorted and binned once you know how it fits together strategically. A strategic perspective helps you to know what to look for in a given situation—what could change the picture meaningfully—and where that information is likely to come from. A strategic framework helps you separate the signal from the noise. Understanding an issue strategically increases your confidence, helps you write faster and more clearly, and reduces "on the one hand/on the other hand" dithering. And the process of researching an issue strategically generates clarity on both what is known and its limits.

An analyst who has weighed an issue strategically will have a far more satisfying discussion with a customer and be able to field most questions with a meaningful insight. Sometimes that insight will be, "We have considered this and simply don't know." But even that is a better answer—and a more time-saving one—than the tactical analyst responding, "I will have to take your question, work on it, and get back to you."

Some of you are reading this and thinking, "The problem is not that I don't understand the importance of strategic analysis. I do! The problem is that good strategic analysis takes so much time to produce." *You must protect that time.* Here is how one of my most important mentors did it in one national crisis.

Winston Wiley was chief of CIA's Persian Gulf analysis when Saddam's forces invaded Kuwait in August 1990. For us working the issue, the next five months were frenetic. Yes, this was before the digital age swung into high gear, but all the digital age pressures I have been describing in this chapter were manifest: an explosion of information coming from around the world; insatiable customers asking for answers *now;* customers asking a level of tactical questions I had never seen before ("Which way does the door open?"); and our support to the warfighters meant that we were coping with an explosion in the number of important customers. The Internet age didn't introduce the concept of information overload—we had it in 1990 with the whole world seized with and producing information on this particular crisis.

Wiley wasted no time with business as usual. He built a new business model for the new situation. From the earliest days of the extended crisis, Wiley was determined to protect our experts from the crush of the most tactical tasks—producing the endless stream of situation reports, answering the most trivial questions. He set up a task force to handle such work. But he held back a small number of experts to do the work that required more expertise and thought. Some of this was, of course, tactical as well. But these analysts developed, honed, and published strategic analysis. And as impressive as they were individually, their dialogue with each other was especially fruitful. They drafted the National Intelligence Estimates and many think pieces. Their intense debates about what Saddam might do guided collection tasking. Their work braced coalition forces for such Iraqi moves as firing Scuds at Israel and flooding the Persian Gulf with oil. And their frequent conversations with the task force analysts also enriched the tactical products. Their work pace was never less than hectic—just as hectic as anything I encountered in the more recent years of the digital age. But thanks to Wiley's organizational approach, they got strategic analysis done.

## Carve Out Time for Tools

Chapter 10 discussed tools that make an analyst's job easier (therefore faster) and tools that will do for the analyst some things he used to have to do for himself (freeing the analyst for more meaningful work). But in this chapter, I have mentioned that analysts complain that it doesn't feel like the tools are helping with the overload of information. Part of this is a shallow response to a feeling: I am busier than ever, overwhelmed even, so the tools aren't helping enough. Part of the dynamic, however, and what I'll discuss here, is that these analysts need more help from their managers aligning priorities.

A leading source of stress and frustration among workers comes when the boss has unrealistic expectations. A leading source of unrealistic expectations by bosses is when they don't really know what it takes to get the job done. Among leaders of analysis, a leading source of unrealistic expectations is that what it takes to get the job done has changed since they were analysts.

Just twenty years ago, analysis was a matter of mastering critical thinking, developing substantive expertise on an issue of concern, analyzing the topic, and delivering the analytic insights to a decision maker. As the information hurricane builds momentum, on top of all the above, analysis is also a matter of mastering the digital age tools of the craft. Again, there is no handling today's information volume without these tools.

This presents the analyst with several challenges. Each tool must be learned to be of service. Some would say, "Well, the tool builders must make their products more intuitive, like Google's search tool, so there is nothing to learn." Believe me, the tool builders know this and strive for such simplicity. But that still misses the point. It is not sufficient that the Google search interface is simple and intuitive. For analysts, connoisseurs of information, even Google's search tool needs to be *learned* in a serious way. Where does it search? What does it miss? How do I get what I need from it? How does it prioritize what it finds? When should I look beyond the top ten, or hundred, hits Google delivers? Similar learning must be invested to determine when to trust Wikipedia or what kind of questions can be handled by the Wolfram Alpha computational knowledge engine. And these are some of the easiest of the digital age tools.

This is serious work and takes time. It also takes trial and error. As I discussed in chapter 10, potentially useful IT tools are being developed at an amazing rate. Many tools require a serious road test to judge their usefulness and much practice to use them well. Yes, sometimes the tool will disappoint you and it will feel like your time has simply been wasted. That comes with the territory. Some of this testing, of course, can be centrally done in a large analytic organization. Having a dedicated team of tool testers is especially good for weeding out the worst tools. But some of the analysts' work is so individual that central testing cannot determine whether it will be a good tool for *me*.

The role of the leader here is to deliver several things. You need to deliver a clear message that this is now a serious part of every analyst's job. Like doctors, they are expected to keep abreast of the tools of their field. Where you can, you must make this part of their job easier, securing technical advisers to help with training (and to screen out the inferior tools). And perhaps most important, you need to reward the work. You need to convey that the activity of learning new tools is not a temporary distraction and not something an analyst is expected to do on her own time. You need to demonstrate that a week trying a tool and then abandoning it is neither a failure nor time wasted. You need to include on every analyst's performance evaluation this requirement: "an expanding mastery of relevant tools."

And you need to remember that part of this effort is to ease the analysts' sense of being overwhelmed. This means you cannot simply add this real work on top of their existing work. Some product deadlines will need to slip. Other products will fall off the bottom of your priority list. Some of you are seduced by a fallacy: if the tool is good, it will make the analyst more efficient, which means the tool will save more time than it takes to learn, which means the analyst actually has more time, so no deadline needs to slip. There are a couple of things wrong with this thinking. First, there is the trial and error I spoke of—not all tools will be acceptable, so the time trying some of them is sunk. Second, some of the tools relieve the analyst of drudge, freeing the analyst for *more meaningful* work but not resulting in *less* work.

The payoff here might seem like a leap of faith, but it will have several manifestations. Analysts will find more relevant information, including information they used to miss, while spending less time in the task of sifting through incoming documents. Analysts will be freed from some low-thought tasks that tools do competently. Analysts will be able to make sense of larger sets of information and a wider array of sources. Analysts will be able to reach customers with information displays that are more clear and persuasive. Analysts will be able to build relevant models—at least if-then logic trees—that will automatically track and flag important indicators. *And your organization's production of useful insights will accelerate.*

A payoff will not be that you and your analysts no longer feel busy. Increasing your production of insights will stoke your customers' appetite for more. But it can be the energizing kind of busy that comes from doing something exciting that people appreciate.

All this can sound like the tools have become more important than the analyst. They are not, and the technophiles among you must not lose sight of this. The most important tool remains the one the analyst carries in his head. The most important cloud is the network of analysts dealing with each other. But the most important supply the analysts consume is information, and the most important thing they produce is information. No mastery of this business is possible without the tools of the information age.

## Grow Experts Faster

This is the third technique to speed up analysis. Experts tend to work more quickly than novices. The master carpenter has tools laid out efficiently, he can grab most without looking, and he works with the confidence that comes from thousands of hours of practice. The master analyst is quick to recognize patterns in situations or to know this situation feels subtly different. The master analyst often has pivotal pieces of evidence in her head, can retrieve other evidence with a few keystrokes, and has that friend in graphics who will produce just the kind of data display she has used successfully with this customer before.

I say experts *tend* to work more quickly because it is not universally true. Every leader of analysts has experienced the expert with speed problems: the expert burned out on his topic; the expert stuck at a work pace that sufficed in 1990 but doesn't suit today's crisis; the expert who refuses to start writing until she has read everything she can find on the topic. I have worked with each of these flawed experts and many more. But on average, a high-performing expert analyst produces valuable insights faster than a high-performing journeyman. So it is relevant to examine whether we can accelerate the process of developing experts as one means of analyzing faster.

I remember CIA Director Mike Hayden once addressing the need to turn new hires into experts at the agency. He endorsed the need, but added, "We have examined how long it takes to produce an expert with fifteen years of experience and it turns out to be about fifteen years." He was referring to the fundamental truth that experience matters and experience takes time. I certainly have met enough "instant experts"—people who claimed to be experts after just a year or two—to know that they don't lack intellect, information, or ideas; rather, they usually lack humility and an intuitive grasp of how things actually work in the world.

But I do believe that there are a few ways to trim Hayden's "fifteen years" down a bit. I'll skip over the obvious but expensive solution of hiring more experts to begin with—if that option is available to you, jump on it.

We did something interesting at CIA several years ago that accelerated one type of analyst development. It began with the recognition that there are two basic types of expertise for any analyst. The first type is the substantive knowledge about the topic. For me as an analyst, for example, this was Middle Eastern military affairs. The second type of expertise is mastery of analytic skills. In 2000, we established a program to expedite acquisition of this second type of expertise. We launched the Career Analyst Program (CAP) to give our new analysts a basic tool kit of analyst capabilities. As CIA's (2007) website describes the program, it "introduces all new employees to the basic thinking, writing, and briefing skills needed for a successful career. Segments include analytic tools, counterintelligence issues, denial and deception analysis, and warning skills." This was much more extensive than the training we had given new analysts previously, and it paid off. I had led the group that had developed and sold the concept of CAP, so I watched its launch closely. After just its first few years, it was quite apparent that it was working. The average analyst at his second anniversary in CIA was demonstrably more capable than was the case before CAP existed. This is just a guess, but I believe we shaved as much as a year off the development of general analytic expertise through this program.

It was an expensive investment. The fact that the program was several months of mandatory full-time training was a dramatic increase over any analytic education we had provided previously. More important, John McLaughlin, the head of CIA's analytic directorate at the time, committed to using some of the directorate's most talented officers to teach CAP—officers who would be missed from our analytic production line. He said he wanted the instructors to be better than those associated with the directorate's previous training. The results were so obviously worth the expense that the directorate soon expanded the model into all its training.

Accelerating the development of *substantive* expertise is also possible but certainly tougher to tackle programmatically. Of all the efforts I have seen, I remain convinced that on-the-job training and time on target matter the most for this type of expertise. If done right, on-the-job training can deepen expertise quickly. Part of doing it right is to consciously *deepen an analyst's learning experience just when he needs it.*

Hank, a senior imagery analyst I worked with, was a master at this and taught me much. He had watched Middle Eastern military developments many more years than I. I also knew (and liked) many other senior analysts who didn't have nearly Hank's impact on me. What did Hank do that they did not?

- Whenever we would discuss some unfolding situation, he would start by talking about what he saw in the latest imagery. I'd be looking at the same imagery, but he consistently saw many details I had missed. Then, without lecturing, he'd tell me why he thought this detail or that was meaningful.

- *How* he thought taught me more than *what* he thought, and he'd always take time to explain it.

- Just as important, he cared what was going on in *my* mind. How did I reach this or that conclusion? This is how he could often detect where I had gone wrong.

- It was always what we refer to today as just-in-time training. We were looking at today's activity. It was concrete, real, of immediate concern, and I was trying to understand it enough to write about it for tomorrow's intelligence publication.

- When we discussed what was likely to happen tomorrow or next month, he would carefully walk me through his analysis. When my projection differed, he'd say, "Well, you could be right, but here's why I think that's less likely."

All this sounds slow—and believe me, Hank's southern roots meant he talked slow—but we did this through countless crises, when neither of us had minutes to spare. Looking back, he taught me a ton, but it came in hundreds of snippets. It wasn't just me who interacted with Hank this way. I know a generation of imagery analysts who still talk about having "learned at Hank's knee."

I mentioned Hank teaching me even during crises. This raises another issue in accelerating the development of expertise: crises are experience incubators. Several factors make them rich in lessons for any analyst. The action loop between the customer and the analyst is shortened. The customer says what he needs, and it is clear that he needs it *now!* So you know quickly whether your analysis met that need. And because events move so quickly, you often know whether your forecasts were right or wrong, useful or irrelevant. Substantively, you learn things that your previous experience might have missed. An example of this for me, something that I learned in a crisis, concerned logistics. I had been doing military analysis for more than a decade when Iraq invaded Kuwait. Suddenly, I had to learn just how many cargo trucks, fuel trucks, and transporters are needed to move an armored division this many miles over that terrain in this time period. I had long known that logistics is critical in military operations, but now I had to learn it in a way that could produce such clear analysis as, "They can be ready to attack in strength along this line in four days—they cannot do it in two."

It is not accidental that so many of the examples I have used in this book come from crises. That first Gulf War was an intense learning experience for me both as a military analyst and as a leader of analysis. Ditto my leadership in counterterrorism after 9/11. The education was so intense that I wanted it for my subordinates as well. Every time there was a crisis somewhere outside of my area in CIA, I would be quick to contribute subordinates to the task force. I'd send analysts and managers. They'd come back exhausted—and smarter.

This chapter is about working at the speed of today's information, but nothing I have discussed for accelerating the development of expertise sounds like an information age solution. Does this twenty-first-century problem have any twenty-first-century solutions? I see nothing transformative out there to develop experts faster, but there are a few things that at least help.

Digestible curated information is available like never before. The first stop on an amazing variety of topics can, of course, be Wikipedia when good enough (facts, analysis, history, opinion) is good enough. But even fresher and more esoteric information is just a few clicks away. If while analyzing Libya in the 1980s I wanted to know, say, how life in Tripoli differs from life in Misurata, I would probably have resigned myself to hours of LexisNexis searching, hoping some journalist had published a relevant press piece in the last decade. Today, I might go to expat-blog.com, enter the search-terms "Tripoli" and "Misurata," and see what turns up that is reasonably current. On the same site, I can even post a question and get a response from someone with on-the-ground experience this week, with amplifications or corrections by another observer. Again, much of this has the just-in-time advantage. That is, when I need it, when my mind is focused on an immediately relevant issue, I can quickly get a dose of background that will deepen my analysis. One of the hardest parts of developing expertise is when you are taking in vast amounts of new information without context. This just-in-time advantage comes with the context of the situation at hand.

Expat-blog.com and Wikipedia are examples of *curated* information. Someone has brought information together from many sources. Some of it is synthesized into a coherent narrative. Some of it simply made the curator's cut and is included (or at least not deleted) because a curator has judged it has some value. But wait! Analysts like their information raw. They don't want someone they don't know/trust pre-digesting it! That is correct and relevant but wrong-headed. Don't think of the info-curator as delivering a take-it-or-leave-it dump of allegations. Think of the curator— even one you don't personally know—as an information ally. If he tells you something useful of which you were unaware, he has *pointed you* to information of potential value. The analyst may still then have to dig for the raw material that the curator uncovered, but it is much easier to find something you now know exists. With today's digital tools and the pointers provided by the curator, you now have a good chance of finding his source material. The good analyst will then evaluate the raw information for herself. And if she cannot find the raw information, the curator needn't be dismissed out of hand. Rather, he can be treated as any other source delivering an allegation second or third hand. The analyst will weigh it, judge it, and decide whether or how to use it, not dismiss it because the source is unproven.

Part of becoming an expert is learning who the curators and other experts are and what they are saying. This, too, has never been easier. Here is a recent example. Because of my research on forecasting, Amazon's curators (actually, curating algorithms) pushed me a suggestion to read *The Predictioneer's Game,* by Bruce Bueno de Mesquita. I had not encountered Dr. Bueno de Mesquita's work before, so I jumped on it (and, of course, I read it on my twenty-first-century e-reader). Another twenty-first-century bit is provided in that book: a link to his website www.predictioneersgame.com, where I can try his prediction model myself. And simply Googling "Bueno de Mesquita" leads me to Moshe Sniedovich's (2011) thoughtful critique of the book in his blog, *Decision-Making under Severe Uncertainty.*

It is easy to see how all this information can be overwhelming, but even the public library always left me with a similar feeling of "so much to read, so little time." Does the twenty-first-century information environment cut in half the time it takes to become expert? I don't think so. Reading Bueno de Mesquita's book took me as long as it would have in 1980. The point is that I can get smarter faster than ever before, perhaps becoming expert in ten or twelve years rather than Hayden's prescribed fifteen, without ever losing the true expert's awareness of how much I don't know.

Let me end this section on accelerating expertise on a cautionary note. In my last few years as a CIA executive, I encountered a surprising challenge in deepening the substantive expertise of our new hires. One day

I was meeting with a large group of young analysts, almost all of them Millennials we had hired in the previous two years. I spoke of my concern that many of our deepest experts were near retirement. I said I wanted these young analysts to do a "Vulcan mind meld" with those folks before they retire. One brave young analyst said, "Yes, you keep saying that and we don't really care for it." I was taken aback, and said, "Oh, I'm sorry. 'Vulcan mind meld' is an old *Star Trek* term, from before you were even born, it means . . . " The analyst cut me off. "We know what it means. But we don't want to be the receptacle for that sacred knowledge. Once I have that degree of expertise, won't I be trapped working on that issue for the rest of my career?"

We need to have an answer for that intrepid young analyst. He speaks for many who are eager to grow, learn, and get ahead in the company but are leery of being pigeonholed. Here is what I would suggest: "David is a world-class nuclear expert who is eligible to retire. He didn't develop that expertise because we tricked him into it. He developed it because he was fascinated by the topic. And he didn't stay on that account because we trapped him. He stayed because he was having an impact. David is doing a job he knows matters. But it has always been his choice, and whether to stay or leave is his choice. We can only impart some of David's knowledge to you if you are interested. If you are, and we do, I'm betting you will see some of what got David hooked on it. But as in so much of life, learning tends more to expand your options than narrow them." Those would be my words as a leader of analysts today. More important, my deeds—my decisions as a personnel manager—would have to show that I am not shackling any analyst to an account he feels is a ball and chain.

## A Fourth Way?

I said I see three ways to speed analysis. Investing in strategic analysis, carving out time for tools, and accelerating the process of growing experts—each of these will help your organization produce quality analysis more quickly. Each of these is an investment involving low risk and real return.

But there is a fourth way, one that sets many analytic leaders' teeth on edge. Sharply reduce editing. Get out of the way of your analysts and let them routinely communicate directly with your most important customers, without the filter of your editing. The effect is not so much to speed up *analysis*. The principal effect is to accelerate the *production* of analysis, getting raw insights from the analysts' brains into the customers' more quickly.

This is certainly a risky proposition, and I'd resist dumping editing altogether. When I worked as an analyst, the editing process taught me my craft. When my supervisors edited a draft, they could climb into my mind, seeing how I thought, what I knew and what I did not, the weaknesses in my reasoning, and the effectiveness of my communications. The best of my editors were no-nonsense types who would say things like, "That's a bullshit assertion! You haven't supported it with anything." Or, "You still haven't told the reader why he should care!" This taught me my craft, taught me to respect the reader, and taught me an intellectual humility I desperately needed. Beyond the education I received from my best editors, I appreciated their quality control.

As a manager, my appreciation of editing even grew. There were many times I would be the second reviewer in an editorial chain. I would see an analyst's draft after it had been first reviewed by the analyst's direct supervisor. But on occasion, the press of business might require that we skip that first supervisor, so that I would be the first to review that same analyst's draft. Frequently, the quality simply would not be what I was used to seeing. Without the supervisor's first scrub, I was seeing weaknesses in logic or presentation that would remind me of the drafts I used to see when I was the line supervisor.

But there are certainly diminishing returns in multiple levels of review. The PDB, our premier daily intelligence product, had an astounding eight layers of review when I retired! A friend who had worked on the PDB staff for years addressed the phenomenon. He said that they had studied the impact of multiple layers of review and conclusively shown that each layer improved the draft, but each layer "only moved it half the distance to the goal line." Besides his point about the diminishing value of multiple layers of review, he was making the profound point that there is no such thing as a perfect draft (the goal). Because every editor can find some way to "improve" a draft, the question becomes, "When do you let the draft go?"

Eight layers of editing certainly is extreme. It is driven by the high stakes of a publication that might trigger presidential action. But whatever is the review norm for your analytic organization, consider cutting it in half. Even if your organization only edits a piece once, allow the editor half the time she normally spends on a draft. Just as important, give your reviewers tight deadlines, so no draft marinates in an in-box. And put a strict limit on the number of times a supervisor is allowed to re-review the same paper. I have seen supervisors send drafts and redrafts back to an analyst half a dozen times until he was satisfied that it was good enough to publish. That is a reviewer who won't let it go until it is good enough but cannot articulate what "good enough" is—or a reviewer lacking the spine to simply kill a piece that falls far short of quality standards.

Cutting review in half will demonstrably increase the mistakes that you publish. That scares many leaders. But it is important to weigh also the cost of a sclerotic editing process when your customers need analysis fast.

You can also mitigate the risk of publishing mistakes by focusing your editing on eliminating mistakes. Eliminating mistakes is one of two things editing does. A good editor catches mistakes, not just in spelling and punctuation but in logic, in flow, and in argumentation. A good analyst learns not to make the same mistake twice. The second thing editing does is help make the draft more effective, a story better told. Catching mistakes is a craft. Storytelling is an art. Editing to eliminate mistakes is faster. Focusing the edit on this part of the task might reduce the risk of publishing mistakes to an acceptable level, while still accelerating the production of analysis. Doing so would also require accepting that not every analytic piece needs to be literature and accepting that not every piece will address every conceivable follow-on question a customer might have.

These are business decisions. We are talking about choices and trade offs. No decision to risk a decline in product quality should be made lightly. As with so many other issues raised in this book, the thing is to find a balance that feels right for your organization and customers. Your product line might have some items that read like the best articles in *The New Yorker,* others that read like a piece from the sports page of a college paper, and others that read like the crime page in a local weekly. Speed editing, even no editing, might be appropriate for one of these and not the others.

# Nurture Your Inner Opportunist

Much of what we have been talking about in this chapter can sound like *coping* with the information hurricane. But don't settle for just coping. To thrive as a twenty-first-century leader of analysis, be an *opportunist.* The information environment offers opportunities that should make your mouth water. There is a bounty of information out there, yours for the taking.

Where are the opportunities? Oh, there are several ports-of-call worth frequent visits. Beyond the ports which have served you so well over the years, and might still be the richest, your analysts are now discovering new ones. There are bits of info previously unavailable. A Libyan with a laptop posts a few blog paragraphs about developments this week in Misurata. A Haitian with a smartphone tweets that riots just jolted Port au Prince. Ayatollah Khamenei's website (yes, he has one) announces something unexpected.

Beyond such new sources of *bits* of information, people—and algorithms—are doing things with *masses* of information for you. A UN economist might post six years of data on energy use in emerging economies. A sentiment mapper might show a trend of middle-class anxiety in a country that otherwise looks healthy. A data miner might publish a correlation between prepaid phone card sales and sectarian violence in Congo.

The timid look at all this as overwhelming. The opportunists see all this as a bounty. The timid see the explosion of information purveyors as a distraction at best and competition at worst. The opportunists see those purveyors as unpaid suppliers. The timid worry about being upstaged by someone with a sexy new approach to analysis. The opportunists hungrily watch others test new approaches and jump on the approaches worth adopting. The timid squirm about not being able to keep up with the information hurricane. The opportunist says, "There is information we are missing, and next year we will find more than we use today, but today we are using more than ever before, today we are doing better analysis than ever before—today we are providing more useful insights than our predecessors ever thought possible."

The speed of information requires nimbleness, initiative, and local solutions to complex analytic problems. The speed of information requires that analysts network together fluidly and at their own initiative. Your job as leader is to encourage that and to eliminate impediments to it.

A last point for the opportunist: be bold enough to flaunt it. Show your customers that your organization thrives in the information hurricane. Show them that your crew is finding bits of information that everyone else missed. Show them that you are making sense of the valuable fragments others dismissed as trivial. Not only do you have the happiest, most productive, most insightful analysts, but also their products contain rare gems and exotic spices.

## KEY THEMES

To deal productively with today's information hurricane, you'll need to remind yourself that you are its beneficiary, not its victim. As the leader of analysts, you will be held responsible to process more information than can be processed, to connect more dots than can be connected, and to consume more than can be digested. The sheer volume contains mostly low-grade ore and you will curse it. But your analysts also will be able to generate more insights than ever before, and it is a great time to lead this enterprise.

Push back against some natural temptations that come with information glut:

- The temptation to fixate on just the best sources of information, "the good stuff." Sometimes the nugget you need will be hidden in an extremist's bloviating blog, in the dirtiest of unfiltered data, or in the desperate Tunisian who just set himself on fire.

- The temptation to "go tactical." When the information comes in volume, there is something interesting to comment on every day. In this environment, it takes a force of will to widen the analysts' aperture, to pull them back to see the forest.

- The temptation to conclude that if you and your analysts just work hard enough, you won't miss anything.

Build an information strategy to deal with the information relevant to your particular line of study.

- Identify the best, most reliable sources. Use them every day.

- Identify the information that is useful only occasionally. Make sure someone is paying attention to that.

- Analyze where useful information should be available or might be acquired with some work.

- Make sure someone is scanning for information you'd be held responsible for but isn't on the narrow topics your analysts are currently focused on.

With the accelerating speed of information, we need to think about whether we can accelerate analysis. Major acceleration may be just a decade away with the drugs, devices, and brain-machine partnerships that are being developed. For the first time, these no longer sound like science fiction to me. In the meantime, I see three ways to speed analysis, at least modestly.

- Make time for strategic analysis. Once your analysts understand issues strategically, even their tactical analysis comes more quickly. And many time-wasting rabbit holes are avoided.

- Make time for new tools. Information technology already is giving analysts the ability to find information, model scenarios, and use data much more quickly. More tools will come along. Just as you expect your doctor to keep up with the advances in medical science, make it part of your analysts' job to learn and experiment with such tools.

- Grow experts faster. I've seen the development of analysts be serendipitous and ad hoc, and I've seen it be thoughtful. The latter makes use of some of your most precious experts to train and mentor their juniors. And it pushes analysts into situations (such as crises) that incubate expertise. This is all expensive for any analytic enterprise, but the payoffs are real.

Finally, be realistic about what you need to deliver in the information hurricane. You can't take advantage of every piece of useful information. You can't be the first to take advantage of every new tool. But you can be better at all this than your competitors.

# Conclusion

· · · · · · · · · · · · · · · · · · · · · · · · · · · · · · · · · · · · · · · · · · · · · · · · · · · · · · · · · · ·

Yes, that's a lot. From understanding your role to understanding your analysts, from enabling a flow of insights to exercising effective quality control, from attending to what your customer wants to delivering what your customer needs, from timeless rules of reason to ever-changing tools of technology, you have a lot to attend to. You're a coach, cheerleader, curator, editor, teacher, midwife, enforcer, and visionary. You're a strategist and a tactician. In short, you're a leader.

How did I do it all—and do it effectively? Well, I didn't. The overachiever in me never got used to that. I look back at my years of leading analysis, from supervisor to executive, and I am filled with pride—and embarrassment. I kick myself for how many things I had to learn the hard way, how many mistakes I made, and how many stupidities I uttered. And I take comfort in the conviction that on balance, I helped more than I hurt. I was right more than I was wrong. And was lucky more than I deserved. No leader is brilliant at everything. A good leader is pretty good at the things that matter the most, most of the time.

The things that served me best as an analyst often helped me as a leader: to keep an open mind; to know that I am probably wrong about something; to be always learning; and to never lose sight of the fact that my best work is only evident in the effectiveness of others.

The analyst's discipline of focusing on the right question also served me well. And as a leader, the question of supreme importance is this: *Is this working?* The answer usually is yes or no. Are we producing useful insights or not? Are our customers hooked on our service or not? Are talented analysts drawn to us or leaving? Do they trust *me*, and do they think I trust them? Does our culture discourage lazy thinking? On analytic issues, are we making progress or not? In forecasting, is our batting average healthy? In warning, are we catalyzing useful action? The answers to such questions might be difficult to face, but they are not hard to come by.

Whenever the answer to such questions is "no," of course, complexity rears its head again. Corrective action must be taken—MUST be taken—but many corrective actions have negative side effects. Investing much more of my time with customers, for example, would mean less time with my subordinates. Pushing the quality pendulum might stifle creativity. Increasing our analytic flexibility (to respond to unforeseen crises) might come at the expense of our ambition to deepen our analytic expertise. In our organizations everything important is connected to everything else. The organization that seemed like a machine, subject to Newtonian physics, looks more like a living body in which physics and chemistry and biology all come into play.

And it is here where I learned to embrace a word I was trained to expunge as an analyst: *feel*. Does this feel right? Does it feel like I have enough information to make this decision? Does it feel like I must act now?

Feelings matter in every human relationship, and you only lead humans. Much of the time I felt like I had to play psychologist, for which I had no training, probing the feelings of others. My subordinates, seniors, and customers were each individuals with complex needs, motivations, and outlooks, and I needed to guess how to deal effectively with each. Beyond individuals, I was also regularly dealing with groups. Tribal and cultural behaviors were on full display, some endearing and some destructive. Group dynamics called on me to play anthropologist, for which again I had no training. To some extent, my training as an analyst again served me well; I accepted that the truth is complex, individuals are complex and groups even more so, and talking to them is the best way to learn what is in their heads. But to an extent uncomfortable for this analyst, I had to pay attention to whether it *feels* like this relationship is working.

A theme of this book has been *balance*. So much of what you do as a leader of people who think for a living requires that you maintain a healthy balance between competing needs. Again, complexity. As difficult as it might be to choose a desirable balance, say between breadth and depth or between speed and quality, the issue is even more complex. In the real world, balance is a 3-D state, not 2-D. It's not a teeter-totter on which just two things are involved; it's an organism in which adjusting the balance between two elements can throw off their balance with a third. Imbalance can begin as a tip in any direction and can hurt your entire effort. Here, my strength as an analyst again might get in the way. Here, I will be tempted to overanalyze, collect more data, model more consequences.

Well, here is another area where you will have to feel. Does my analytic enterprise *feel* in balance—three-dimensional balance? Experience taught me that a healthy balance doesn't really feel like anything. But *imbalance* does. It is noticeable. If you've ever balanced a broomstick by its tip, you did it by making tiny corrections as soon as you felt a slight lurch in any direction. You became sensitive to that slight feeling, reacted to it instinctively, and adjusted before it got serious.

In leading analysis, what is serious imbalance? A negative answer to any of the yes-no questions I presented above (e.g., Are we producing useful insights or not? Does our warning catalyze useful action?) is a sign of dangerous imbalance—imbalance you will feel and feel desperate to correct. But you needn't wait for such extreme signs to check your balance. As with the broomstick, usually a little imbalance can be fixed with a little correction. You can find early indicators of trouble if you build a rapport with those precious subordinates and customers who will be brutally honest with you. For some of the things I talked about in chapter 3, "Shaping the

Environment," and chapter 9, "Analysis as a Business," you can set up systems to monitor indicators—360-degree feedback and customer surveys are easy examples. Digital data about customer clicks and time spent on your products is gold. Being sensitive to such indicators does not mean you have to make a correction for every bit of negative feedback you get. Rather, it means you are actively paying attention to the health of your enterprise, deciding when to act and when to simply keep an eye on something.

If you collect and listen to the early indicators of imbalance, you will find that corrective actions often can be painless. A simple note to the workforce, a meeting with the right individuals, waiving one of your rules—any of these might do the trick. When you are sensitive to imbalance, you learn to avoid overcorrection. You also learn not to procrastinate to take action. Rather, you diagnose quickly, choose your action, and then adjust as you go along. Your instincts will improve with experience. Your analyst training that the truth often lies deeper will serve you well, avoiding shallow diagnosis of the problem. But you will have to act before your inner analyst is confident that the truth has been found.

Many of us get so absorbed by the pace of business and the momentum of what we are trying to do that we don't pay enough attention to the early indicators of imbalance. When we receive negative indicators, our instinct first is to debate their validity and second is to request more data. Committing to be open to such information is easier if you embrace three assertions:

- I am missing something important in my organization.

- Not all my actions are brilliant.

- I cannot define reality by myself.

Balance would be difficult enough if you were standing still. But a theme of this book has been that the very craft of analysis is moving, expanding, evolving. In the face of all this change, it helps to reconnect with what is constant: the *purpose* of analysis. As I've said, Jack Davis noted decades ago that the purpose of analysis is "to narrow the range of uncertainty" for those who must decide. The tools, techniques, and approaches used in analysis have expanded tremendously since he said this, but that purpose of analysis remains the same.

And like a spinning ice skater spotting a fixed point to keep his balance, the leader of analysis can use this constant purpose as a focus of stability. It provides a binary check on your unit's work in general and on each analytic product: Are we—or is this product—narrowing the range of uncertainty for our customer? Again, the answer is usually a simple yes or no. And if the answer is frequently negative, it is a sign that balance is off. If everyone in your team keeps an eye on this core purpose, they self-correct, helping the balance of the whole.

As their leader, you don't need to be perfect. Get it right most of the time, on the things that matter most, and the people you are privileged to lead will be better than they were. Your customers will conclude they need your product. In a business where you simply cannot get everything right, avoid every surprise, or anticipate every threat, you will still be able to conclude, *Yes, this is working!*

# Bibliography

Abrashoff, Capt. D. Michael. 2012. *It's Your Ship: Management Techniques from the Best Damn Ship in the Navy.* 10th ed. New York, NY: Grand Central.

Acerbi, Alberto, Vasileios Lampos, Philip Garnett, and R. Alexander Bently. 2013. "The Expression of Emotions in 20th Century Books." *PLOS ONE.* http://www.plosone.org/article/info:doi/10.1371/journal.pone.0059030.

Anderson, Chris. 2011. "Film School." *WIRED* 19, no. 1: 112–17.

Anthony, Scott. 2012. "The Four Worst Innovation Assassins." *Harvard Business Review,* April 18. https://hbr.org/2012/04/the-four-worst-innovation-assa.

Ariely, Dan. 2008. *Predictably Irrational: The Hidden Forces that Shape Our Decisions.* New York, NY: HarperCollins.

Ball, James. 2013. "Nate Silver: 'Prediction is a really important tool, it's not a game.'" *The Guardian,* May 3. https://www.theguardian.com/world/2013/may/03/nate-silver-prediction-important-tool

Bilton, Nick. 2013. "Disruptions: Data Without Context Tells a Misleading Story." *New York Times,* February 24. http://bits.blogs.nytimes.com/2013/02/24/disruptions-google-flu-trends-shows-problems-of-big-data-without-context/

Bruce, James B. 2008. "Making Analysis More Reliable: Why Epistemology Matters to Intelligence." In *Analyzing Intelligence: Origins, Obstacles, and Innovations,* edited by Roger Z. George and James B. Bruce. Washington, DC: Georgetown University Press. Kindle edition.

Buckingham, Marcus, and Curt Coffman. 1999. *First, Break All the Rules.* New York, NY: Simon and Schuster.

Bueno de Mesquita, Bruce. 2009. *The Predictioneer's Game.* New York, NY: Random House. Kindle edition.

Burton, Robert. 2008. *On Being Certain: Believing You Are Right Even When You're Not.* London, UK: St Martin's Griffin.

Bush, George. 1998. *A World Transformed.* With Brent Scowcroft. New York, NY: Alfred A. Knopf.

Butler, Declan. 2013. "When Google Got Flu Wrong." *Nature.com,* February 13. http://www.nature.com/news/when-google-got-flu-wrong-1.12413.

Catmull, Ed. 2014. *Creativity, Inc: Overcoming the Unseen Forces that Stand in the Way of True Inspiration.* New York, NY: Random House.

CIA (Central Intelligence Agency). 2007. "Training Resources." CIA Intelligence & Analysis. https://www.cia.gov/offices-of-cia/intelligence-analysis/training-resources.html

CIA (Central Intelligence Agency). 2009. *The Work of a Nation:* The Center of Intelligence. https://www.cia.gov/library/publications/resources/the-work-of-a-nation/86402%20Factbook-low.pdf

Chabris, Christopher, and Daniel Simons. 2009. *The Invisible Gorilla.* New York, NY: Random House.

Collins, James C. 2001. *Good to Great: Why Some Companies Make the Leap and Others Don't.* New York, NY: HarperCollins.

Collins, James C., and Jerry I. Porras. 2002. *Built to Last: Successful Habits of Visionary Companies.* New York, NY: HarperCollins.

Commission on the Intelligence Capabilities of the United States Regarding Weapons of Mass Destruction. 2005. *Report to the President.* http://govinfo.library.unt.edu/wmd/report/report.html#overview.

Cooper Ramo, Joshua. 2009. *The Age of the Unthinkable: Why the New World Disorder Constantly Surprises Us and What We Can Do About It.* New York, NY: Little, Brown and Company.

Davis, Jack. 2008. "Why Bad Things Happen to Good Analysts." In *Analyzing Intelligence: Origins, Obstacles, and Innovations,* edited by Roger Z. George and James B. Bruce. Washington, DC: Georgetown University Press. Kindle edition.

Dennett, Daniel C. 2013. *Intuition Pumps and Other Tools for Thinking.* New York, NY: W. W. Norton.

De Pree, Max. 2004. *Leadership Is an Art.* New York, NY: Currency.

Domingos, Pedro. 2015. *The Master Algorithm: How the Quest for the Ultimate Learning Machine Will Remake Our World.* New York, NY: Basic Books.

Dyer, Jeff, Hal Gregersen, and Clayton Christensen. 2011. *The Innovator's DNA: Mastering the Five Skills of Disruptive Innovators.* Brighton, MA: Harvard Business.

Ellenberg, Jordan. 2015. *How Not to Be Wrong: The Power of Mathematical Thinking.* New York, NY: Penguin Books.

Ferren, Bran. 2008. "Leadership Speaker Series, Harvard Center for Public Leadership." *YouTube* video, 1:55:34. http://www.youtube.com/watch?v=GxbB18QoYO4.

The Flu Trends Team. 2015. "The Next Chapter for Flu Trends." *Google AI Blog,* August 20. https://ai.googleblog.com/2015/08/the-next-chapter-for-flu-trends.html.

Frick, Walter. 2015. "What Research Tells Us About Making Accurate Predictions." *Harvard Business Review.* https://hbr.org/2015/02/what-research-tells-us-about-making-accurate-predictions.

Gates, Robert M. 1996. *From the Shadows.* New York, NY: Simon & Schuster.

George, Roger Z., and James B. Bruce, eds. 2008. *Analyzing Intelligence: Origins, Obstacles, and Innovations.* Washington, DC: Georgetown University Press.

Ginsberg, Jeremy, Matthew H. Mohebbi, Rajan Patel, Lynnette Brammer, Mark S. Smolinski, and Larry Brilliant. 2009. *Detecting Influenza Epidemics Using Search Engine Query Data.* http://static.googleusercontent.com/media/research.google.com/en/us/archive/papers/detecting-influenza-epidemics.pdf.

Gleick, James. 2011. *The Information: A History, A Theory, a Flood.* New York, NY: Pantheon Books.

Goffee, Rob, and Gareth Jones. 2007. "Leading Clever People." *Harvard Business Review,* March: 72–79.

Goodell, Thaxter L. 2002. "Cratology Pays Off." *Studies on Intelligence,* November: 19–28.

Google Flu Trends Data. 2015. https://www.google.org/flutrends/about/.

Hackman, J. Richard. 2011. *Collaborative Intelligence: Using Teams to Solve Hard Problems.* San Francisco, CA: Berrett-Koehler.

Hawkins, Jeff. 2004. *On Intelligence.* New York, NY: Times Books-Henry Holt and Co.

Hayden, General Michael V. (2007). "Statement for the Record to the Senate Select Committee for Intelligence." *Central Intelligence Agency.* https://www.cia.gov/news-information/speeches-testimony/2007/statement_011107.htm

Heath, Chip, and Dan Heath. 2010. *Switch: How to Change When Change Is Hard.* New York, NY: Broadway Books.

Heath, Chip, and Dan Heath. 2013. *Decisive: How to Make Better Choices in Life and Work.* New York, NY: Crown Business. Kindle edition.

Helgeson, Sally. 1990. *The Female Advantage: Women's Way of Leadership.* New York, NY: Currency.

Herbert A. Simon. 2018. In *Wikiquote.* https://en.wikiquote.org/wiki/Herbert_A._Simon.

Heuer, Richards J., Jr. 1999. *Psychology of Intelligence Analysis*. Washington, DC: Center for the Study of Intelligence.

Heuer, Richards J., Jr., and Randolph H. Pherson. 2010. *Structured Analytic Techniques for Intelligence Analysis*. Washington, DC: CQ Press.

Hoffman, Bryce G. 2012. *American Icon: Alan Mulally and the Fight to Save Ford Motor Company*. New York, NY: Crown Business.

Horowitz, Ben. 2014. *The Hard Thing about Hard Things: Building a Business When There Are No Easy Answers*. New York, NY: HarperCollins.

Howe, Jeff. 2008. *Crowdsourcing: Why the Power of the Crowd Is Driving the Future of Business*. New York, NY: Crown Business.

Johansson, Frans. 2006. *The Medici Effect*. Boston, MA: Harvard Business School Press.

Johnson, Steven. 2010. *Where Good Ideas Come From: The Natural History of Innovation*. New York, NY: Riverhead Books.

Kahneman, Daniel. 2011. *Thinking Fast and Slow*. New York, NY: Farrar, Straus and Giroux.

Kandel, Eric. 2006. *In Search of Memory: The Emergence of a New Science of Mind*. New York, NY: W. W. Norton & Co.

Kerr, James. 2013. *Legacy: 15 Lessons in Leadership*. London, UK: Constable.

"Kevin Kelly and Steven Johnson on Where Ideas Come From." 2010. *Wired* 18, no. 10. https://www.wired.com/2010/09/mf-kellyjohnson.

Kidder, Rushworth. 1995. *How Good People Make Tough Choices: Resolving the Dilemmas of Ethical Living*. New York, NY: HarperCollins.

Kidder, Rushworth. 2005. *Moral Courage: Taking Action When Your Values Are Put to the Test*. New York, NY: HarperCollins.

Klein, Gary. 2003. *The Power of Intuition: How to Use Your Gut Feelings to Make Better Decisions at Work*. New York, NY: Currency Books.

Klein, Gary. 2013. *Seeing What Others Don't: The Remarkable Ways We Gain Insights*. New York, NY: PublicAffairs.

Kotter, John P. 1999. *John P. Kotter on What Leaders Really Do*. Brighton, MA: Harvard Business.

Krames, Jeffrey A. 2002. *The Jack Welch Lexicon of Leadership*. New York, NY: McGraw-Hill.

Lambeth, Benjamin S. 1984. *Moscow's Lessons from the 1982 Lebanon Air War*. Washington, DC: Rand.

Leetaru, Kalev H. 2011. "Culturomics 2.0: Forecasting Large-Scale Human Behavior Using Global News Media Tone in Time and Space." *First Monday* 16, no. 9. http://firstmonday.org/ojs/index.php/fm/article/view/3663/3040

Levy, Steven. 2011. *In the Plex: How Google Thinks, Works, and Shapes Our Lives*. New York, NY: Simon and Schuster.

Levy, Steven. 2012. "The Rise of the Robot Reporter." *Wired,* May 2012.

Logan, David, John King, and Halee Fischer-Wright. 2008. *Tribal Leadership: Leveraging Natural Groups to Build a Thriving Organization*. New York, NY: HarperCollins.

Lohr, Steve. 2012. "The Age Of Big Data." *New York Times Sunday Review,* February 11. http://www.nytimes.com/2012/02/12/sunday-review/big-datas-impact-in-the-world.html.

Lomas, Natasha. 2016. "Meet Articoolo, the Robot Writer with Content for Brains." *TechCrunch.com.* https://techcrunch.com/2016/06/28/meet-articoolo-the-robot-writer-with-content-for-brains/.

Lotan, Gilad. 2011. "Breaking Bin Laden: Visualizing the Power of a Single Tweet." *SocialFlow,* May 6. http://blog.socialflow.com/post/5246404319/breaking-bin-laden-visualizing-the-power-of-a-single.

Lowenthal, Mark M. 2009. *Intelligence: From Secrets to Policy.* 4th ed. Washington, DC: CQ Press. Kindle edition.

Lundin, Stephen C., Harry Paul, and John Christensen. 2000. *Fish! A Proven Way to Boost Morale and Improve Results.* Westport, CT: Hyperion.

MacEachin, Douglas. 2007. "The Record Versus the Charges: CIA Assessments of the Soviet Union." *CIA Center for the Studies of Intelligence.* https://www.cia.gov/library/center-for-the-study-of-intelligence/kent-csi/vol40no5/html/v40i5a08p.htm

MacKenzie, Gordon. 1998. *Orbiting the Giant Hairball: A Corporate Fool's Guide to Surviving with Grace.* New York, NY: Viking Penguin.

Mang, Charles C. 1998. *The Leadership Wisdom of Jesus: Practical Lessons for Today.* San Francisco, CA: Berrett-Koehler.

McChrystal, Stanley. 2015. *Team of Teams: New Rules of Engagement for a Complex World.* New York, NY: Penguin.

McGregor, Jena. 2015. "The XPrize Founders How-To Guide for Going after Big, Bold Goals." *Washington Post,* February 19. http://www.washingtonpost.com/blogs/on-leadership/wp/2015/02/19/the-xprize-founders-how-to-guide-for-going-after-big-bold-goals.

Medina, Carmen. 2008. "The New Analysis." In *Analyzing Intelligence: Origins, Obstacles, and Innovations,* edited by Roger Z. George and James B. Bruce. Washington, DC: Georgetown University Press. Kindle edition.

Medina, John. 2008. *Brain Rules: 12 Principles for Surviving and Thriving at Work, Home, and School.* Seattle, WA: Pear Press.

Mellers, Barbara, Eric Stone, Pavel Atanasov, Nick Rohrbaugh, S. Emlen Metz, Lyle Ungar, Michael M. Bishop, Michael Horowitz, Ed Merkle, and Philip Tetlock. 2015. "The Psychology of Intelligence Analysis: Drivers of Prediction Accuracy in World Politics."

*Journal of Experimental Psychology: Applied.* http://dx.doi.org/10.1037/xap0000040.

Milley, Anne H. (2010). *Analytics: The Beauty of Diversity.* Video, Predictive Analytics World Conference, Washington, DC. http://www.rmportal.performedia.com/node/1345.

Morell, Michael J. 2008. "Strategic Intent of the Directorate of Intelligence: Analytic Insight, Anytime, Wherever Needed" (vision statement, CIA, October 16, 2008).

Mudd, Philip. 2015. *The HEAD Game: High Efficiency Analytic Decision Making and the Art of Solving Complex Problems Quickly.* New York, NY: Liveright.

National Commission on Terrorist Attacks Upon the United States. 2004. *The 9/11 Commission Report: Final Report.* Washington, DC: Government Printing Office. http://www.9-11commission.gov/report.

National Guard Bureau. 2000. "Operation Desert Shield/Desert Storm Timeline." *DoD News,* August 8. http://archive.defense.gov/news/newsarticle.aspx?id=45404

National Intelligence Council. 2012. *Global Trends 2030: Alternative Worlds.* www.dni.gov/files/documents/GlobalTrends_2030.pdf.

Olson, James M. 2006. *Fair Play: The Moral Dilemmas of Spying.* Lincoln, NE: Potomac Books.

Perkins, Dennis N. T., 2000. *Leading at the Edge: Leadership Lessons from the Extraordinary Saga of Shackleton's Antarctic Expedition.* New York, NY: AMACOM.

Pillar, Paul. 2011. *Intelligence and U.S. Foreign Policy.* New York, NY: Columbia University Press.

Pole, Andrew. 2010. "How Target Gets the Most out of Its Guest Data to Improve Marketing ROI." Predictive Analytics World Conference, October 19–20, 2010. http://rmportal.performedia.com/node/1373.

Provost, Foster, and Tom Fawcett. 2013. *Data Science for Business: What You Need to Know about Data Mining and Data-Analytic Thinking*. Sebastopol, CA: O'Reilly Books. Kindle edition.

Reichenbach, Hans. 1968. *The Rise of Scientific Philosophy*. Berkeley: University of California Press.

Rosling, Hans. 2006. *The Best Stats You've Ever Seen*. TED video, 19:46. http://www.ted.com/talks/hans_rosling_shows_the_best_stats_you_ve_ever_seen.html

Ryan, Kathleen D., and Daniel K. Oestreic. 1998. *Driving Fear out of the Workplace: Creating the High-Trust, High-Performance Organization*. San Francisco, CA: Jossey-Bass.

Sandberg, Sheryl. 2013. *Lean In: Women, Work, and the Will to Lead*. New York, NY: Alfred A. Knopf.

Shirky, Clay. 2010. *Cognitive Surplus: Creativity and Generosity in a Connected Age*. New York, NY: Penguin. Kindle edition.

Siegel, Eric. 2013. *Predictive Analytics: The Power to Predict Who Will Click, Buy, Lie, or Die*. Hoboken, NJ: John Wiley & Sons. Kindle edition.

Silver, Nate. 2012. *The Signal and the Noise: Why So Many Predictions Fail, but Some Don't*. New York, NY: Penguin Books.

Silver, Nate. 2016. "Who Will Win the Presidency?" *FiveThirtyEight*. https://projects.fivethirtyeight.com/2016-election-forecast/

Simons, Daniel. 2007. "Inattentional Blindness." *Scholarpedia* 2, no. 5: 3244. http://www.scholarpedia.org/article/Inattentional_blindness.

Sims, Peter. 2011. *Little Bets: How Breakthrough Ideas Emerge from Small Discoveries*. New York, NY: Free Press.

Sinek, Simon. 2009. *Start with Why: How Great Leaders Inspire Everyone to Take Action*. New York, NY: Portfolio/Penguin.

Sniedovich, Moshe. 2011. "Criticism of Bueno de Mesquita's Theories." *Decision-Making under Severe Uncertainty* (blog). http://decision-making.moshe-online.com/criticism_of_bueno_de_mesquita.html

Stefansen, Christian. 2013. "Flu Trends Updates Model to Help Estimate Flu Levels in the US." *The Official Google.org Blog*, October 29. http://blog.google.org/2013/10/flu-trends-updates-model-to-help.html.

Stefansen, Christian. 2014. "Google Flu Trends Gets a Brand New Engine." *Google Research Blog*, October 31. http://googleresearch.blogspot.com/2014/10/google-flu-trends-gets-brand-new-engine.html.

Stone, Brad. 2013. *The Everything Store: Jeff Bezos and the Age of Amazon*. New York, NY: Little, Brown and Co.

Surowiecki, James. 2004. *The Wisdom of Crowds: Why the Many Are Smarter than the Few and the Collective Wisdom Shapes Business, Economics, Societies, and Nations*. New York, NY: Random House.

Taleb, Nassim Nicholas. 2007. *The Black Swan: The Impact of the Highly Improbable*. New York, NY: Random House.

Taleb, Nassim Nicholas. 2012. *Antifragile*. New York, NY: Random House.

Taleb, Nassim Nicholas. 2013. "The Fourth Quadrant: A Map of the Limits of Statistics." In *Thinking*, edited by John Brockman. New York, NY: HarperCollins.

Tenet, George. 2007. *At the Center of the Storm: My Years at the CIA*. With Bill Harlow. New York, NY: HarperCollins.

Tetlock, Philip. 2005. *Expert Political Judgment: How Good Is It? How Can We Know?* Princeton, NJ: Princeton University Press.

Tetlock, Philip, and Dan Gardner. 2015. *Superforecasting: The Art and Science of Prediction*. New York, NY: Crown Business.

Tolstoy, Leo. 2010. *War and Peace*. n.p.: Superior Formatting. Kindle edition.

US Government. 2009. *A Tradecraft Primer: Structured Analytic Techniques for Improving Intelligence Analysis.* Washington, DC: GPO. https://www.cia.gov/library/center-for-the-study-of-intelligence/csi-publications/books-and-monographs/Tradecraft%20Primer-apr09.pdf.

Watts, Duncan. 2011. *Everything is Obvious\* (\*Once You Know the Answer).* New York, NY: Crown Business.

Yardley, Jim. 2012. *Brave Dragons.* New York, NY: Alfred A. Knopf. Kindle edition.

Zenger, John, and Joseph Folkman. 2009. *The Extraordinary Leader: Turning Good Managers into Great Leaders.* New York, NY: McGraw-Hill.

Zinni, Tony. 2009. *Leading the Charge: Leadership Lessons from the Battlefield to the Boardroom.* London, UK: Palgrave MacMillan.

Zinni, Tony. 2014. *Before the First Shots Are Fired.* London, UK: Palgrave McMillan.

# Index

creative desperation in, 88
defined, 76
failure-aversion limitation, 82
inhibiting factors, 82
negative outcome, 89
study guide, 94–95
See also Creative analysis
Intellectual bullies, 23
*Intelligence* (Lowenthal), 133
Intelligence Advanced Research Projects
Activity (IARPA), 121
Intuition:
in expert analysis, 66–67
*versus* lazy thinking, 8
*Invisible Gorilla, The* (Simons &
Chabris), 104
Irritants of analysts, 20–28, 32–33, 66

Johnson, S., 79
Joseph, Bob, 158

Kahneman, D., 120
Kelly, K., 93
Kidder, R., 136
Klein, G., 41–42, 66, 87–89

Lake, Anthony, 126
Lazy thinking, 7–9
*Leadership Is an Art* (De Pree), 153
Leading analysis:
analytic fluency, 4–5
Black Box information, 7
expert analysis role, 8
"good-enough" analysis, 10–11
intuition, 8
lazy thinking, 7–9
managerial failure, 1–2
manalyst approach, 2
process management, 5–7
responsibilities of, 4–7
standards, 9–11
study guide, 12
substantive analysis, 1–2, 4–5
thorough analysis, 11
uberanalyst approach, 2–3
Link charts, 180
Liquid-network approach, 84, 86
*Little Bets* (Sims), 84, 93

Long-term forecasting, 113
Lowenthal, M., 133

Manalyst approach, 2
McLaughlin, John, 210–211
Medina, J., 46–47
Meeting agendas, 46
Megatrends, 117–119
Military conflict predictions,
110–111, 114
Miscik, Jami, 164–165
Misquoted analysis, 23
Mistake elimination *vs.* insight
generation, 40–44
Monday morning quarterbacks, 25–26

Narrative Science, 183
National Intelligence Council, 117–119
*National Intelligence Daily,* 143–144
National Security Act (1947), 145
Need-to-know status, 26–28
*New York Times,* 181

Office of Terrorism Analysis, 15
Olson, J., 133
OpenStreetMap, 68
Operational tradecraft, 40
Outside-In Thinking, 65
Oxford Analytica, 159

Pandora, 186
Parris, Mark, 126
Peer influence, 18–19
Pherson, R., 65
Pixar Animation, 77
Porras, J., 164
*Power of Intuition, The* (Klein), 66
*Predictioneer's Game, The* (Bueno de
Mesquita), 213
Predictive analysis:
characteristics of, 109–115
complexity of, 107–108
in elections, 109–110
expertise in, 122, 129
fictional global scenarios, 118–119
gambling analogy, 122–124
game theory approach, 108
for historical pivot points, 115–119